JAPAN'S
🔲
SECRET
🔲
WAR

ROBERT K. WILCOX

Marlowe & Company
New York

Grateful acknowledgment is made for permission to reprint excerpts from "Nuclear Weapons History: Japan's Wartime Bomb Projects Revealed" by Deborah Shapley. Copyright © 1978 by *Science*. Reprinted by permission.

Library of Congress Cataloging in Publication Data

Wilcox, Robert K.
 Japan's secret war.

 Bibliography: p.
 Includes index.
 1. Atomic bomb—Japan—History. I. Title.
QC773.3.J3W55   1985   355.8′25119′0952   84–22628
ISBN 1–56924–815–X

Printed in the United States of America

BOOK DESIGN BY ANN GOLD

JAPAN'S
SECRET
WAR

In memory of Derek deSolla Price, without whose help this story would not have been told

And to my children, Robert and Amaya, whom I pray will emerge unscathed from the growing nuclear threat.

PREFACE

by Professor Derek deSolla Price, Yale University

"The first scientific and military evaluation team after that first mushroom cloud was aghast at the horror of the scene. As far as the eye could see the core of a city had been vaporized; hundreds of blocks of city had vanished with only small pieces of fused scrap to attest to former buildings. Beyond the core around ground zero, it was even more horrible as survivors with the flesh melted from them told of the flash, the fire storm, the rage of explosions. Beyond that again were the defoliated hills and the blackened letters HOLLYWOOD. . . ."

Can you imagine an alternative world history in which the last phase of World War II was marked not by Hiroshima and Nagasaki but by the totally unforeseen atomic bombs on Los Angeles and San Francisco? The Japanese were well aware by the end of the war that the Allies were bent on battering them into submission and ending their desperate island-by-island fighting. The United States, on the other hand, was winning, and the European war was already over. The United States had not been invaded, bombarded, and pillaged in this century, and there was no thought of a war that was other than on foreign fields. I cannot imagine the horrors of a United States that had experienced the atomic bombs on its own soil. The total killing and destruction, the panic and disorganization would have been incredible.

This book is an exploration of a story about just such a possibility that is so horrendous that nobody, American or Japanese, wants to believe that there could be any truth to it. Again and again the basic evidence that "something" was going on in Japanese wartime research on the atomic bomb has been published and documented, and each time the evidence has excited no more than curiosity and authoritative evaluations that nothing of any importance could really have been going on. Now Robert Wilcox has ferreted out further evidence that much more was going on, first in Japan and then continuing in North Korea. Now I, for one, cannot escape the possibility that the atomic bombing of California (with the bombs delivered by kamikaze pocket submarines) might have been an actuality if the war had continued and Truman had not made the decision to end it all with the American bombs.

Could the Japanese really have done it? How long would it have taken to do it? Could Truman have had any sort of secret information about this possibility? At present we simply do not know the answers to these questions, but more information is coming in as the massive wartime files are pieced together, and one day we will know. The overriding questions at the present are what difference it all makes and why there is this strange reaction of so many people that they would rather hear nothing of it. Have all of us academic researchers and Wilcox himself been pressing too near to some monstrous secret story that governments must at all costs still conceal? I think probably not, but the phenomenon is real nonetheless and needs an explanation.

I believe that in telling this story, we are doing battle with not one but three huge psychological hang-ups shared by those of deep caring and compassion. In the first place, it seems that this story may be a way of justifying the otherwise unforgivable use of our atomic bombs which instigated a whole generation of terror of nuclear holocaust in which I grew up and still live. In the second place, we have the postwar hate/love relationship between the United States and Japan, which was associated with the reconstruction, rehabilitation, and coming into effective rivalry of that nation. Thirdly, we have the deep revulsion of the physics community of the United States from its "original sin" (as J. Robert Oppenheimer called it) in playing its key role in developing the bomb. All psychological efforts were made by the scientific community in those postwar years to save all that was beautiful and useful in its science by showing off the benefits of our friend the atom in leading us to a new world, now sadly tarnished, in which nuclear energy would save us all from famine and want.

It puts me in a quandary to realize that by supporting the cause that the historical truth must come out, I might unwittingly betray my colleagues who share my concern about the use of nuclear weapons, share my love of science in general and nuclear physics in particular (though I would like to ban all nuclear power), and worry about fanning any reemergence of national hatreds of any sort. Let's say the story that Wilcox is telling is all true and perhaps only the tip of an even vaster iceberg, what difference does it all make? It matters a lot to me, for the moral issues become in a way clearer and more universal.

We must realize that the use of nuclear armaments is a question for the whole world's population, not just for a particular nation or, worse still, the ruling powers of one nation. At all times we must believe that we are as likely to be nuked as to nuke the enemy, and the same goes for any sophisticated weapons system of which we believe we have the monopoly. If weapons can exist, it must be presumed that they will be developed and used in desperate war by anyone. What is odd is not that Japan may have had the atomic bombs nearly ready to go, but that it turned out that the Germans had never come near the mark even though the foundations of the atomic age had been laid in German laboratories by 1939. What is even odder is that the story of the Japanese bomb runs to North Korea and thence to the Soviet Union. Did it have anything to do with the Soviet development of the bomb so soon afterward?

I respect the doubts of colleagues who feel in their bones that this story that my graduate student Eri Yagi and I discovered almost by accident more than twenty years ago has to be a false alarm. But I fear it is not. Something was going on, and that something looks more and more significant the more we find out. Just after the discovery I had the good fortune to be able to ask Robert Oppenheimer and several other high-placed and knowledgeable people what they thought about the story we had published. None of them knew anything of the matter and assured me that it must have been relatively insignificant and not known to Truman. Twenty years later I cannot believe that any longer. They may have known nothing, but the Japanese effort existed and reached a maturity in North Korea. No longer can we maintain that a Japanese bomb just couldn't have happened. Obviously it "nearly" did. The only questions are how near and what does it do to our judgment on the one case we have of atomic warfare.

ACKNOWLEDGMENTS

A lot of people factored into this research. John Taylor of the Modern Military Branch, National Archives, was always supportive and helpful. He pointed me in the right directions and let me know when something important was at hand. He is an asset to the Archives and I was lucky to have his help. I would also like to give special thanks to my mother, who continually aided in the processing of the manuscript; my wife, Bego, who has never faltered in her support of my writing; and my agents, Jim and Elizabeth Trupin, of Jet Literary Associates, who believed in this project even when it seemed it wouldn't get done.

In addition, I want to thank all the persons I called upon for interviews or correspondence, who are mentioned in this book. It was gracious of them to comply with my intrusion. There is also a large number of persons who are not mentioned in the book who nonetheless gave time and/or knowledge and help. I wish to thank them as well. They include: D. C. Allard of the Naval Historical Center, Washington, D.C.; Mara Bustelo, my translator in Spain; Edwin Coffee and Edward J. Reese at the National Archives; Harry Cooper of "Sharkhunters," Fox Lake, Illinois; José Fernandez, Ana Rosa Nuñez, and my brother-in-law, Joe deAmezola, all of Miami, for Spanish translations; Irene A. Kelly, Harry Kelly's widow, for her hospitality and access to her husband's files; Laurie Rackas of Cable News Network, Washington, D.C., for her insightful reports on this matter; Edward Rumpf, Chester L. Somers, Bob Kennedy and his daughter Beth, Bob Johnston, editor of the *Portsmouth Periscope,* John Whiteman of the *Portsmouth Herald,* and James Vizigian, all of whom provided, along with Bob Norling, valuable information on the *U-234;* Susana Sigg, who did special research for me in Washington; Tani H. Taniuchi and especially Aki Tohdoh, my Japanese translators in Miami; and David A. Smith, State and Military Records, and Paulette Dozois of the Prime Minister's Archives, Public Archives, Canada.

For help in Japan, I wish to thank: Hiroyoshi Kurihara, Science Counselor, Embassy of Japan, Washington, D.C.; Sumio Shimodoi, president of the Sanyo Co., Hiroshima, and his business manager, Yoshio Negishi; Ko Shioya, editor-in-chief of *The Reader's Digest,* Japanese Edition; Hiroshi Okashita of the Japan Atomic Energy Research Institute; Isao Zamoto and Ken Koizumi of TBS Britannica; Yuzo Endo, Central Research Institute of Electric Power Industry; Tamiyo S. Togasaki, librarian, The International House of Japan; Harold William Merzenich and Norihisa Toda, directors of Atlantis Kingdom America; Emiko Sawai, Ikuko Shibata, and Fumiko Hatanaka. I was a stranger in a strange land and these people aided me in various ways. I am grateful and will always remember the experience.

Finally, I would like to thank my editor at Morrow, Doug Stumpf, who helped shape the work.

I have always assumed that the Japanese would have done whatever they could to develop the atomic bomb during the war, and if they had had it, would have used it. I have always assumed that any country that could have had the bomb during the war would have used it, the Nazis, the Soviets, and the Japanese. So we were not unique.

—Edwin O. Reischauer, Harvard professor
and former U.S. ambassador
to Japan, in *Science* magazine

INTRODUCTION

Shortly after World War II had ended, American intelligence in the Pacific received a shocking report: The Japanese, just prior to their surrender, had developed and successfully test-fired an atomic bomb. The project had been housed in or near Konan (Japanese name for Hungnam), Korea, in the peninsula's North. The war had ended before the weapon could be used, and the plant where it had been made was now in Russian hands.

By the summer of 1946 the report was public. David Snell, an agent with the Twenty-fourth Criminal Investigation Detachment in Korea (later he became a *Life* magazine correspondent), wrote about it in the *Atlanta Constitution* following his discharge. He had interviewed one of the many sources for the story: a Japanese officer on his way home from Korea who said he had been in charge of security for the project.

Paraphrasing the officer, Snell wrote:

In a cave in a mountain near Konan men worked, racing against time, in final assembly of "genzai bakudan," Japan's name for the atomic bomb. It was August 10, 1945 (Japanese time), only four days after an atomic bomb flashed in the sky over Hiroshima and five days before Japan surrendered.

To the north, Russian hordes were spilling into Manchuria. Shortly after midnight of that day, a convoy of Japanese trucks moved from the mouth of the cave, past watchful sentries. The trucks wound through valleys, past sleeping farm villages. . . . In the cool predawn, Japanese scientists and engineers loaded genzai bakudan aboard a ship at Konan.

Off the coast, near an islet in the Sea of Japan, more frantic preparations were under way. All that day and night, ancient ships, junks and fishing vessels moved into the anchorage.

Before dawn on August 12, a robot launch chugged through the ships at anchor and beached itself on the islet. Its passenger was genzai bakudan. A clock ticked.

The observers were 20 miles away. This waiting was difficult and strange to men who had worked relentlessly so long, who knew their job had been completed too late.

The light in the east, where Japan lay, grew brighter. The moment the sun peeped over the sea there was a burst of light at the anchorage, blinding the observers, who wore welder's glasses. The ball of fire was estimated to be 1,000 yards in diameter. A multicolored cloud of vapors boiled toward the heavens, then mushroomed in the stratosphere.

The churn of water and vapor obscured the vessels directly under the burst. Ships and junks on the fringe burned fiercely at anchor. When the atmosphere cleared slightly the observers could detect several vessels had vanished.

Genzai bakudan in that moment had matched the brilliance of the rising sun to the east.

Japan had perfected and successfully tested an atomic bomb as cataclysmic as those that withered Hiroshima and Nagasaki.

The bomb was being developed by the Japanese Navy for use in kamikaze planes, the officer told Snell through an interpreter. The planes were to be thrown against American troops when they landed on Japan's shores.

"But time had run out," Snell reported and added:

The observers sped across the water, back to Konan. With the advance units of the Russian Army only hours away, the final sense of a *Götterdämmerung* began. The scientists and engineers smashed machines, burned papers and destroyed completed genzai bakudan.

Before Russian columns reached Konan, dynamite sealed the secrets of the case. But the Russians came so quickly that the scientists could not escape.

The scientists were taken to Russia and tortured, the officer said. But they wouldn't talk. "Our scientists will suffer death before they disclose their secrets to the Russians." He knew, he said. He had just talked to one in Seoul who had escaped and was, like himself, being repatriated.

American military officials were confused. They knew the Japanese had been working on an atomic bomb but believed they had not advanced beyond theory. Now they were confronted with numerous reports to the contrary. All reports said essentially the same thing. It was hard to believe there was not some truth to it. "It is felt that a great deal of credence should be attached to these reports," concluded Colonel Cecil W. Nist about Konan in his G-2 intelligence summary of May 1–15, 1946, intended for top-level eyes in Washington only.

It had been reported that Korea, especially the North, had uranium deposits. A top-priority team was immediately dispatched to the peninsula to determine just how much. What followed was the frantic aftermath of a story that had begun years earlier and continues today in its implications for Japan's stance on defense and nuclear arms. But the story is not just about Japan's atomic bomb project. What eventually unfolded also encompasses spies, secret weapons projects, and clandestine missions that traversed the globe. In short, it became a story of a secret war, a story that until now has never been told.

How far had the Japanese gotten? What were the personal stories behind the effort? An article in *Science* magazine, dated January 1978, said the chief Japanese scientist involved was one Yoshio Nishina, a colleague of Niels Bohr, the famous Danish physicist. Nishina had been at cross-purposes on the project. His friendship with Bohr and other Westerners had kept him from committing himself fully. But his loyalty to Japan had caused him to drive his men relentlessly. The effort had ruined him. After the Hiroshima bomb had been dropped, he had headed the investigating team sent in by the Japanese Army. Understandably, after such radiation exposure, he had died of cancer in 1951.

The *Science* article implied there were a lot of unanswered questions about the Japanese bomb project. While American authorities always maintained the Japanese had neither the talent nor the resources to make a bomb, they had nevertheless sent a special investigating team into Japan right after its surrender to find out if they were right. The team concluded they were. But then occupation troops mysteriously and ruthlessly destroyed all of Japan's cyclotrons.

If the Japanese posed no threat, why such destruction? And why wasn't the project part of standard World War II history? I decided to call one of the experts quoted in the article: Derek deSolla Price, Avalon professor of the history of science at Yale University. Price was probably the first Western scientist to look into the story. In 1962 he and a Japanese history of science graduate student, Eri Yagi, now a professor at Tokyo University, placed a letter to the editor in the November issue of the *Bulletin of the Atomic Scientists,* the antinuclear proliferation journal noted for the clock on its cover ticking away to nuclear doomsday. The letter outlined what the two had learned from the writings of several Japanese scientists who had participated in the project, including the fact that the Japanese Army had given Nishina 1.5 million yen for the project in 1944 alone. The two historians also asked readers for more information.

Since they were addressing the world's physics community, they expected to get a large number of responses. "It produced nothing," said Price. Yagi, he intimated, experienced pressures from her countrymen, and they subsequently dropped the project.

Price suggested some possible new angles on the story. It was his conjecture, he said, that the Japanese had found out about our A-bomb project early in the war. There were similarities between their and our projects that, to his mind, couldn't be explained otherwise.

This is a startling theory. The American atomic bomb project, called the Manhattan Project, was supposedly one of our most closely guarded secrets during the war. For years it was assumed no unauthorized person had known about it until we dropped the first bomb on Hiroshima on August 6, 1945. Then, in 1950, investigations revealed that Klaus Fuchs, a European scientist involved in the Manhattan Project, had passed some of its secrets to the Russians. The Germans are also reputed to have gotten bits and pieces.

If the Manhattan Project was broken by the Russians and Germans, why not by the Japanese as well?

Furthermore, conjectured Price, contrary to the widely held view, the United States may have known about the Japanese project before the end of the war, and this information might have influenced President Harry Truman's decision to use the bomb on Japan.

Price told me he did not think I would ever be able to prove Truman had known. He himself had tried, he said, and gotten nowhere. It would have been the kind of information labeled "For the President's Eyes Only," probably not even written down. But he gave me a few leads in case I decided to pursue the subject and wished me good hunting. "You'll probably have to go to Japan if you want the full story."

I wasn't ready for that yet. But I had an idea that a trip to

Washington might help. A lot of new information about World War II was coming out. The time was right.

One of the most important developments in recent World War II history has been the opening of previously classified intelligence files. The so-called Magic documents are an example.

Magic was a triumph of code breaking. Because of the operation, the United States was able to listen in on most of Japan's secret communications throughout the entire course of the war. We knew practically every move the Japanese were going to make. We were often able to learn the objectives and positions of Japanese military units, such as their combat fleets and submarines. Just such information was the crucial factor enabling us to win the Battle of Midway, the turning point in the Pacific war. The pre-Midway intelligence enabled us to pinpoint their attack fleet in the open ocean and thus surprise it. After Midway, the Japanese went on the defensive and never regained the advantage.

The British, too, had a Magic. It was called Ultra, as in *Ultrasecret*. With it, the British were able to listen in on Germany's secret conversations. Partly as a result of Ultra, the British received information about when and where the Germans were going to bomb England. They also knew where German combat ships were. Consequently, Ultra deserves a large share of the credit for the British victory in the Battle of Britain in the European war, which some consider the turning point.

Only a few people knew of Magic and Ultra during the war: the code breakers, a few top-level government officials, and the two heads of state. In America the interceptions, as they were called, were deciphered, arranged into summaries, and then condensed into a single daily document which itself was locked in a case and deposited on the president's desk. Generally it was seen by only a few cabinet members and himself. If it contained information that had to be discussed with others, that information was said to have been obtained from an "impeachable" source; no one would ask any questions.

I went to Washington with the hope that the Magic documents would hold the key to the story. John Taylor, a researcher at the Modern Military Branch of the National Archives, was assigned to help me. I was lucky. Taylor was knowledgeable and enthusiastic. His office, on the top floors of the archives, retained some of the atmosphere that must have been present when the code breakers themselves were doing their work: Ceilings were low; security measures to protect the files were in effect; archivists hurried about, dispensing the knowledge that made them experts in particular fields.

It turned out Taylor had worked with the writer of the *Science* article, Deborah Shapely, and therefore knew something of the Japanese A-bomb work. In fact, even before I asked him, he went to his desk and returned with a United States Strategic Bombing Survey (USSBS, pronounced us-bus) report on the subject. It was from a special Manhattan Project mission that had gone in with the first occupation troops to investigate Japan's A-bomb progress. But the report was only a few pages long and told me nothing new. And Taylor didn't know of any references to the subject in the Magic documents.

That did not mean there were none. Some 10,000 pages of Magic documents were now in the archives, he advised, and more to come. They were not indexed or catalogued. It would take a long time, but I could go through every one of them. No telling what I would find; the few people who had gone through them before had been looking for other things. They could have missed any material on an atomic bomb. In the documents it was probably not labeled as such.

In addition, he said, there were at least five other sets of documents that might contain pertinent information, each one of them more voluminous than the Magic files. These included the massive Office of Strategic Services (OSS) files. The OSS had been our espionage organization during World War II (it was the forerunner of the CIA). These records also included USSBS files which contained the material from a giant study we made immediately after World War II of everything we had done abroad. Both USSBS and OSS records were housed on entire floors of the huge National Archives building.

Furthermore, said Taylor, another entire building was filled with the records of the U.S. occupation of Japan. They had been indexed only by broad categories, unlike the detailed indexing of the OSS and USSBS files. The building was in Suitland, Maryland, outside the District of Columbia. One could go there and look at boxes packed with official papers that were just as they were when they had been hastily shipped home from Japan after the occupation. It would be like finding a needle in a haystack. But the possibility of success was perhaps more real there than anywhere else. The Suitland files, which consisted of acres and acres of boxes with thousands of papers in each, were untouched.

I told Taylor of a new A-bomb lead I learned of in the September 11, 1978, *Miami Herald*. It was one of the first stories to come out of the newly declassified Magic documents. SPANIARDS RAN SPY RING FOR JAPAN IN U.S., the headline said. The article had been written by a *Washington Post* reporter who visited the archives only a few days after the documents had arrived. It described a ring of spies code-named TO (pronounced "toe"), the Japanese word for "door."

The TO spies were mostly Spanish nationals and diplomats, said the article. They had relayed information through the Spanish Embassy in Washington to Madrid, and from there it had been sent to Tokyo and Berlin. Messages had included information about convoys, troop movements, American strategy, and weapons development. The convoy information had resulted in the sinking of Allied ships, and TO had been such a thorn in America's side that we tried to kill its chief (who was not named) in Madrid.

Was this how the Japanese had found out about our A-bomb program if, indeed, they had?

Taylor brought in the first Magic volumes. They were called "Diplomatic Summaries"—capsulizations of intercepted messages between Tokyo and various embassies. I started going through them. At first I didn't seem to be getting anywhere. The pages contained a hodgepodge of information grouped under general headings: "Military," "Economic," and "Psychological and Subversive." The only order was chronological.

At the top of each summary was the date. Then after one of the four headings there would be something like: "Berlin: Japanese Ambassador [Baron Hiroshi] Oshima has sent Tokyo a report entitled 'America's Defense Measures' which includes the following. . . ." The report would be summarized and Oshima's comments printed verbatim, perhaps with a note from the summarizer explaining what the ambassador meant in view of other deciphered intercepts in Magic's possession.

I could imagine these summary makers working late into the night, waiting anxiously for the intercepts, then sitting down to figure them out. Their reports were well written, first-rate jobs of condensation and clarity. It was easy to see why famous novelists like Britain's Graham Greene and Ian Fleming had worked in intelligence. One had to have rare talents, including a mind that could see through the clutter.

Once in a while I'd come upon an isolated reference that made me feel I was close to hitting pay dirt. For instance, I came across a summary that said, "A German communication quotes an article in a Japanese newspaper to the effect that a cyclotron equal in size to the one in the United States, which is the world's largest, . . . will be completed in the shops of Ishikawajima Dockyards by the end of the year."

So we knew they were working on an atom smasher! I looked hard for more. But there was nothing. And there was no clue to our reaction.

The cyclotron reference was in a July 19, 1942, summary. Another one, a few months later, said, "According to a military officer [presumably he was American, but the Japanese did not state whether he had knowingly or unwittingly given the information to them], a bomb has been developed in a chemical laboratory, which, upon bursting, produces a temperature of 1,000 degrees over a wide area."

Was this our planned A-bomb?

And so it went. I'd note anything that might at some later date have a bearing on my search, and periodically, running into something like the above, my hopes were raised. But this was rare and after a week the most impressive thing emerging from my notes was TO.

In the beginning the TO references made no more impact than anything else. They were isolated bits: a report that U.S. ships had left New York Harbor, specifications of a new airplane we were building, and so on. Magic didn't seem to know much more about it.

The TO references were usually under the "Psychological and Subversive" heading. I began to look for them whenever I came to it. By the time I finished going through all the volumes for 1942 (approximately four), I had a sizable file. A typical item read:

Madrid, Ambassador [Yakichiro] Suma sent the following communication to Tokyo on July 14 (1942):
   "To Intelligence—New York.
   "Extremely Urgent
   "A convoy of 45 ships assembled from various places left San Francisco this morning bound for Australia, carrying tanks and troops."
   Note: As previously reported, the evidence in our files is believed to establish that TO intelligence is intelligence collected by a Spanish spy ring. . . . The Navy Department informs us that no convoy for Australia left San Francisco on July 14, but has given us information as to recent sailings from West Coast ports which might have led an

intelligence agent to the conclusion expressed in the above report. . . .

Other reprinted TO reports were just as fragmentary. It was obvious Magic had not yet gotten a handle on the ring itself. The summaries gave no more than the reports and occasional notes bearing on their accuracy. But when I started looking at the volumes for 1943, the picture suddenly changed. A summary dated January 24, 1943, was the longest I'd seen up until that time: eighteen pages. Entitled "Summary of Information Received by This Branch Concerning the Organization and Operation of the 'TO' Intelligence Net in the United States," it finally put the net in focus.

"Three days after Pearl Harbor," it began, "the Japanese Foreign Office sent out a circular to its representatives in various parts of the world, pointing out that 'with the outbreak of war against England and the United States the position played by our organization for gathering information is of increasing importance.' " The Foreign Ministry asked the embassies in neutral countries to set up espionage nets, and less than a month later the Japanese ambassador in Madrid, Yakichiro Suma, cabled back that with the help of Spanish Foreign Minister Ramón Serrano Súñer, he had been able to elicit the services of a Spaniard who had been a Nazi spy in England. In Suma's words, he was a "cavalier," strong-willed, quick-acting.

Although the original summary had named the TO chief, his name had been blocked out in the copy supplied to the National Archives. Apparently the National Security Council had decided the man's identity should not become public knowledge.

But the Spanish press saw the newspaper stories about TO that had come out when the Magic documents were declassified. Putting various facts together, they identified the man as Ángel Alcázar de Velasco, a former bullfighter and Falangist who was still alive in Madrid. An article in the December 1978 edition of *Historia* showed him grinningly acknowledging his part.

The summary I was reading continued: "At this time at least six TO agents have entered the United States and a seventh agent is to leave Spain for this country next month." TO sources mentioned in the intercepts included: "a major in the office of the Chief of the Air Branch,' 'a certain Army officer,' . . . 'a certain Jewish officer in the Aviation Department,' 'my informant in the Air Corps,' . . . 'my friend in the Navy Department,' . . . 'a supervisor of floating piers in New York.' . . ."

It seemed the United States had infiltrated the ring with a double agent; one of the TO spies apparently was dealing with the American Embassy in Madrid. TO's intelligence was sent back by radio, by diplomatic pouch, and through the use of invisible ink between the lines in stories supposedly filed by Spanish newspaper correspondents. Many of the messages were inaccurate, the summary advised, but some were "correct and of some importance." Japan was spending a lot of money on the ring and had plans to enlarge it.

The archives at Suitland, Maryland, were a searcher's nightmare: a vast warehouse of file boxes from the occupation—9,000 linear feet of them, with little or no indexing. The archivists could tell you where boxes of records from different occupation departments might be, and they could show you shipping lists that roughly described what a group of boxes contained, but then you were on your own. The gold was out there. But on which mountain? Beneath which rock?

The economic and scientific section seemed the logical place to start. No telling how many boxes there were; it seemed like hundreds. I narrowed the number down to twenty or thirty and started digging. Many of the boxes had not been opened since they were packed back in 1952, when the occupation ended. Potentially each held a blockbuster. But I made little progress. I found only peripheral material: administrative files about Nishina and other scientists; an occasional enticing but usually brief report about uranium in Japan or in one of its occupied countries.

Then, out of the blue, while going through a file labeled "Magazine and News Articles," I found what appeared to be the typed manuscript of a newspaper story which began, "Japan developed and successfully tested an atomic bomb three days prior to the end of the war." It was copyrighted 1946 by the *Atlanta Constitution,* and it was written by David Snell (who was not otherwise identified).

I read on: "She destroyed unfinished atomic bombs, secret papers and her atomic bomb plant only hours before the advance units of the Russian Army moved into Konan, Korea, site of the project. Japanese scientists who developed the bomb are now in Moscow, prisoners of the Russians. They were tortured by their captors seeking atomic 'know-how.' "

The story was the kind I had been looking for. Was it true? Where was Konan? The next line told me it was in North Korea—under

Russian control. It has not been open to the West since before World War II.

In the fifth paragraph Snell wrote: "I learned this information from a Japanese officer, who said he was in charge of counterintelligence at the Konan project before the fall of Japan. He [the officer] gave names, dates, facts and figures on the Japanese atomic project, which I submitted to United States Army Intelligence in Seoul. The War Department is withholding much of the information. To protect the man who told me this story, and at the request of the Army, he is here given a pseudonym, Capt. Tsetusuo Wakabayashi." Snell speculated that the capture of the Japanese project by the Russians explained why soon after the war Russian Premier Joseph Stalin had said, "America will not long have a monopoly on atomic weapons."

I have already mentioned the most important details of the Snell story: how the bomb was test-fired on an island off North Korea; how work on it was split between a factory in Konan, where major components were made, and a cave in the mountains north of Konan, where a select few assembled the bomb; and how the Russians had overrun Konan before a second bomb could be built.

But other parts of the story also sparked my interest. They corresponded with what I had learned elsewhere about the Japanese A-bomb program, thus making the uncorroborated aspects of the story more credible in my eyes. For instance, construction of Nishina's cyclotron was mentioned as one of the first steps in the program. This was little known even in Japan—especially in 1946. And the story gave me some new details about how the program might have advanced. "When task forces and invasion spearheads brought the war ever closer to the Japanese mainland," it said, "the Japanese Navy undertook the production of the atomic bomb as a defense against amphibious operations. Atomic bombs were to be flown against Allied ships in Kamikaze suicide planes."

That made sense. I knew how desperate the Japanese had been to thwart the coming Allied invasion. They had developed all kinds of fantastic schemes to throw the enemy back into the sea in what they called the "defense of the homeland." It was their last chance.

The navy project started about midway through the war, according to Snell's informant. It was centered in Nagoya (the first time I had heard that city mentioned in connection with the project). "But its removal to Korea was necessitated when the B-29s began to lash industrial cities on the mainland of Japan. I consider the B-29 the primary factor in the defeat of Japan," the Japanese officer declared. "The B-29 caused our project to be moved to Korea. We lost three months in the transfer. We would have had genzai bakudan (Japanese for atomic bomb) three months earlier if it had not been for the B-29."

The officer said Japanese intelligence had learned "at least a year before the atomic bombing of Hiroshima" that "there was a vast and mysterious project in the mountains of the eastern" United States. Was this the Manhattan Project's uranium separation plant at Oak Ridge, Tennessee? Professor Price had conjectured that the Japanese knew of it. "On the other hand, Allied intelligence must have known of the atomic project at Konan, because of the perfect timing of the Hiroshima bombing, only six days before the long-scheduled Japanese naval test."

Was all this simply the lie of a Japanese soldier whose pride had been hurt by defeat and who wanted his conquered country to save face? Or was it American propaganda intended to quash criticism over using the A-bomb? Or was there something to it? Whatever the answer, I couldn't dismiss it.

First I tried to locate Snell. I found him in *Who's Who in the South and Southwest.* He was listed as a former *Life* magazine correspondent living in Houston. He had a long list of credits: reporter on the *New York World-Telegram; Life* correspondent in Europe, Africa, and Middle East; author of syndicated column called "Dateline America"; a writer for Time-Life Books; president of International Writers Ltd.; many awards, including the prestigious George Polk Memorial. He was a distinguished journalist. He had to be taken seriously.

Snell stuck by his story. He said he still remembered the Japanese officer gesturing broadly to indicate the size of the explosion. But unfortunately he could not tell me the informant's real name. "I've lost my files, and I simply can't remember," he said apologetically. "It was a long time ago."

He said the story caused quite a stir when it ran in the *Constitution.* He remembered Ralph McGill, the editor then, having to defend it. But it was quickly forgotten because Konan was under Russian domination, and the only information coming out of the area was that the Russians would not allow anyone near it and were dismantling its plants and shipping them back to Russia. Edwin Pauley, the only Western observer allowed in North Korea after the war, had verified that. During the Korean War, Snell said, American soldiers in the Konan area came upon a mysterious mountain installation that he felt backed up his story. Scripps-Howard newspapers had written about it. But then we were defeated at the Chosin Reservoir, which housed one of the dams feeding power to Konan, and silence closed in again. Snell said he was sorry he couldn't be of more help.

It didn't surprise me that Snell's files had been lost. He said he had thrown them out when he had moved. I throw files out that are even five years old. These were thirty years old. I checked every aspect of his story that I could: the names of the military detachments he mentioned as being in Korea; other minor details that might reveal inconsistencies. All were correct, and a search through the archives turned up additional support. Formerly secret reports showed that stories about "an atomic discharge" and a "high-energy bomb" to be used against aircraft and ships had circulated in Japan before the surrender. Konan turned out to be the hub of one of the largest industrial complexes in Asia. It was a vast munitions emporium sheltered, by virtue of its obscurity, from Allied bombing. It was the only Japanese-controlled area with enough power for the gigantic industrial problems that would have been involved. Suitland even yielded formerly classified documents saying there was uranium near it. This was the logical place for an end-of-the-war atomic bomb project.

Then I uncovered the clinchers—a series of formerly top secret intelligence documents that said U.S. forces throughout South Korea had gotten the same reports that Snell had. The first was a summary of a report. The date was not clear—either 1945 or 1946—but the facts were. It said succinctly, "Atomic experiments were conducted in a chemical plant located at Hungnam. Machinery were destroyed by the Japanese before the Soviets occupied the area."

More digging in the same box turned up a lengthier summary. Dated May 21, 1946, it had come from the U.S. Army's chief of staff office in Korea. It said:

Of increasing interest have been recent reports dealing with an apparent undercover research laboratory operated by the Japanese at . . . Hungnam. . . . All reports agree that research and experiments on atomic energy were conducted. . . . The two chief scientists were Takahashi, Rikizo and Wakabayashi, Tadashiro [whom I had never heard of]. The recent whereabouts of these two individuals is not known, inasmuch as they were taken into custody by the Russians last fall. However, before their capture they are reported to have burned their papers and destroyed their laboratory equipment. . . . Some reports . . . say . . . the Russians were able to remove some of the machinery.

Further reports stated that the actual experiments on atomic energy were conducted in Japan, and the Hungnam plant was opened for the development of the practical application of atomic energy to a bomb or other military use. This section of the . . . plant . . . was always heavily guarded. . . . These reports received separately are surprisingly uniform as to content. It is felt that a great deal of credence should be attached to these reports as summarized.

The summary was signed "Cecil W. Nist," a G-2 colonel.

It was just as Snell had reported it, and according to footnotes, there were more reports. But when I asked to see them, I was told that they were still classified. I would have to put in a Freedom of Information Act request to the Central Intelligence Agency, which might or might not grant me access. I would certainly not hear for many months, probably years. There was a huge backlog, and agencies like the CIA were not quick to comply with FOI requests.

It didn't matter—at least for the time being. I felt I already had enough confirmation to begin treating Snell's story seriously.

"You penetrated our atomic bomb program?"

Ángel Alcázar de Velasco nodded. It had been in 1943, he said. "The information was that the American work on a nuclear weapon was very advanced but they had a long way to go. There were even notes about the detonator. It was similar to one already in use by the Germans. A Spanish doctor got the information—an M.D.—a refugee from Spain."

I hadn't expected to hear this so quickly. It took me by surprise.

It had been relatively easy to find Alcázar de Velasco in Madrid in 1980. I had called Spanish journalists who had interviewed him when the first TO stories broke in 1978. One of them had given me his address.

Some say he still works as a spy, although his best spy days appeared to be behind him. He certainly still acted like one. When we knocked on the large wooden door to his central Madrid apartment, he yelled in irritation that he was not yet through with his morning bath. Could we go have some coffee across the street and come back in half an hour? We complied. But no sooner had we done as ordered than he entered the back of the little café and was watching us from a seat at its far end. Apparently he thought we wouldn't recognize him. But I had seen some recent pictures. I told my translator to go along with the game.

After we had returned to the apartment and introduced ourselves, he was fairly cordial. He was over seventy now. His hair was kinky, gray, and long, extending out Harpo Marx-style, like a turban on his head. But he was lean and spry and wore a nice tan suit. The interview began with him, at my request, telling a little about his background. He explained how he had become a spy and met the Japanese, among them Yakichiro Suma, who was to be his contact. They had subsequently wanted him to cover the American West Coast when his agents had discovered the Manhattan Project. I had planned to save that subject for last, figuring it might be touchy.

"Well, what happened?" I pushed.

He said the report had come sometime in "early" 1943. He couldn't be exact. It had also involved photos and some sort of "explosion"—not any test-firing of the bomb, he added when I pointed out that the first test-firing had been in 1945, but some sort of preliminary. "The material I saw was on the *early* plans about making the atomic bomb."

He said he had forwarded it to the Japanese in Berlin, bypassing Suma (who, he said, got only the "unimportant stuff"), and they had told him to get more. Whether he actually did get any further reports was not clear. When I pressed for clarification, he changed the subject, discussing the system of agents he had in the American Southwest. It was a network of three, who, in turn, had their own agents and who worked for the Germans as well. They ranged from Houston to Phoenix and were very active down in Mexico. A favorite spot for crossing into the United States was Juárez-El Paso, just 250 miles south of Los Alamos, New Mexico, where the Manhattan Project had set up its bomb-building plant.

The crossings occurred at night. Alcázar de Velasco himself made several trips across, once "just to get a look at the enemy," another to attend to a problem with one of his agents in Houston. Some of his agents did not know their information was going back to the Japanese. They thought they were working solely for the Germans. He went to Mexico via the Caribbean by German submarine.

But Los Alamos hadn't officially opened until March 1943, I pointed out, trying to get him to get back to his A-bomb espionage. That didn't matter, he said. The report had come around that time.

He was adamant. He became annoyed when I continued to question him on the point. I decided to back off since he had assured me of another session the following morning. We went on to other subjects.

The next morning the topic of the atomic bomb again came up. He told me a strange story: The Japanese finally contacted him and told him to get "samples" from around the area of the explosion. The date again was uncertain. He claimed it was 1943, but other things he said indicated it could have been later. Since the area was guarded and inaccessible, the Japanese asked him to send two "Chicano boys." They sent special money for the operation. The boys came back with the soil samples, and his agents put them in medicine bottles. When he notified the Japanese in Berlin, he was told the samples were too important to be sent back by regular channels. They wanted him to go to Mexico, pick up the samples, and hand them over to Japanese agents who would meet him. They sent more money.

The Germans were tiring of ferrying him around for "unspecified reasons," he said, but the Japanese finally arranged to have him taken to Mexico via submarine. He met the Chicano boys with the samples and they went to the Majestic Hotel, one of Mexico City's oldest. It was downtown. Two Japanese were waiting for him. They had come from Mazatlán, a Pacific port notorious for its high concentration of Japanese spies, most of them posing as fishermen, as these two were. He says he thought they were chemical engineers, although he wasn't sure.

He and the Japanese exchanged code words. Prior to meeting them, Alcázar de Velasco had deposited the boys and the samples in a room in the hotel. The agents didn't ask for the samples; they asked for the boys. He went and got them. The agents "made a very thorough medical check," he said. "Nails and skin were examined. They took blood from the boys' fingers, arms, and ears. They touched them with [some sort of solution] on the skin." (I later read in *The Secret History of the Atomic Bomb*, edited by Anthony Cave Brown and Charles P. MacDonald, that a white corpuscle blood count was the principal test to determine if a person had suffered overexposure to radiation.) After that, the Japanese asked for the samples but wouldn't go near them. "That scared me since I'd been carrying them." For the first time, he said, he began to realize the significance of what was happening; they were looking for radioactivity, he guessed. He realized that from the beginning the Japanese had intended to have unsuspecting persons exposed so they could be tested.

As the agents examined the boys, he said he made small talk. He told them that the Americans already knew about two of his agents on the East Coast, but that all this was according to plan. The East Coast ring had been set up as a decoy. It was supposed to be discovered. "You need to give the enemy some information so they won't be looking elsewhere." He never asked the agents their names because "You don't do that in the spy service. They'll just tell you lies." When they finished, they all went to a cabaret and then parted, never to see each other again. Alcázar de Velasco claimed that because of the tests, the Japanese decided the United States would not finish the bomb in time for the war.

All this occurred in early 1943, he insisted. He remembered, he said, because it was during the rainy season. He had to assist the two Japanese at one point across a muddy street. But the Mexican rainy season is from May to September. So at the earliest, it was probably around the summer of 1943. Further inconsistencies in what he told me made it apparent that the meeting could have taken place anytime between May 1943 and late 1944. (There was an explosion on May 4, 1945, in connection with the Los Alamos project. It was the detonation of uranium by TNT as a preliminary to the first atomic bomb test in July. But that, too, seems too late to fit Alcázar de Velasco's claims.)

The main points of Alcázar de Velasco's testimony, at least, did not seem improbable to me. He had claimed his men knew about our A-bomb project in at least two books. The first was one of his own, *Memories of a Secret Agent,* recently published in Spain and available only in Spanish. In it, he described his one and only meeting with Adolf Hitler to discuss a communiqué from one of his spies. The spy was code-named Sebastian.

The meeting, he wrote, took place in June 1943. Sometime prior to that, Sebastian, who was never identified by his true name, sent an urgent message stating, "I know for sure that the United States has finished the study of a new and terrifying weapon made of atoms." It added that the "first experiment had been very successful."

This conforms to the chronology of our A-bomb program. By January 1943, we had indeed finished all preliminary studies on making the bomb. And a vital experiment had been performed. On

December 2, 1942, Enrico Fermi had produced the world's first chain reaction. We knew the bomb could be made, and we knew how.

Wilhelm Canaris, head of the Abwehr (military intelligence), met Alcázar de Velasco prior to the meeting with Hitler and told him that Hitler would not be happy with Sebastian's report. He did not want to believe that America was so far advanced. Alcázar de Velasco's German plane had been shot down on the way to Berlin, forcing him to parachute out. He was slightly injured and now—in light of Canaris's information—very nervous.

The führer was flanked at his desk by two SS men. As Heinrich Himmler read Sebastian's report out loud, Hitler got up and paced, repeatedly asking questions about Sebastian's reliability. While Sebastian had sent the message two different ways, Alcázar de Velasco didn't tell Hitler that. Instead, he said, "I am sure of Sebastian, but in this business you never can be completely sure. Your agents are always subject to traps."

Apparently that was what Hitler had been waiting to hear. The führer walked back to his desk and slammed his fist down. "That is the truth!" It was a shout of finality. The discussion was over. "I expected him to say more," concluded Alcázar de Velasco, "but he simply gave a wave of his hand."

This is consistent with what we know from other sources about Hitler's attitude toward the atomic bomb. Among the reasons Germany's program did not go far were Hitler's lack of interest and his prejudice. He frequently referred to nuclear physics as Jewish physics and disdained it for that reason. He also, according to such sources as Albert Speer, the Reich's armaments minister, did not fully understand the potential of an atomic weapon. Rather, he wanted weapons that would be ready quickly—new tanks and planes.

Another pertinent story by Alcázar de Velasco is found in the 1979 book *Spanish Spies,* published in Madrid and also available only in Spanish. In it, Alcázar de Velasco told author-historian D. Pastor Petit that his deepest regret regarding World War II was that he did not take seriously enough the atomic bomb reports he got. However, in neither book I've cited did he mention the Mexico City rendezvous. In fact, Petit's reference comes almost out of the blue. There is no preceding information about Alcázar de Velasco's atomic bomb espionage.

Was he lying? Just trying to impress me and the others? When I wrote him asking for documentation on his claims, he wrote back:

"There are no documentary proofs because if there were, we would not have done our job correctly." Alcázar de Velasco does have some corroboration beyond his own words. Both Ladislas Farago and J. C. Masterman, high up in Allied intelligence during World War II, wrote that the Germans found out about our atomic bomb project and that Alcázar de Velasco was a cunning and dangerous agent. The late Farago, who worked for American intelligence, wrote about him in *The Game of the Foxes;* Masterman, a leader in British intelligence and also dead, in *The Double-Cross System in the War of 1939 to 1945.* The FBI has perhaps 10,000 pages of files on Alcázar de Velasco and TO (which it calls Span-Nap). I had still not received them under my Freedom of Information Act request when I conducted my interview. All I could get was a phone report that the files contained "real hot stuff."

Neither Farago nor Masterman connected Alcázar de Velasco to atomic bomb espionage. But since he was part of the German network, even using German spies, he could have learned of any such espionage or even been its source. Farago said that by 1942 the Axis network in America consisted mostly of Spanish spies. The "explosion" Alcázar de Velasco told me about could have been Fermi's pile. A foreign agent could have thought, or called, it an explosion. His agents were not physicists. Perhaps confusion, rather than lying, led to the inconsistencies that peppered Alcázar de Velasco's story, perhaps a little of both. But the story had a ring of truth. The details were unusual. If the samples he claimed to have turned over to the Japanese had been gathered prior to May 1945, then they probably would not have been radioactive and thus might have led the Japanese to the conclusion he said they reached: that the United States was far from completion of the project. I was to hear this conclusion often in the Japanese sources.

But the most important corroboration regarding what Alcázar de Velasco told me was this: However they had learned it, the Japanese, according to the testimony of several high-ranking Japanese generals, had in fact learned in early 1943 that America was progressing successfully with its atomic bomb project. This is precisely when Alcázar de Velasco said he passed along the report. According to *The Emperor in the Showa Era,* published in 1968 and one of the few Japanese books to discuss that country's project, Premier Hideki Tojo himself had the information.

Compiled from interviews with participants in the project, this book quotes "the General Groves" of the Japanese project, Toranosuke Kawashima, as saying Tojo called him into his Tokyo office and stated, "The atomic bomb projects of the United States and Germany are progressing. If we are behind, we will lose the war. I want you to step up our program to make it." Tojo told Kawashima, who was then unfamiliar with Japan's project, to see General Takeo Yasuda for particulars.

Other sections of Japan's military were reported to have heard about the U.S. project at approximately the same time. Alcázar de Velasco was the only spy I could find who claimed to have passed along such intelligence. Since, at the same time, TO was helping sink "many" ships and providing other important intelligence to both the Germans and Japanese, I decided to take him at his word—at least for the time being.

Surprisingly, a good number of the Japanese scientists and military men I hoped to see were still alive in 1980. Many were reluctant to talk to me. I finally obtained an interview with Sumi Yokoyama, who had been Nishina's wartime secretary and now supervised the Nishina archives. Soft-spoken but strong-willed, she had become the force behind the post-wartime Rikken. Founded in 1917, it was the largest and most important private scientific organization in Japan, and, after the war, began manufacturing and supplying radioisotopes to be used as atomic tracers for medical purposes. But she really did not want to talk to me. "Frankly speaking," she wrote in a note I found in my box at the International House, "I worked for Dr. Nishina . . . but I was young . . . and not a scientist. . . . I am sure it will be better for you to see scientists first."

I could not argue with that. After a short exchange of pleasantries she took me outside, along a tree-shrouded path, which looked probably much the same as when Nishina was alive. Birds chirped from overhead branches and uniformed schoolgirls skipped by. Soon we approached a cream-colored two-story barrackslike building almost hidden in the greenery. It had housed Nishina's second-story office. Hidehiko Tamaki was waiting, she suddenly said. He came frequently to research a book he was writing.

Tamaki had been a key man in Nishina's project. And since Price's graduate student, Eri Yagi, had been shown Tamaki's report to the Japanese Air Force, it was he who, in a roundabout way, had been responsible for alerting Price to the Japanese project.

Nishina's office really wasn't very big—about the size of an elementary school classroom. But it was cool and comfortable, with wooden walls and a big leather couch. Banks of file drawers stood about. Nishina's old desk and blackboard were at the far end.

Tamaki came in, smiling. Two other elderly men were with him. They stayed in the background. Tamaki was short and fat with bushy salt-and-pepper eyebrows. Miss Yokoyama introduced us and left. Tamaki pointed to the couch and called for tea.

We sat and sipped for a while. Nobody said anything. I waited expectantly for my translator, a young Japanese girl, to start the interview. I was later to find out that in Japan, one doesn't start talking immediately, especially when older East meets younger West. My companions were staring off into space in contemplation and I, frankly, was getting anxious.

Finally, I started questioning. Tamaki didn't want to talk. He would not look at me. He seemed irritated that I believed there had been a program to produce a bomb. Nishina wanted only to make atomic power, he repeated. When I switched to asking him about Nishina's personality, he warmed a little. Nishina loved Bohr, reading research papers, and solving puzzles—probably in that order. He played a pretty good game of chess, too. And when he tackled a scientific problem, he abandoned everything else.

Later, several weeks after the interview, I was told by Miss Yokoyama that Tamaki had decided he didn't like me. "He's just a novelist," he had said disdainfully of me. That was that. I probably wasn't going to get much more from Tamaki, and perhaps it was my own fault. I had not intended to be rude, but I had come right out and told him what I was interested in. And I had persisted. In Japan that can be frowned upon.

Nevertheless, I had come out of the interview with some new information, especially about Konan. I had already accumulated quite a file on the place and a little on its creator, Jun Noguchi. Most of it had come from USSBS and OSS archives.

Konan had been a major U.S. Navy target toward the end of the war. We knew only that it was a huge industrial and munitions complex. A lot of my information was pre-World War II: reports from spies or informers who described sailing by it or sneaking into it. The Japanese would not let anybody get near. But slowly, through aerial photography and interrogations of refugees and prisoners of war, the United States had put together a reasonably accurate picture.

Noguchi, the industrialist who had built Konan, however, was a real mystery. I could find hardly any information about him, only vague references to a kind of "king" of the area who was treated with great deference. When I asked Tamaki about Konan, he said Nishina had once had a meeting with army generals in which he had protested that there was not enough electricity in Japan to produce atomic power. One of the general's responses, he said, was "Don't worry, we'll get the power in North Korea." Noguchi was the man who "controlled the power" in Korea, Tamaki said. He had "established it" before the war.

My previous investigations had shown Noguchi to be elusive, if nothing else. The sources mentioned him, but usually in only the most cursory ways. He was the "war party" developer, the "militarist" collaborator, the "exploiter." Prewar studies of Korea by the Institute of Pacific Relations, a defunct organization of scholars formed in 1925 for the "scientific study of the peoples of the Pacific," warned of his munitions manufacturing. Even the hazy glimpse of the man I had been able to get from such sources as a fifty-page formerly secret 1942 OSS report, entitled "Japanese War-Effort Plants, the Noguchi Konan Enterprises," left no doubt that had Noguchi been so inclined, his complex easily could have supported an atomic bomb project.

Konan had a refinery capable—had the Japanese found the necessary material—of converting raw ores into pure uranium. It certainly had the industrial plants and power to conduct large-scale U-235 separation—had pilot separators been set up there. The OSS report described the dams feeding the sprawling complex as the "greatest" hydroelectric system "in the empire." Northern Korea was "Japan's Muscle Shoals," it said, likening the area to America's Tennessee Valley Authority and Grand Coulee Dam, which powered the United States' main separation effort. The two mountaintop reservoirs which were the heart of the system—the Chosin and Fusen—generated at least 600,000 kilowatts between them. According to *Atomic Quest* by Arthur Compton, one of the scientists involved, our own separation plants at Oak Ridge required only 250,000 kilowatts —not even half the amount coming into Konan.

Other intelligence reports indicated that northern Korea was one of the world's leading producers of graphite, the moderator which Fermi had used in his first reactor, the late 1942 breakthrough in the U.S. program. And Konan was close to Japan's possible uranium supply. My searches at Suitland had turned up numerous reports of uranium ores being mined by the Japanese in Korea, the most tantalizing of which named a town where Noguchi's parent company in

Korea, the Korean Nitrogen Fertilizer Company, had one of its major synthetic fuel operations.

According to a formerly secret Military Intelligence Section (MIS) report of the Far Eastern Command, numbered 1710 and dated January 1947, "German sources" had told U.S. interrogators in June 1946 that "uranium deposits" had been found in coal mines near Chuul, North Korea, a settlement just north of Eian. Eian, perhaps 125 miles up the coast from Konan, was a Noguchi-owned town. Postwar intelligence from the area disclosed that three Koreans who had worked there told U.S. interrogators that there had been "nine buildings and workers quarters" outside the mine—an unusually large cluster—and that when the Russians took over the mine, they immediately restricted access to it. Other reports said there was a plant "capable of refining rare element minerals" near Eian, and the Noguchi synthetic fuel factory there contained, late in the war, a special section called the "gas department" which was restricted to all but a few Japanese. The section, said the informants, had unusual "high-pressure equipment," and its product was "stored underground in the hills."

All this reminded me of Snell's story: "In a cave in a mountain near Konan men worked, racing against time. . . ." America's project had been fragmented—different jobs performed in different areas. Japan's might have been that way, too: theory worked out at home; large-scale separation and bomb assembly carried out at Konan, Eian, and mountain caves near them.

Northern Korea was the only place in the empire with enough power, especially at the end of the war, for an atomic project. It was safe enough from bombing and invasion to house one. It was in the midst of Japan's best possible uranium supply, meaning that the ore did not have to be shipped back to the embattled home islands, a destination it probably never would have reached.

Eventually, I turned up no fewer than ten sites in Korea where U.S. intelligence reported that the Japanese had mined uranium ore during the war. Most of the sites involved secondary ores—fergusonite, euxenite, monazite—found throughout the peninsula's many streams and gold mines. But at least one of them was reported to have been pitchblende—the primary ore. And according to a document I found at Suitland, Noguchi was one of the primary handlers of the ores.

This document, *Atomic Bomb Mission Japan, Final Report, Scientific and Mineralogical Investigation,* was the work of a Manhattan

Project mission sent to Japan in September 1945, just days after the formal surrender, to find out what progress the Japanese had made in developing an atomic bomb. A similar mission, called Alsos (the Greek word for *grove*) had gone into Germany with the invading troops and had discovered, to its relief, that the Germans had not come very close to creating an atomic weapon. The mission to Japan stayed there roughly a month, interrogating many scientists, including Nishina, Arakatsu, and many of the others involved in the project. It even made a trip to Korea after learning that much of the activity had occurred there. Noguchi and his company were mentioned throughout the mineralogical section of the document. By the time the mission's geological detachment had reached Seoul, however, most of the Japanese mineralogical records had been burned. But there was evidence that pointed to much digging for uranium ore, and one of the chief diggers and refiners had been Noguchi's company "Nitchitsu," an acronym of the name in Japanese of the parent company, the Japan Nitrogen Fertilizer Company.

Robert D. Nininger, the mission's head geologist, learned from the Korean Bureau of Mines that Nitchitsu had processed almost all the uranium-bearing ores consumed by the Japanese during 1944—574 of the 641 tons of monazite and 1.5 of the 2.1 tons of columbite. Nitchitsu was the government's main supplier of rare metals, which would have included uranium. And unlike all other mining and refining companies there, which were tightly controlled by the government, it shipped its ore solely "at Navy direction"; it was accountable only to the admirals.

According to the Snell story, the navy had been responsible for the Konan project. Furthermore, the mission report quoted Bunsaku Arakatsu, who was the head of the navy project, as saying there was heavy water for his work in Korea.

Several persons I was to talk to in Japan told me Noguchi was making heavy water in Korea.

In Japan I met another important man—Yoichi Yamamoto, an engineer who had worked with the army project, code-named "NI," especially in trying to find uranium. Miss Yokoyama had said she did not like him. But I wanted to talk with him anyway.

He met me at the station. His head was shaved. The war had changed him. He was now a practicing Buddhist. He was not proud of his NI involvement. He blamed Nishina for Nagasaki (probably why Miss Yokoyama did not like him). Nishina knew Hiroshima had been hit by an atomic bomb, he said. But he was so ashamed America had produced one when he had not that he had not told the generals until after Nagasaki. If he had, charged Yamamoto, Japan would have surrendered earlier and the bombing of Nagasaki could have been avoided.

But surprisingly, Yamamoto said the Japanese who died at Nagasaki, even Hiroshima, did so for a purpose. If the atomic bombs had not been dropped, "millions more [from both sides] would have died." Japan was preparing to defend the homeland at all costs, he explained. As terrible as they were, the American bombs averted an even worse bloodbath.

After he had got all that off his chest, he told me about NI. He had been assigned to the project in June 1944, the same month American troops were landing in France. Nishina had told him to hunt for uranium. The Eighth Army Technical Lab, of which he was a part, had decided to concentrate on samarskite in Ishikawa. It contained "20 percent" uranium, he said. With schoolchildren digging around the clock, they eventually came up with 750 kilograms of the stuff. But it was never used. The program, at least in Japan proper, had dissipated by that time.

Yamamoto knew Noguchi had factories at Konan, and "they had heavy water there." But he knew nothing of a Konan atomic bomb project. He thought the heavy water might have been used in connection with making jet fuel. This agreed with material I had received from the Japanese Defense Agency.

Japan's interest in jet planes had started in 1942, when it learned the Germans were building a jet for "reconnoitering and bombing America." It "has rockets under its wings so it can make a fast getaway," Ambassador Oshima had cabled Tokyo from Berlin about a German jet in February 1943.

By 1944 the Japanese had bought the plans for two German jets: the Messerschmitt 262, a two-engine fighter-bomber that first appeared over Europe in the summer of that year, and the chunky little Messerschmitt 163 Komet, which never really became operational because of its volatile rocket fuel. An entire Komet had been sent by submarine to Japan, along with plans and German technicians for both jets. But only the plans had arrived. After the secret cargo had been discharged at Singapore, the plans proceeded to Tokyo by plane. The Komet and technicians went by a ship, which was sunk by an American submarine.

But when the "Defense of the Homeland" plan was formulated, the two jets, nevertheless, were designated among the primary weapons—along with the "death ray," "uranium bomb," and suicide squadrons. An OSS report I found (numbered M-552, and dated February 1, 1945) implied that the jets, in addition to being used in the conventional manner to intercept B-29s, might also be manned by suicide pilots delivering A-bombs; that was what Snell's informant had told him.

In the absence of the actual jets to copy, the Japanese decided to make their own versions. The navy, almost devoid of ships by this time, was the prime mover in the scheme. It called its copies the Shusui (Me-163) and the Kikka (Me-262). The Japanese "attempted to produce the plane from the blueprints," wrote Jerome B. Cohen in *Japan's Economy in War and Reconstruction*, published in 1949. "Original plans contemplated the production of 155 planes by March 1945, 1,200 by September 1945 and 3,600 by March 1946."

Eventually, using Magic, War Department, and OSS files and the few books I could find commenting on the subject, I was able to amass references and documents relating to the jets. These, as well as some of what I had been given at the Defense Agency, revealed conclusively that Konan was the main site for producing the special hydrogen peroxide-based fuel required by the jets. "The high command was relying quite heavily on the propellants for [B-29] interception," said a summary of USSBS Report No. 385. "The entire project received the highest priority and great initial strides were taken in the erection of production plants."

If Konan was a main base for the secret jet plane project, might it not also have been the center of a secret uranium bomb project, to which, through the homeland defense plans, it was directly connected? Snell's informant had told him the bomb was being readied for B-29 interceptions.

Yamamoto had no answer for that question. "All planning was done in secret," he said. "I could not even keep documents concerning what little I was involved in."

But another veteran I was soon to meet knew more about the two projects. I had run into Matao Mitsui's name while researching the navy's atomic bomb project—the one initiated by the fleet and headed by Kyoto's Professor Bunsaku Arakatsu. Mitsui, who had risen to the rank of captain, had been graduated from Kyoto University in explosives and chemicals. His work as an expert for the navy had resulted in his assignment to Arakatsu's Kyoto project. He had also been one of the directors of the jet fuel effort.

"I was there at the jet's first flight," he told me when we sat down for an interview in Tokyo. He appeared younger than I knew he was, spoke English well, and seemed willing to help in any way he could. The first test had been of a Shusui, in July 1945. The squatty plane shot up from the Yokosuka Naval Air Base near Tokyo to 9,000 feet, he said. But then its engine quit. The problem, he said, was in the fuel tank. The outlet leading to the jet's engine was too high. In the steep level of climb, the fuel had dropped below it, and the engine's gas supply was cut off. The plane dipped over and crashed. The tank had to be redesigned. By the time the problem was corrected the war had ended.

The Kikka met a similar fate. Test flights revealed flaws in its two turbojet engines. Corrections were not completed until after the surrender.

But the effort to make fuel, like the effort to find uranium for NI, had gone on unaffected by delays at the other end. Of course, jet fuel production had its own problems. Although the Japanese had received the basic propellant formulas from the Germans, the death of the German technicians had left them to work out all problems by themselves. As a result, overall production never approached the goals that had been set.

In addition, an earthquake late in 1944, floods in early 1945, and the relentless Allied bombing doomed the effort on the mainland. About the only place where jet fuel was produced in quantity, said Mitsui, was at Konan. But that work was handled independently, he told me, and he did not know much about it. He assured me he knew of no A-bomb project there. But there "could have been," he agreed. Everything was so secret.

The more he thought about it, the more he became puzzled. "Noguchi *was* making heavy water," he volunteered. But then he shook his head with a smile. "I didn't know about any atomic bomb project there." As far as he was concerned, the fleet A-bomb program had ended in July—the same month the Shusui had crashed.

My next appointment was with representatives of Nihon Chisso —what Noguchi's company (Nitchitsu) is currently called. Shoji Kamata, apparently the company's historian, along with his other company duties, did most of the talking. He, too, said he had never heard anything about an atomic project at Konan. But he had written a company history containing a section about the jet fuel project. It is supplemented by an account written by former Admiral Hideo Hasagawa, commander of Konan at the end of the war, a copy of which I was given by Defense Agency historical section archivists. Konan was the navy's Korea headquarters. The jet fuel project was code-named NZ by the navy. The fuel was intended not only for jets, according to Admiral Hasagawa, but for V-1 or V-2 rockets like those "the Germans used in bombing London." NZ workers were told that the outcome of the war hinged on what they were making.

The fuel consisted of three basic chemicals: hydrogen peroxide, hydrazine hydrate, and sodium permanganate. Hasagawa wrote: "To produce the fuel, we needed lots of electric power. . . . In Japan, there was little power . . . [but] at Konan, there was lots. . . ."

Also essential were electrical conductors made out of platinum, an extremely precious metal. Platinum was the only substance strong enough to withstand the huge and powerful electric arcs used in the making of the chemicals.

To get the platinum, the government instituted a huge collection program. Not only were most industrial stores taken, but families gave up heirlooms, and individuals donated personal jewelry, even dentures. "We collected 60 percent of all the platinum in Japan at that time," wrote Hasagawa, who declined to see me when I was in Japan.

How much fuel was produced is a matter of debate. According to Hasagawa, the propellant was made "very well and in great quantity." Kamata says only seventeen tons were made. They were stored, he writes, in "underground shelters" near the coast. In any case, the war ended before it could be used, and when it became obvious that Konan was going to be overrun by the Russians, Hasagawa ordered that the NZ operation be destroyed (except for the platinum electrodes) and the propellant dumped into the sea.

Hasagawa wrote that the platinum he ordered saved weighed "504.4 kilograms" and was worth $200 million. It belonged to the Japanese people. After the war they would be penniless and starving and would need it very much. "I knew we were not supposed to do anything without the Russians' permission, but I decided to bring it back to the Japanese people."

So with the Russians landing on an airfield servicing Konan, a Captain Nakao took off in a fighter loaded with the precious metal. Hasagawa lied to the Russians, enabling Nakao to get away. The fighter crash-landed near Tottori on the eastern coast of Honshu. (He didn't say why the crash occurred.) The United States confiscated the platinum, charged the Japanese with hoarding, and took it home. But both Hasagawa and Kamata said much, if not all, of it was returned and became the basis of early war relief.

Back at Konan, there had been a slipup, and NZ had been only partially destroyed. The Russians found out about the propellant project and the platinum. They began torturing Hasagawa and NZ engineers, demanding more information about both. "If I had told them, they could have gotten the platinum back," wrote Hasagawa, "so I said nothing. I was tortured with fire and water. When I passed out they would throw me in a cell until I regained consciousness, then torture me again." They also threatened to kill his wife.

Kamata wrote: "Mr. Takahashi was tortured so harshly that he fainted several times." He, too, apparently did not talk.

Eventually, all at NZ—Hasagawa, Takahashi, Wakabayashi, several more—were tried for destroying Russian property and given five- to seven-year sentences in Siberia. "In January 1946, I [Hasagawa] and 5 others from Nihon Chisso were taken to Vladivostok to start a new life in Siberia. We were not treated as human beings. I was given one bowl of soup and 200 grams of bread a day —even when the temperature was 60 degrees below zero." He was sentenced to hard labor.

Reports from other repatriates were more detailed: "We worked eight hours a day, yet, due to the cold and hunger, one after another fell. About 15 prisoners of war died daily due to malnutrition. Once, there were two to three hundred corpses piled up in front of our barracks and many patients were groaning inside. It was hell on earth. . . ."

He was not freed until 1954, and the terrible conditions caused him to lose an eye, Hasagawa wrote. But there was a consolation: "I am proud to say that at the end of the war, Japan's navy was more advanced in the field of rockets than Russia and America."

It was an impressive story, similar in its recounting of the last days at Konan to Snell's account of the alleged atomic bomb project. Had NZ created the atomic bomb stories? Was the A-bomb project really just a jet fuel project which, because of its secrecy, had been mistakenly taken for an atomic project?

Leaving Chisso, I was becoming less and less optimistic about finding anyone who could confirm an atomic bomb program at Konan. But I was still not satisfied. There were too many unanswered questions. Why had U.S. intelligence picked up so many consistent reports from different Japanese who had worked at Konan? If NZ had been housed there, had there been any other secret projects? Konan was certainly big, militarily important, and secret enough to have had others. And what would others who had actually been involved in the projects say? Asking atomic bomb questions of Chisso, which in the 1970s was taking heat as the source of poisonous mercury discharges that caused deformities in the children of residents of Minamata, was like asking the cigarette companies whether smoking caused cancer. I needed to *talk* to those who actually had been involved in the projects at Konan and who had no vested interest in what I was trying to determine.

I arrived home on June 1, 1980. I began to consolidate all the material I had amassed. In the meantime, I began writing to every conceivable person and agency that might be able to shed light.

This led to many Freedom of Information Act requests. I went from agency to agency asking for documents about TO, Alcázar de Velasco, the Japanese attempt to make an atomic bomb, the various scientists involved. It is a lengthy process. There are thousands ahead of you; the agencies, not wishing to comply, try to discourage you at every point. I was dealing with two of the toughest—the CIA and FBI—as well as with many military branches. One also needs money to have files searched, copies made, etc. There are ways to minimize the costs, but that takes more letters, more time, more craftiness. And often your appeals are denied for the flimsiest of reasons. By the time I started writing in earnest I had not received the first document. But I couldn't wait.

It is plain in the 160-page Atomic Bomb Mission report that its members sent back to the United States many Japanese and Korean documents dealing with the projects and the search for uranium. These documents were translated and may still exist somewhere— if they have not been destroyed. When they were shipped home, information concerning the atomic bomb and Russian access to atomic bomb material was extremely important. Almost certainly it was classified so that it could never be publicly disseminated through the normal channels. And in view of the destruction of the cyclotrons in Japan, the authorities may have made doubly sure that the full story was hidden.

I believe that the United States and Japan purposely covered up the story in order to protect what were perceived then as national interests. The United States wanted an ally that could help against

Russia and was, perhaps, embarrassed that it had not been more fully informed of the Japanese project. Japanese officials did not tell the full story for fear of being prosecuted as war criminals and of being scorned by their own people who had suffered two atomic bomb attacks. The Japanese scientists complied for the same reasons, although their consciences have led them to make piecemeal disclosures since that time.

Since I returned from Japan, the U.S. and Japanese penchant for covering up questionable World War II activities (in some cases, out-and-out atrocities) has been amply demonstrated.

In February 1982, the UPI reported: "High levels of radiation exposure to soldiers at atomic test sites 25 years ago were kept hidden by a set of phony records, a former Army medic said Sunday . . . [and] he was warned that if he told anyone of his experiences, 'I could be charged with treason under the National Security Act.' "

In May 1982 the AP reported: "Rep. Barney Frank (D-Mass.) has called for a congressional investigation into reports that State Department officials secretly smuggled hundreds of Nazi war criminals into the United States"—thus enabling them to escape prosecution —"in exchange for Soviet intelligence information. The . . . operation 'is the most appalling mixture of moral insensitivity and incompetence I have seen,' said Frank. . . ."

Most pertinent were the widely disseminated revelations in spring 1982 that the Japanese had conducted hideous biological experimentations on American prisoners and others in Manchuria during the war. While Nazis were being sentenced to death for the same things in Europe, the United States decided it would cover up the Japanese atrocities so that the information on human experimentation, which was considered militarily important at that time, not fall into the hands of the Russians.

The grisly details were published in the *Bulletin of the Atomic Scientists*. POWs were injected with diseases. Limbs were frozen solid. They were tied screaming to posts and fragmentation bombs were exploded beside them.

Only after the story of the Manchurian atrocities had been published in practically every newspaper in the West did the government admit that the stories were true. Even as I write, the Japanese, Koreans, and Chinese are arguing about a Japanese World War II cover-up. New history books published in Japan have deleted mention of mass murders, rape, and pillaging committed by Japanese forces which invaded China in the 1930s, according to a *Miami*

Herald story, dated August 7, 1982. The Chinese have lodged a formal diplomatic protest over the deletion, and the Japanese are "considering it." Atrocities against Koreans are said to have been left out, too.

As Professor Price said in *Science* magazine, "Japan's attempt to acquire an atomic weapon during World War II changes the moral and ethical relationship between Japan and the U.S. . . . The story has been that the Americans were guilty and the Japanese were innocent and blameless; that the Americans developed this terrible new weapon and proceeded to commit an atomic rape of the then-help-less Japanese. . . ."

While I was looking for a translator in Japan, I had lunch with Yumiko Mikame, a quick-thinking and very attractive young Japanese woman, who seemed, after only a little bit of talk, to be the answer to my problem. She was also an activist who was very much involved in the Hiroshima peace movement—highly antinuclear.

As she listened to me explain more about what I was after, I felt the atmosphere get cold. "Just what, Mr. Wilcox," she suddenly said, "is your purpose in writing this story? Are you going to try to justify what America did at Hiroshima and Nagasaki by saying the Japanese would have done it, too?"

The question caught me off guard, I had not expected it here at lunch, and I did not have a quick answer.

"Well, I should think that knowing what the Japanese themselves did on the atomic bomb would help your organization," I said. "You want to know what went on in your own backyard, don't you? If you or someone you provided did the translating for me, you could ask your own questions. It's always better to be informed." She seemed to accept the answer.

The fact that the Japanese had a continuing nuclear bomb program from 1939 on, and possibly got farther than Germany, means that history, especially nuclear history, has to be rewritten. Deborah Shapely, author of the *Science* article that reopened the story, wrote:

The project is highly significant to the history of nuclear weapons, to Japan's subsequent self-denial of nuclear weapons, and to the relationship that developed between Japan and the United States after the U.S. atomic bombing of the cities of Hiroshima and Nagasaki. . . . But the historical importance of the project lies not in the fact that Japan failed but that she tried, and that Japan's post-war attitude, that she, as the one nation victimized by atomic weapons, is above seeking to acquire them for herself, is not historically accurate. The historical record shows—on the basis of the eagerness of her military and the willing cooperation of her scientists—that if other factors had made a bomb possible, the leadership—which by the end of the war were placing their own youth in torpedoes to home them on the advancing U.ى. ᵃeet —would not have hesitated to use the bomb against the United States.

That kind of analysis angered contributors to the *Bulletin of the Atomic Scientists* and members of other groups dealing with the impending doom of nuclear buildup and with Asian scientists. The atomic scientists responded with an article by MIT's Charles Weiner, entitled "Retroactive Saber Rattling?" It denounced the "press story" impression "that Japan may have posed a potential nuclear threat against its enemies in the war and that the Japanese have pulled a 'curtain of silence' over the subject." An article by John W. Dower in the April–June 1978 *Bulletin of Concerned Asian Scholars* did the same thing.

The *Science* article said only that the Japanese did, after all, have a project and wondered if there wasn't more to the story. Clearly there is. And to argue that a few obscure references, mostly to a minuscule program that died in 1943, constituted a public airing of the program is to miss the point. Only when all the facts are known will the true implications to science and the world be known.

Herbert F. York, director of the program on science, technology, and public affairs at the University of California at San Diego and an expert on the history of atomic weapons and arms control, touched on some of the deeper questions involved in the same *Science* article:

Two points. First the Japanese story completes the set, that every nation that might plausibly have started a nuclear weapons program did so: Germany, Great Britain, the United States, the Soviet Union, France, and, we now know, Japan. So the case has been weakened of those who have argued that governments, or more precisely, the generals, emperors, and presidents, can hold back from this decision and say "No." The decision to develop nuclear weapons is not a fluke of certain governments, but a general, technological imperative.

A second point I would make—and this cannot be proven on the basis of the Japan story alone—is that it is not the generals, emperors, or presidents who are the driving force behind a country's development of nuclear weapons. It is the cadre of scientists and engineers, who go to their governments and say, "Look what we can do. If you give us this and this, you will be that much closer to having a nuclear bomb if you should ever want one." I believe that this is happening in other nations of the world today.

What happens when scientists take the nuclear road is very important. The future of the world may depend on it.

PART

ONE

1

The stocky little director of Japan's Army Air Force Technical Research Institute, Lieutenant General Takeo Yasuda, was worried. As an electrical engineer he had done so well at Tokyo University that his professors had asked him to stay and teach. But the army offered more opportunity. Still, he had kept abreast of the latest research in nuclear physics. Fission—the splitting of the atom to release energy—had caught his interest. Since its discovery in Germany in late 1938, he had been acutely aware that a bomb of incredible power might be made from uranium. Uranium atoms gave off neutrons when they fissioned. Those neutrons could split other atoms and so on. If done in a lightning-fast chain reaction, a gigantic explosion would result. Yasuda considered this so important that he had sponsored special lectures on it, making attendance by his young officers mandatory.

Now, in the spring of 1940, he saw the United States—increasingly regarded as Japan's enemy—becoming secretive about its atomic research and embargoing shipments of uranium. Previously there had been extensive discussion of fission in American scientific journals. Suddenly there was silence. What was going on? Had the Americans—or British or Germans, for that matter—started working on a bomb?

Yasuda shifted in his chair. The United States was strong enough without a superweapon. It was time to stop wondering and start acting. For that reason he had summoned Tatsusaburo Suzuki, one of his young staff officers, to come to his Tokyo office. Suzuki, a former artillery specialist, was born in Nagoya, a porcelain center where uranium was used for coloring. As a child he had demonstrated a superior aptitude for science and had been sent to Yasuda's alma mater, Tokyo University. He had graduated with an emphasis in physics and X rays.

Suzuki probably would have been the man summoned even if he had not attended the same school as Yasuda (the military was very cliquish). Japan had competent nuclear physicists at the time—but not many. Barely eighty years had passed since it had decided to adopt Western science in order to industrialize and thus protect itself from the West. The majority of scientists were civilians, who were regarded by the military as rather undisciplined and as having questionable loyalties. Many had been schooled in the West. Suzuki, on the other hand, was one of the few army physicists. He was first a soldier, then a scientist.

But this did not mean he was unenthusiastic about science. Fission had been discovered the year he'd been graduated. It dominated discussions among his colleagues. He considered it the most important development in his field and vital to his country's defense. He eagerly anticipated Yasuda's assignment.

Suzuki's meeting with Yasuda that April day was the first step in what was to become Japan's World War II atomic bomb project. Yasuda ordered Suzuki to make a preliminary report on the feasibility of producing a uranium bomb, as it was often called then. The twenty-nine-year-old officer was to take his time and address the pertinent questions: Could such a bomb be made? How and with what resources? And so on. Years later, in response to a question from his shocked daughter about how he could have initiated such a horrible secret project—one that, in the hands of America, had caused such suffering to his people—Yasuda answered, "Japan is a small country, so it is limited. We cannot make as many airplanes as America. So we cannot win the war by doing the same things as she does. To win a war, we needed something special, like an atomic bomb."

Suzuki lost little time seeking the aid of his former Tokyo University professor, Ryokichi Sagane. Sagane, although only thirty-five years old, was a rising star in Japanese physics and already had an international reputation. It would be to Sagane that U.S. scientists would drop from a B-29 a letter urging immediate surrender following the atomic bombing of Hiroshima in 1945. But that was five years in the future. Sagane had studied cyclotrons and fission at the University of California at Berkeley under Ernest O. Lawrence, who had won a Nobel Prize in 1939 for his invention of the cyclotron. He was now working in the U.S. atomic program, which, as Yasuda had guessed, was just beginning. After leaving California, Sagane had gone to England, where he had studied at the famous Cavendish Laboratory at Cambridge. He then returned to Japan to begin construction on the largest cyclotron outside the United States, a 220-ton, sixty-inch device at the Institute of Physical and Chemical Research, known later to Americans simply as the Rikken (the word was formed from the sounds of the first letters of the institute's name in Japanese). The Rikken already had in operation a smaller, twenty-six-inch cyclotron, built in 1936. Sagane told Suzuki that a bomb could be produced and that Western scientists, including Lawrence, were probably working on one.

Among those also conducting fission experiments at the Rikken was Tameichi Yazaki, a Japanese physicist who had, like Sagane, spent time in America. Suzuki consulted him as well. Yazaki had worked with Enrico Fermi, the Italian physicist and 1938 Nobel Prizewinner who went on to spearhead the American A-bomb effort. It was Fermi who had unwittingly started the quest for the bomb when, in 1934, he had bombarded uranium with neutrons and been the first to observe a fission, although at the time he had not recognized the event as such.

Everything was new then. Even the neutron, a tiny subatomic particle with no charge, had been discovered only two years before. Until its discovery nobody believed an atom could be fissioned, but its lack of charge enabled it to approach and split an atom without being repelled.

By the time Fermi determined exactly what he'd observed fascism had driven him from Italy to New York's Columbia University, where he worked on the chain reaction—the next major step in making the bomb or atomic fuel. In December 1942 he became the first to create a controlled atomic reaction (power-producing, but nonexplosive), a breakthrough that would throw the U.S. A-bomb program into high gear. According to a memoir written by Suzuki, Yazaki told him, "Fermi will complete the bomb."

After his consultations with the Rikken scientists, Suzuki believed an atomic bomb could and should be made, and there was no time to lose. He believed Japanese scientists could figure out the specifics. They told him there were calculations to be made and practical engineering problems to be solved. It might take awhile, but they were up to it.

As far as uranium went, nobody knew exactly how much would be needed, but most believed there could be enough, if not in Japan proper, then in one of the colonies—Korea, for instance.

Korea, taken right after the defeat of Russia in 1905, was virtually enslaved by Japan. It was rich in resources and could provide anything the Japanese wanted—and cheaply—labor included. The head geologist at the Rikken, Satoyasu Iimori, had just returned from Korea, bringing back minerals from which he was refining uranium. In 1936 he had found uranium-bearing ores in Japan proper.

In addition, Suzuki himself was especially interested in the possibility of using atomic power to run ships, maybe even planes. Japan was horribly deficient in petroleum and had to import all its oil. Atomic power offered a stupendous solution, but one would have to learn how to control the chain reaction—to use its heat before it reached the critical, explosive stage. (Fermi did this late in 1942). The neutrons, of course, were the key. They caused the chain reaction. If one could control their emission so that they would not cause enough fissions in rapid succession to explode, only enough to produce heat, one had a viable fuel. The controller would be a substance that absorbed neutrons. There were several of them, and Suzuki decided cadmium, a silvery white metal used in making alloys and plating, might do well. (It was a visionary guess. Cadmium was later used in the successful U.S. program.)

It was six months before Suzuki was done researching and writing. When he turned in his report in October 1940, Yasuda was pleased. It verified his beliefs and put the issue into perspective. There was little doubt that a uranium bomb could be decisive to the outcome of the war, and building one was feasible, although how long it would take was still a question. Work on it could be explained as an attempt to produce atomic fuel. Yasuda had the report copied and circulated.

It met with varied responses, including skepticism. Military planners above Yasuda's level were more receptive to short-term projects —weapons they knew could be in the field in months. Admittedly the problems of making a bomb or atomic fuel were substantial. It might take years. In addition, Japan's scientific community was not, as a whole, receptive to theoretical physics. After all, Hantaro Nagaoka, generally regarded as the Father of Japanese Physics, had been so hounded after he had invented the famous Saturnian model of an atom—showing it as a planet with electrons revolving—that he had abandoned it. His colleagues dubbed it metaphysics.

But by the spring of 1941—one year after Yasuda had assigned

Suzuki to the A-bomb question—relations between the West and Japan had so deteriorated that the general was finally able to get the project funded. The Rikken, located on the outskirts of Tokyo, got the contract.

The amount of money allocated was not much compared to what was being spent for the same purposes in America. Across the Pacific, at least six universities had already been enlisted to work on an unofficial atomic bomb project. But the Japanese program had moved from idea to actuality. It had been born and was growing, and the United States, which was already beginning to worry seriously about what the Germans were doing in the field, knew nothing about it. The common assumption was that the Japanese did not have the men or resources to mount such a project.

2

In April 1941, nine months before the United States and Japan went to war, General Yasuda sent Suzuki to the Rikken's director, Masatochi Okochi, to discuss who at the institute should head the uranium bomb project. They settled on Dr. Yoshio Nishina, perhaps the country's foremost physicist at the time.

Like Yasuda, Nishina had attended Tokyo University. His degree in electrical engineering had led him to nuclear physics (the atom, after all, was the basic unit of electricity). Following Nishina's graduation in 1918, he went to Europe at the urging of his teacher, Nagaoka, the dean of Japanese physicists until his death in 1950. (In Japan, age and seniority are more highly valued than they are in America.) Nagaoka had studied under Cambridge's Ernest Rutherford, who won a Nobel Prize in chemistry for his mapping of the atom's structure—the same thing Nagaoka was noted for in Japan. Following Cambridge, Nishina went to Copenhagen and Niels Bohr's Institute of Theoretical Physics. The Nobel Prizewinning Bohr was, along with Albert Einstein, one of the greatest living theoretical physicists of the century. He and Nishina became close friends, so close that Bohr's children called Nishina "uncle."

Nishina spent eight years in Europe, from 1921 to 1928. From Rutherford he learned all about the atom. From Bohr he learned quantum mechanics, the "new physics," which was replacing classic Newtonian physics, providing the framework for so many later discoveries. During that time Nishina made his unique contribution: He authored, along with Sweden's Oskar Klein, the Klein-Nishina formula which enabled scientists to compute the scattering of cosmic rays. Nishina thus became recognized internationally as an expert on cosmic rays.

In 1928, following a month's tour of American universities, he returned home to Japan to continue his study of cosmic rays and to introduce quantum mechanics. He became the "Father of New Physics" in Japan. In recognition of his accomplishments, he was given his own laboratory at the Rikken in 1931. Because of the free, unstructured teaching approach he brought from Europe, his lab quickly became popular with Japan's young physicists. Here discussion with the teacher was encouraged rather than forbidden. By 1938, 100 full-time researchers were working in his lab. Nishina built the country's first cyclotron—the twenty-six-incher at the Rikken—and began, with Sagane's help, construction of the sixty-incher, which was to weigh 220 tons when completed in 1944.

Most significantly, Nishina was instrumental in getting the Rikken to build a nuclear research laboratory and also in convincing Japan's Society for the Promotion of Scientific Research, one of the country's major research-funding organizations, to create an Atomic Nucleus Subcommittee, which Nishina chaired.

The nuclear lab was his pride and joy. As an electrical engineer he loved to tinker with the cyclotrons. The lab also had a cloud chamber for tracking subatomic particles and other important pieces of equipment used in nuclear studies. Suzuki visited it often. According to one student—Shinichiro Tomonaga, who, many years after the war, won a Nobel Prize—it looked like a "factory" with "a monster of a crane . . . and a gigantic high-tension apparatus [the completed cyclotron] . . . attached to it."

Like many other nuclear physicists at the time, Nishina, upon reading about the discovery of uranium fission in early 1939, had plunged into fission experimentation. In 1940 and 1941 he wrote no fewer than four papers on the subject. They appeared in the *Physical Review* and *Nature,* and included "Fission Products of Thorium by Neutrons," "Fission Products of Uranium by Fast Neutrons," and "Some Experiments on the Relative Cross Sections of Reaction Produced by Fast Neutrons."

Nishina did so well in his fission experimentation that he actually discovered a new uranium isotope: U-237. Normal uranium—the kind one gets out of the ground—is called U-238. The *U,* of course, stands for "uranium"; the *238* is its atomic weight, which is the sum of the number of protons and electrons making up its nucleus. By bombarding the normal uranium with fast neutrons (as opposed to slow, or thermal, neutrons), Nishina changed it into U-237. It had lost one of its particles. The result—U-237—was an isotope, uranium that was chemically the same as U-238 but atomically different. This new isotope was unstable, meaning it might fission more easily than elements made up of a stable number of atoms, such as U-238. Nishina published his findings in an article in the *Physical Review* entitled "Induced (Beta) Activity of Uranium by Fast Neutrons." The date was May 3, 1940. At almost the same time American researchers published the same discovery, prompting Arthur H. Compton, one of the leaders of the American atomic bomb project, to state in his 1956 book *Atomic Quest* that the Japanese work in 1940 was "running parallel to ours."

Each new discovery of this kind was another milestone in the development of the bomb. When the West began to restrict publication of nuclear research in the last half of 1940, Nishina and his colleagues were put in the dark.

The Rikken, where Nishina worked, was a huge complex by Japanese standards. Located in what in 1980 would be the Sengoku section of the city, it consisted of more than fifty buildings, including research labs, ore refineries, and storage warehouses. In typical Japanese fashion, there were trees all around. It did not resemble an American factory; rather, it was like a barracks area with little ponds and greenery.

The cutoff of information from the West wasn't as stifling as it could have been. The Rikken had been created in 1917 in response to an earlier cutoff during World War I. Its directors had prepared for Western censorship. There were many libraries, and they had subscriptions to science journals from around the world, many of which picked up information not being published by the United States.

Nishina's office was on the second floor of one of his labs. It was filled with books from the West. They included thirty volumes of the *Proceedings of the Royal Society* (British), the *Physical Review* (American), and German and French journals and encyclopedias, as well as works of Goethe and Shakespeare. Nishina read and spoke English, German, Danish, and French. Western classics were among his favorites. There was a blackboard for teaching, which he chalked regularly, and, beneath the office's east window, a small couch on which he napped in the afternoons. Above his desk hung a picture of him and, in full uniform, the emperor's brother, who was smiling and had his arm around Nishina's shoulders.

Nishina was a chubby man with a handsome smile and a short temper. He laughed a lot and shouted a lot. He would conduct daily meetings in his office with his young assistants, who sat before him in chairs arranged in a semicircle. Contrary to the stiff-backed, tight-lipped, authoritarian style of most Japanese labs of his day, Nishina liked back-and-forth banter, an exchange of ideas. He had learned this style from Bohr. He also preferred theory to application, so that once an idea had been shaped sufficiently to be applied, he preferred to go on to something new.

By July 1941, five months before Pearl Harbor, the money from the army had arrived, and Nishina considered the project officially started. He created a file for it among his others and eventually called in a young assistant, Hidehiko Tamaki. Tamaki, thirty-two, a graduate of Tokyo University, was an atomic physicist who had impressed Nishina when the two had worked together on cosmic rays. Tamaki later wrote two books, *From Periodic Law to Ultrauranium* and *Nishina,* a biography for children. He also, by 1980, held a chair in physics at Japan's Chiba University. In 1941 he was simply a promising young researcher.

Nishina's feelings at this time about making an atomic bomb are unclear. Tamaki said that he went into the project only with the intention of developing atomic power. But the Japanese Army obviously wanted an atomic weapon and it's hard to believe that in its dealings with him, that was not made clear. Nevertheless, it does appear that Nishina did have strong feelings against war with America. When the bombing of Pearl Harbor was announced over the radio, he is reported by some of his researchers to have reacted to the news by calling the Japanese leaders fools. "Don't they know they can't beat America?" But Pearl Harbor was still months away, and Nishina was intrigued with the prospect of unleashing atomic energy.

He outlined the situation to Tamaki.

Uranium fission, as Tamaki well knew, had opened up the possibility of a new type of bomb. The army had done a preliminary study indicating the bomb was feasible. The military was also interested in atomic fuel. Now they—those at the Nishina lab—were going to have to get down to specifics. Tamaki was to start from scratch. What did they have to know and do to produce a bomb? A large body of international literature was already available to help. Tamaki would also have access to the cyclotron, the researchers in the lab who had been working on the problem, and other experts outside the lab should he need them. But he had to be careful about going outside the lab; this was a military project and therefore had to be kept secret. Under no circumstances was he to tell anyone he contacted for information the reason for his inquiry.

Some of the things Nishina knew already were: If the Japanese were ever to produce a bomb or atomic fuel, they probably had to get a lot of uranium. This was because isotope U-235, present in natural uranium only in very small amounts, caused fission. (It was Nishina's friend Niels Bohr who had first theorized this.)

To extract the isotope, they were going to have to devise a completely new method of separation. They couldn't separate the two chemically—the normal way of separating mixed substances—because isotopes had the same chemical makeup as the element they were part of. The only differences the two had were atomic—the number of protons and electrons in the atoms of each. But Nishina's lab, as well as others in Japan and elsewhere, had recently been working on the new field of isotope separation.

Once the researchers had devised a separation method, they would have to figure out exactly how potent a concentration of U-235 would be needed. Pure U-235 would be best. Only a small amount would be needed for an explosion. But it would also be extremely difficult to accumulate. Luckily, it appeared, they wouldn't have to go that route. All they needed to do, published reports had indicated, was enrich the U-235 content of natural uranium by 10 to 20 percent and they might have a critical mass—explodable uranium in which a chain reaction was ready to ensue.

They needed to calculate the critical mass in order to have the correct measurements not only for an eventual bomb casing but also so they wouldn't accidentally amass it beforehand and blow up Tokyo. In fact, such an accident could never happen because in order to cause an explosion, the mass has to form in millionths of a second —something that could not happen accidentally. But neither Nishina nor Tamaki was certain about anything at this point. All they knew was that something in the neighborhood of 1 kilogram to 100 kilograms of fissionable material might go. The higher the enrichment, the smaller the mass.

Determining the critical mass was itself dependent on a variety of other calculations and variables. Perhaps most important was how many neutrons were emitted when a U-235 atom fissioned. It was the neutrons, with their unique ability to split atoms, that caused the needed chain reaction. But nobody knew how many neutrons came out of each U-235 fission; they knew only that the average was between two and three. A violent explosion involved trillions of fissions. With a number that large, they had to be more accurate. "Two or three" wouldn't do. If the number was two, the critical mass would be much bigger than if it were three, or any number in between (as, in fact, it was—2.5, to be precise). They could use the cyclotron and cloud chamber to solve that problem. The cyclotron could fire neutrons at uranium, causing fission, and the cloud chamber would show how many neutrons came out.

These were the major problems of physics and chemistry the researchers would have to confront before designing a bomb. There were other less important questions. But if the major ones could be solved, they would be well on their way toward producing first atomic fuel and then the bomb itself.

Fuel was the logical first step in any atomic bomb program at the time. It was the first big step that America was aiming for (Fermi's experiments). It allowed one to put much of one's theoretical speculation to the test. If Nishina could build what is today called a reactor —an assemblage of fissionable uranium that is approaching critical mass—it would provide a way to test many of the theories he had to come up with.

For instance, it would show the chain reaction in operation (approaching, but not reaching, criticality) and consequently all the attendant mechanisms, such as the neutron emission. Both the reactor and a bomb depend on a chain reaction. The difference is that in a bomb the chain is uncontrolled and incredibly swift, resulting in an explosion. In a reactor it mounts slowly, controllably, resulting only in the production of heat. And through the use of substances which absorb neutrons, like Suzuki's cadmium, it can be stopped or cut back at any time.

No one had ever built a reactor. Its basic principle was simple: Congregate enough fissionable uranium to get the chain reaction going. The problem was how much. How enriched? Only hard work would give the answers.

However, Nishina and probably Tamaki knew one fact that would aid them in building a reactor. Certain substances had the ability to "reflect" neutrons. This was important because if they could encase their fissionable uranium in one of these substances, the reflecting, or bouncing back, of the escaping neutrons increased the chances of their having more fissions in the mass. This meant they could use smaller, less enriched amounts of uranium.

Such substances were called moderators. They were elements with very light atomic weights, such as carbon. They worked because their nuclei were so small that they would not split or absorb neutrons, but instead would bounce them back where they came from, in the manner of colliding tennis balls.

One of the best moderators known was deuterium, also called heavy water. Heavy water is ordinary water which has been heavily electrolyzed. The burning off concentrates the deuterium, an isotope present in the water in minute amounts. Heavy water had been discovered only in 1932, and because it was so hard to make (great masses of water had to be electrified for long periods to get a small amount of it), there wasn't much around. Actually there was not much use for it except as a moderator.

But Nishina had got hold of some. From where it is not clear. After the war he told American investigators that it was from Norway, one of the few places known in the West to be producing heavy water before the war. (But there are indications Nishina had got it in Japan or maybe Korea. In the tumultuous postwar days he lied to the investigators about other matters.)

Norwegian heavy water was to become a focal point of concern to the Allies throughout most of their race to produce an atomic bomb. When the British learned in October 1941 that the plant producing the Norwegian heavy water was in Nazi hands, they became so alarmed that they immediately began planning an annihilate-at-all-costs assault. That was only three months after Nishina had called Tamaki in. But the British and the Americans had no idea that the Japanese had any heavy water, let alone an atomic bomb project.

Nishina told Tamaki how they might use heavy water in making a controlled reaction, and Tamaki went to work.

3

The Japanese industrialist Jun Noguchi surveyed his empire, and on this day, December 8, 1941, he had reason to feel euphoric. Japanese war planes had, with devastating effect, attacked the American fleet at Pearl Harbor. Japan's undeclared war in Asia—already a decade long—was assured of continuing. The gamble he had taken nearly twenty years before was paying off in a way he had never dreamed. He was standing on a plateau overlooking Konan, Korea.

To his left were rugged hills rising to steep mountains perhaps 20 miles inland; to his right was the unpredictable Sea of Japan—one moment a peaceful dream of fog and calm waters; the next, a torrent of storm and rain. In front of him, snaking between the mountains and the lowland rice paddies that clung to the coast, a gritty swath of smoky, noisy factories stretched in three giant patches, one 68 miles long, nearly 200 miles to the northeast, extending almost to the Russian border. It was the largest industrial complex in Asia, a nearly uninterrupted chain of smokestacks, smelting furnaces, huge bubbling vats, and roaring goliath-size machinery powered by the largest hydroelectric system on the continent. All of it was his brainchild, his stupendous creation.

The system was dependent on three mighty rivers. The largest was the Yalu, which lay to the west and flowed between Korea and Manchuria. Its tributaries, the Fusen and Chosin, had been dammed by Noguchi at their highest points in the mountains. They now flowed east toward the Sea of Japan. Together the three rivers delivered more than 1 million kilowatts of power to the many hydroelectric stations feeding the complex. This was an unheard-of concentration at the time. All of Japan produced only a little more than 3 million kilowatts, and nowhere did it have 1 million kilowatts in one area.

Konan was the hub of this complex. Among its many products were explosives: gunpowder, dynamite, nitroglycerin, and magnesium. It had the largest fertilizer factory in the world as well as chemical and synthetic oil and gasoline plants. All were essential to the war effort. America was a formidable enemy. The armies would now need more of these products than ever.

Noguchi's pride swelled as he stood there on the hill. He knew the complex would become even more important now not only because of its products but because of the immense electric power it generated. As the war intensified, demands on industry in the home islands would increase. Konan would handle special projects, secret projects, projects needing huge amounts of power and rare industrial resources. The army had already told him so.

Noguchi was not just thinking about the profits he would make. He was a patriot, and he took pride in being of use to his emperor. Already there was talk about using his complex to help build a uranium bomb.

Dotting the mountains beyond the complex were the many mines he owned. Korea was rich in geological resources, much more so than Japan, which had begun to depend on it heavily for raw materials. Among the peninsula's most plentiful minerals were gold, copper, silver, iron, lead, tungsten, coal, magnesium, graphite, mica, and the rare earth elements such as yttrium, hard to find anywhere. (Geologists had even reported finding uranium there, although its significance was not yet fully appreciated.) Convinced that there was much more to be found, Noguchi had a near monopoly on extraction and use. Because he was in partnership with the military, which controlled Korea, he was the only private industrialist in the area allowed to mine and process raw materials without having to go through the local authorities. He had struck a deal with them that the other, more conservative industrialists, would not. But it helped build his empire. Every day his trains brought hundreds of tons of freshly mined ores to the complex's huge separation plants, where the ores were refined and shaped into the materials of war. The surprising thing was that few beyond his militarist collaborators knew what the vast complex really was. Its war production was a carefully guarded secret—so secret, in fact, that unauthorized ships were not even allowed to approach its docks, let alone tie up there.

Konan and its vast extension were the materialization of a Noguchi dream. Although a small man, even by Japanese standards, he had made up for it with a fierce will and industrial acumen. Born in 1873, he had not come from a rich or powerful family, a handicap for anyone with his aspirations. Mitsui, Mitsubishi, Sumitomo, Yasuda were the giants of Japanese industry. They were huge conglomerates, not only of industry but of banking and finance as well. And because they had been so long in power, Japanese society was structured to keep others out.

But Noguchi was not to be denied. From an early age he had known what he wanted. Graduating from Tokyo University in 1896 with a degree in electrical engineering, he took a job with the Japanese branch of Siemens, the worldwide German firm specializing in industrial technology. He traveled around the world seeking new processes for the company. Two years after being hired, he got a rare chance to break out on his own. An Italian newspaper reported a way to manufacture nitrogen that was cheaper and less complicated than the old process. Fertilizer, vital to Japan's food supply, was one of the main products utilizing nitrogen. Noguchi recognized that the new method might revolutionize the industry. Through contacts he learned that Mitsui wanted the rights. He knew he had to act fast and had been saving his money for just such a chance. Without telling his German employer, he went to Italy and bought the patent. He beat Mitsui's representative by two days.

Mitsui, though angry, was also impressed, for Noguchi was only twenty-six years old. It decided to finance the young entrepreneur in his efforts to establish the process in Japan. His first company, the Japan Nitrogen Fertilizer Company, was formed in 1908. A year later, in 1909, he erected his first factory. It was at Minamata on Kyushu—across the bay from Nagasaki.

His rise was rapid. A loner, a self-made man, the sole person in control of his company, he didn't have a conservative board of directors to restrict him. In 1910 he erected another factory, this time in Osaka. In 1914 he built still another in Kumamoto. By 1919 electricity had become a costly item in his budget. It was needed not only to run machines but also to execute the processes. The nitrogen, for instance, was made by boiling other chemicals, a method which drew huge amounts of electricity. By the end of that year Noguchi had erected his first electrical power plant, at the same time buying rights to a new German process for manufacturing ammonia.

He now had a huge requirement for raw materials. Buying them was also eating into profits already diminished by the mounting debt he was incurring to his backers, the Mitsui and Mitsubishi banks. In 1920 he formed the Japan Mining Company, a step toward eliminating the problem. The same year he erected a second power plant, and three years later he constructed a huge chemical factory at Nobeoka.

Most of these sites were far south of the industrial centers around Tokyo. Noguchi was a man who liked privacy. Korea—darkly mountainous, sparsely populated, embracing ancient, little-known ways—now caught his eye.

After the Japanese won Korea from the Russians in 1905, they quickly set about exploiting it. Korean labor was cheap. New laws encouraged Japanese investment while excluding all others. The big industrial families saw the peninsula primarily as a rice bowl, a place to grow Japan's food. But not Noguchi. From the beginning he marveled over the potential for power that its rivers offered. He realized that once those rivers had been harnessed, they would provide more electricity than any comparable area in the Japanese Empire.

Konan, just a sleepy hamlet then, was the closest undeveloped settlement near the rivers, and the only one with a port. Noguchi arrived in 1923. By 1926 he had founded the Korean Hydro Electric Company and begun damming the Fusen.

Noguchi's plan was ambitious. The Fusen, as well as the Chosin, flowed northeast along a gentle gradient toward the upper reaches of the Yalu, away from Konan. He could have put power plants along that route, as well as along the Yalu (as he eventually did), and generated enough electricity for his needs. But he wanted much more. The slopes facing Konan were steep, dropping thousands of feet in only a short distance. Small runoff rivers from the Fusen and Chosin cascaded over them. He decided to dam the Fusen and Chosin at their highest suitable elevations and create mountaintop reservoirs. He would then dig tunnels from the reservoir bottoms to the runoff rivers at points just before they made their steep plunges. The effect would be like monster water tanks with drains to Niagara Falls. When the plug was pulled, the weight of the reservoir would force the water through the tunnels with tremendous pressure. The runoffs would become raging torrents, and the sheer drops they cascaded over would intensify them. There would be so much power available that he could easily put three and four generating plants along the route.

While his crews were blasting the tunnel from the Fusen, they discovered one of the richest magnesium veins in the world. Magnesium, a silvery white metal, was in great demand by the Japanese military, which was just then beginning to win control of the government and undertake a war of expansion through Asia. One of the lightest metals known, it was valuable for aircraft construction, and because in powder or strip form it ignited into a white-hot almost-impossible-to-extinguish flame, it was ideal for flares, tracers, and incendiary bombs.

Noguchi struck a deal with the army. He would supply the magnesium they wanted in return for a free rein in the conquered territories. Soon they discovered they had more than magnesium in common. Nitrate, the chief ingredient in fertilizer, was also the chief ingredient in explosives. Nitroglycerin, for instance, combined nitric acid and jellied fat. Three years after the magnesium discovery, the giant Korean Nitrogen Fertilizer Factory at Konan erected a munitions plant next door. As quickly as Noguchi could build them, munitions plants sprouted northward along the complex.

The security-conscious military decided to keep Konan a secret. It became a clandestine supply base, with fertilizer as a perfect cover. Economic reports talked only of nitrogen and rice paddies. Since economists seldom traveled to such a remote area, it was generally accepted that Japanese farms were among the most nitrogenized in the world. Very few Japanese knew what was going on at Konan.

Noguchi was happy to go along with this deception. By 1939, when war broke out in Europe, he sensed that he and Japan were set on an irreversible course. He had already started building the Yalu power stations, owned factories and mines in China and Manchuria, and had so expanded in Japan proper that he was now being called one of the select new *Zaibatsu,* the name reserved for the titan families of Japanese industry and commerce. He sincerely believed his rise was for the good of Japan, and he didn't want either his course, or Japan's, to be jeopardized.

His major fuel-producing plants were in the extreme north, near Russia and the rich Korean coalfields. The process they used was new: making gasoline from coal oil. Japan, more than any other country, was dependent on foreign oil. Noguchi was a key in the militarist plan to eliminate this dependence. His technique was the first to make gasoline synthetically, and he was constantly on the lookout for new processes.

One of the latest he had acquired was a new method of making heavy water. Thousands of gallons of H_2O were electrolyzed in huge tanks. The electrolysis burned off most of the hydrogen (H), and when only millimeters were left, it was nearly pure deuterium, present in water in the amount of about 1 part per 6,700. He was making it in both Korea and Japan.

Allied commandos would soon die in efforts to stop Nazi production of deuterium. Now Japan, Germany's partner in the war, was producing it, too. And the Allies did not know it.

4

The message was terse: "Come to Calais. Important matter to discuss." It was right after Pearl Harbor, and the recipient was Ángel Alcázar de Velasco, a press attaché in London's Spanish Embassy and one of Germany's best spies in England. He sensed that the "important matter" would have something to do with the Japanese. Alcázar de Velasco had passed information to the Nazis about Britain's largest Pacific warship, the battleship *Prince of Wales,* and it was hard to believe the information, which involved its position, had not played a part in Japan's sinking of the ship only a few days later.

He wadded up the message and destroyed it. That night, off Poole, approximately seventy-five miles southwest of London, he met the familiar rubber raft and was rowed out to the waiting German submarine, code-named Raphael. By dawn he was in a Calais hotel used as a headquarters by the occupying Nazis and was talking with his German intelligence chief.

"I don't know the particulars," the chief confirmed. "They'll have to tell you. But the Japanese want to put a spy ring in the United States and we've recommended you."

Alcázar de Velasco, a former bullfighter and adventurer, was certainly not unnerved by the prospect. He hated America, and he was due recognition of his past accomplishments, including two intelligence coups that had brought the praise of Hitler himself.

An original member of Spain's pro-Axis Falangist party and a graduate of the Abwehr's Berlin intelligence school, he had been sent from Madrid to London in the fall of 1940, following so-called neutral Spain's secret agreement to help the Germans against Britain. His fellow spies included Spaniards posing as journalists and diplomats; Welsh, Irish, and Scottish separatists; and a top-level informer in Winston Churchill's inner circle. With their aid he had been able to supply the Luftwaffe with the first and eagerly awaited confirmation that its bombers were truly hurting English cities. He had given the German Army the valuable news that it had almost destroyed the British at Dunkirk.

Alcázar de Velasco had only one reservation: "I'll have to clear it with my superiors in SIM [Spanish intelligence service]."

"We've already done that," replied the chief. "Go to Madrid, and the Japanese will contact you."

He did as he was told. So that no one would suspect anything unusual, he had been instructed to stay undercover at the house of his friend and mentor pro-Nazi Spanish Foreign Minister Ramón Serrano Súñer. Serrano Súñer, Francisco Franco's brother-in-law, was one of the most powerful men in Spain at the time. He was trying to steer Spain further into the Axis orbit.

Days passed in which Alcázar de Velasco heard nothing from the Japanese. He had been told it might be so. For a man like him, the confinement was acutely unpleasant. Although he might have been able to feed his thirst for esoteric knowledge in Serrano Súñer's extensive library, he did not enjoy inactivity.

Born in Mondéjar, Guadalajara, in 1900, he had acquired a taste for cloak-and-dagger episodes at the early age of seven. His village had been involved in a local squabble. Needing to get a secret message to one of their leaders in the mountains, villagers had lifted him onto a horse at night and sent him galloping. The horse died of exhaustion, but he got through. In reward, he had been given one and a half pesetas—twice the money a full-day laborer would get.

"Nobody had ever treated me like that before," he later recalled. "Deep down I realized this was to be my life."

By age twelve, he says, his nerves had been steeled enough to enable him to do what others around him most admired: to fight a bull. Although he was an amateur, he was cited for his style and daring. As soon as he could, he became a professional. By 1928 he was known as Our Young Gypsy of Madrid and was fighting in the most important bullrings in Spain. Not until an unlucky season in 1932 was he forced to give up the art. His chest and legs still bear the scars he received then.

As he grew older, he became more flamboyant. His hair flourished grandly from his head. His small dark eyes penetrated when he spoke, darted in seemingly clandestine awareness when he was silent. With classic Spanish machismo, he draped his coat over his shoulders as if it were a cape. Combined with his reputation from the ring, this flamboyance attracted admirers. Some were rich and powerful. They opened doors for him.

He had always had a sharp and probing mind. He had a thirst for knowledge, including knowledge about himself. With the money and influence he had acquired he entered the University of Salamanca and received a degree in letters and philosophy. He was to become an accomplished writer, author of articles and books. But the answers he found about himself were not the usual ones. They came mainly from the occult.

He became a supremacist, a calculating anti-Semite, a depender on astrology. The world, he decided, was destined to be ruled by an elite of reincarnated supermen, one of whom was he. Their chief obstacles were the Jews. (Curiously, in his beliefs, certain Jews were among the supermen—aberrations or karmic penalties in the reincarnations. This was how he explained why Jews always appeared to him to be in positions of power.) Omnisciently the planets directed the struggle. Satan, an Aryan messiah, and black magic became the catchwords of his beliefs.

Having quit bullfighting, he entered politics and became an original member of the Falange, the Spanish fascist party. The Falange preached empire and conquest and domination over the Latin world. Its central goal was restoration of the Spanish colonies, especially South America, Cuba, and the Philippines. Its members dreamed of the days of the Armada and hated Britain and the United States for having wrested from it its last vestiges of empire. "Spain's position as spiritual center of the Spanish world is her claim to preeminence in world affairs," proclaimed the Falangist literature which, as the party's first director of press and propaganda, Alcázar de Velasco helped write. "We demand the lands governed by our conquerors, which are nations baptized with famous Spanish names, names which the pirates cannot even pronounce."

It was a call to war.

In 1934, while working for the Falange, he met a German named Wilhelm Oberbiel, a director of the Hitler Youth and an official in the Abwehr. Oberbiel was a member of the führer's inner circle and deeply occultist. "In William I found all the knowledge I needed," Alcázar de Velasco wrote. "We discussed the serpent [the Jews] and how it was trying to make slaves of the world." Oberbiel ascribed his knowledge to the Abwehr, and Alcázar de Velasco asked him if he could become a member. He left for Berlin shortly thereafter.

Having graduated from the Abwehr's spy school, he returned to Spain during 1936, the prelude to the civil war. Describing that murderous summer in his award-winning book *The Spanish Civil War*, British historian Hugh Thomas writes that Alcázar de Velasco may have been one of the assassins of José Castillo, an anti-Falange socialist, and that Alcázar de Velasco was awarded the Falange's silver medal of valor for his part in the "victory." When General Franco seized power, he demanded that all Falangists transfer their allegiance from the party to himself. Alcázar de Velasco refused and he was sentenced to death.

When a break occurred at the prison, Alcázar de Velasco used it as an opportunity to get a reprieve. At great personal risk he locked the prison's gates, preventing most of the prisoners from escaping. He did this in part out of loyalty to the party, which by then had gone solidly over to Franco. When the generalissimo heard about it, he commuted Alcázar de Velasco's sentence. By the end of the civil war he was back in the reorganized Falange.

In 1940, with Germany locked in struggle with a desperate Britain and Spain officially neutral but unofficially helping the Nazis, Oberbiel asked Alcázar de Velasco to go to London. It was the return to adventure he had been seeking, and the Germans promised to pay him handsomely.

The plan called for him to work from within the Spanish Embassy. To get the needed diplomatic accreditation, he boldly approached Britain's special ambassador to Spain, Samuel Hoare. Britain knew Spain favored Germany and wanted to change its position. Hoare was aware of Alcázar de Velasco's earlier opposition to Franco. Alcázar de Velasco lied, telling him that if he could get a visa as Spanish press attaché he would secretly work to overthrow the Spanish dictator in favor of a pro-British government. Alcázar de Velasco's real boss, Spanish intelligence, aware of the trick from the beginning, readily arranged for the appointment.

Once in London, he worked feverishly setting up the espionage ring. He had access to the best Axis spies. Welsh, Irish, and Scottish separatists were mainly used for sabotage. When German bombers struck, they attacked surreptitiously from the ground. The British thought the added explosions had come from the air. It was a clever way of destroying targets planes could not hit.

It was nearly a week before the Japanese finally brought word to Alcázar de Velasco that they were ready to see him. He was told to go to the office of German intelligence in Madrid, a building disguised as a business. When he arrived, Yakichiro Suma, the Japanese minister to Spain, was there, smiling, with hand outstretched to greet him.

It had been only a short while since Suma, a tall career diplomat with a taste for art and a penchant for wearing cowboy hats at bullfights, had received a circular from Tokyo asking him to supply Japan with intelligence from Britain and the United States. "With the outbreak of war, [your post is] of increasing importance," the circular had said. He had replied, "To ask Spain to gather information of benefit to us would be a rather delicate matter . . . but I believe it could be managed if handled in the right way."

The minister, in Alcázar de Velasco's recollections of their first meeting, squeezed his hand and said something like "I want to compliment you on the job you've done for the Germans. I, of course, knew of your career in the bullring, and you certainly have matched that in these . . . shall we say . . . even more dangerous activities."

The two went to private chambers, where the minister did not mince his words. "We want you to work for *us* now. It may be harder, but I assure you we'll pay you well. . . ."

The spy expected as much. When it was his turn, he replied, "I'm honored, but I'll have to discuss it with my superiors."

He made a phone call. His superiors already knew about the deal. He returned with a "yes."

"I'll talk to Tokyo as soon as possible," said the obviously pleased Suma. They decided to conclude their meeting with a visit to a brothel. Brothels were practically the only places in Madrid at that time "you could be assured were not bugged," says Alcázar de Velasco.

Later Suma, who had been a consul general in China and chief of information at the Japanese Embassy in Washington, wired Tokyo that through the efforts of Serrano Súñer, he had met the man who was going "to help Japan out by planning the means of gathering intelligence reports from inside the United States." He is "one who will do anything on earth for his friends and those he likes; of strong character, but rather quixotic and hot-headed," the minister said of Alcázar de Velasco.

By that time his new spy was on his way to Berlin.

5

The army, sponsors of the program at the Rikken, was not the only military service interested in the uranium bomb. The Japanese Navy had been following developments in nuclear physics even longer than the army.

For one thing, the navy had an informative friend in Dr. Tsunesaburo Asada, the bright, relatively young (forty-one years old, when the Pacific war started) head of Osaka University's physics department. A 1924 graduate of Tokyo University he had returned from two years in Germany in the mid-1930s to begin, among his other activities, giving lectures at the Navy Technical Research Lab at Yokosuka. The lectures emphasized many of the latest scientific discoveries that the navy might use in war. From 1937 on Asada had emphasized the new discoveries in atomic physics to his navy audiences. He had urged development of both the bomb and atomic fuel. (Later Asada was a major figure in Japan's attempt to put a "death ray" in its skies. This was to be a kind of microwave shooter that would stop engines in flight. In addition, he developed Japan's proximity fuse, a device that enabled bombs and shells to detonate in the vicinity of a target, rather than only when hitting it. The fuse thus greatly increased a weapon's ability to do damage; America's version would help detonate the atomic bombs above Hiroshima and Nagasaki.)

In 1939 a rumor circulated that a turbine engine had been driven with atomic power in California—the rumor was false, but it caused a major stir. The navy was especially interested in atomic fuel. Its ships might be able to cruise indefinitely on it. Then, in 1940 or early 1941, a navy officer, Lieutenant Tutomu Murata, translated an article from a German technical journal that warned of an American "superbomb." The translation was widely circulated. With the U.S.

embargo on uranium shipments and its sudden silence on nuclear research, the navy was finally forced to act. Sometime in the summer or fall of 1941 the institute where Asada had been lecturing ordered Yoji Ito, a navy captain and a scientist, to look into the bomb's and fuel's feasibility.

Ito, an electronics expert who had just returned from Germany where he had been studying radar, was highly regarded. That was why he had been sent to Germany. In the book, entitled *The Entire Story of Secret Weapons,* which Itoh wrote after the war, he said he had already realized the importance of the "matter of uranium." So he cleared a space on his desk for nuclear weaponry.

His initial task was to interview experts. Among the first he visited was Sagane—probably on the advice of Asada. The Tokyo University professor told him the same thing he had told the army's Suzuki: The United States is probably building a bomb, so you had better build one, too. Sagane even seems to have advised Ito to start looking for sources of uranium; Japan, contrary to preliminary reports, probably did not have the quantity on the mainland needed to make a bomb or fuel, whereas America probably did. Ito next consulted Juichi Hino, another Tokyo University professor, who told him essentially the same thing.

Lieutenant Commander Kiyoyasu Sasaki, head of the institute's electrical research section, was also brought in; Ito's superiors thought he needed another man to help. Together the two wrote a report saying a "uranium engine" was feasible and that research into it might yield various other benefits, such as a new way to produce "luminous paint" and "artificial radium." They did not mention a bomb in the report, wrote Ito, because they had decided to look into that matter on a larger scale. Their bosses, the admirals, said Ito, did not want to state in writing their main interest. Of course, he wrote, it was the bomb.

The report led to the formation of a large "committee of experts" to consider the problem formally. It consisted of almost every noted nuclear physicist and electronics scientist in Japan, including Nagaoka, Sagane, Hino, Asada, his Osaka University colleague Seishi Kikuchi, who was also prominent in later radar and "death ray" research, and Nishina himself. There were eleven experts in all, and Nishina was made the committee's chairman.

The date of the committee's first meeting is in debate. *Imperial Tragedy,* written by Thomas M. Coffey and one of the very few books in English to touch on Japan's A-bomb project, states it was only a few weeks after Pearl Harbor. *The Day Man Lost,* written by the Pacific War Research Society, says it wasn't until July 8, 1942. Both books paint the same picture of the committee's first meeting.

Ito presided. A group of high-level navy officers were present. He reminded everyone of the need for secrecy and then asked for opinions from the experts. Asada said that since America could probably produce a uranium bomb, Japan ought to try for no other reason than self-defense. Nishina said the job would be difficult, but he believed it would be "worth trying." He is not reported to have told the navy that he was already working for the army on such a project. This is not surprising in view of the strong animosity between the two services. Even so, the navy quickly made it clear it did not want to work with the army, at least for the time being. Only if there was a need, said Ito, might they go to the army.

The problems involved in making the bomb were discussed. Kikuchi pointed out that finding enough uranium would be difficult. Nishina said he had several tons of uranium ore at the Rikken (undoubtedly what Iimori had brought back from Korea), and there were possibilities, he understood, of getting more from Korea. He added that he understood that in Shanghai the army had about 800 kilograms (1,760 pounds) of uranium oxide (not an ore, but the element itself) from South Africa. It might be available, he said.

Asada pointed out that even if they found enough uranium, they would still have to figure out how to enrich or separate enough U-235 to get an explosion. Then they'd have to develop a mechanism that would explode it in bomb form. A host of difficult calculations would have to be worked out in the meantime. Pressed for an answer on whether they could solve all these problems, Nishina said maybe, but warned the officers not to look for a quick solution. Unsure of details, he may have been waiting for Tamaki's report.

Germany, it was agreed, probably wouldn't be able to produce a bomb because of its expulsion of all its "Jewish scientists." But since most of those scientists had gone to the United States, America probably could. There were a lot of patriotic statements made about Japan and its scientists' ability to perform. Nishina, it is reported, was strangely silent.

Monthly meetings of the group continued for more than a year. At least ten were held. Little consensus developed. Some, like Kikuchi, who had pushed the project initially turned against it, saying that on second thought the problems were too great. Others, like

Nishina, grew more confident of eventual success—but not in time for the current war, which everyone expected to end quickly. Summarizing the committee's conclusions, Ito wrote, "Obviously it should be possible to make an atomic bomb. The question was whether or not the United States and England could really do this in time for this war, and whether or not Japan could do so ahead of them. . . . The general line of thought [was] that it would probably be difficult even for the United States to realize the application of atomic power during the war."

The report gave the impression that the navy wanted to withdraw from the project. Indeed, many of the scientists on the committee went home from the final adjournment in May 1943 believing that to be the case. In fact, the opposite was true. For even as the committee deliberated, the ordnance branch of its fleet command, the most powerful branch of the navy, secretly advanced money for a uranium bomb project to a scientist who was not part of the Physics Colloquium (as the committee came to be known) but was probably as well qualified as even Nishina to head it.

That scientist was Bunsaku Arakatsu, a personal friend and former pupil of Albert Einstein, who had theorized the great energy in the atom. Einstein's letter to Franklin D. Roosevelt had convinced the president to start the American project. Arakatsu was to become as important a figure as Nishina in the Japanese atomic bomb program. In fact, in the later years of the war he appears to have become more important than Nishina.

Born in 1890 and graduated from Kyoto University in 1918, Arakatsu had gone in 1926 to study physics at the University of Berlin. It was there that he studied under Einstein. "I often visited his house," Arakatsu wrote in a memoir. "He influenced me greatly in physics and in my way of thinking." Prior to going to Europe, he had written his thesis on Einstein's famous $E = MC^2$ theory—the formula that first theorized the incredible energy that could come out of the atom.

After a year in Berlin Arakatsu went to the Technische Hochschule in Zurich, Switzerland. Then, like Nishina, he went to Cambridge and Rutherford's Cavendish Laboratory. Returning to Japan, he could speak and write English and German.

Unlike Nishina, who was interested in many aspects of physics, Arakatsu seems to have focused almost exclusively on the atom's nucleus. In 1934, when the world's nuclear physicists had just begun to study what happened when an atomic nucleus was bombarded with atomic particles, Arakatsu constructed a particle accelerator from little more than a book and some scrap metal. Modeled after the Cockcroft-Walton machine, which later won a Nobel Prize for its inventors, it was Japan's first accelerator, an indispensable tool for studying nuclear physics. Realizing heavy water's value as a moderator, Arakatsu began manufacturing it the same year. This was only two years after Harold Urey had discovered the hydrogen isotope.

By 1936 Arakatsu was already disintegrating nuclei with his Cockcroft-Walton machine and making careful observations of what happened. He had a cloud chamber—one of the first in Japan—to observe the tracks of the various particles emitted in the disintegrations. Particle emission, specifically neutron emission, was at the heart of making the chain reaction.

With the discovery of uranium fission by Otto Hahn and Fritz Strassmann in 1938, many scientists, Arakatsu among them, zeroed in on the uranium nucleus. What was intriguing about it was that the uranium nucleus gave off the neutrons which in turn might produce the chain reaction—something that opened a whole new Pandora's box to the physicist and the world.

The basic problem at the time was that nobody knew precisely how many neutrons were emitted. Therefore, no one knew if the chain reaction would be self-sustaining or if because of the small number of neutrons coming out of each atom, it would simply fizzle before any appreciable energy was released.

Using his accelerator, Arakatsu began bombarding the uranium nucleus and finally arrived at an average figure of 2.6 neutrons given off each fission. It meant that an explosion probably was possible. It was as good a study as had been done anywhere and was published in the October 6, 1939, *Review of Physical Chemistry of Japan.* When the United States sat down to begin its own bomb-related calculations, Arakatsu's work was consulted.

In 1937 Arakatsu had been made a primary researcher in the Atomic Nucleus Subcommittee of Japan's Society for the Promotion of Scientific Research. The society was one of Japan's chief research funders, similar to the National Science Foundation in the United States. Nishina, a friend of Arakatsu's, was the head of the subcommittee.

Arakatsu's trademark, according to a friend, was a waist-length leather jacket. His handwriting was decorative and artistic, and he signed his name with great flourish. Perhaps it was this sort of showmanship, frowned upon by Japan's rigid scientific circles, that kept him from being asked to participate in the Physics Colloquium. But perhaps his absence was by design, for his accomplishments certainly had not gone unnoticed by the fleet command.

The navy first became aware of Arakatsu before the war with America began. He gave lectures at Kyoto University on fission and the possibility of making an atomic bomb. Matao Mitsui, then an officer with fleet ordnance, attended some of the lectures. Mitsui and his boss, Captain Megumu Iso, were aware of the growing possibilities of the bomb, and when Arakatsu published more on uranium fission—especially the April 1941 article "Photo-fission of Uranium and Thorium by Gamma-rays" (in the *Proceedings of the Physico-Mathematical Society of Japan)*—they passed the work along to their admirals in hopes of stirring up interest. It worked. Arakatsu became, in the fleet's eyes, the recognized Japanese expert in the field. Sometime in 1942, as the naval headquarters' experts' committee was convening, the fleet directed Iso and Mitsui to approach Arakatsu on the possibility of starting a secret project. Not even colloquium members were to know.

Arakatsu accepted. He was given approximately 6,000 yen ($1,500), three times as much as members of the colloquium. He was already deep into the theoretical work on producing a chain reaction. To aid him, he had a talented group of researchers, notably Hideki Yukawa, who in 1949 became the first Japanese ever awarded a Nobel Prize in physics. Since 1939 Yukawa had been calculating the energy of fission. He was one of the best theoretical physicists in the world, and Arakatsu could use him as he wished.

The Japanese Navy was still heady with Pacific victory when Arakatsu was first contacted. It had nearly destroyed the Americans at Pearl Harbor, and it ruled most of the ocean south of Japan. It told the Kyoto scientist to take his time. The war wouldn't last very long, said the admirals. He could work at his own pace.

But the army and navy victories were soon to end. By the time the experts' committee disbanded, the navy's priorities would be markedly changed.

6

$\mathbf{B}$erlin was alive with activity in early 1942. America's entry into the war and the realization that Britain was not going to be defeated easily had caused major shifts in Nazi planning. Alcázar de Velasco saw confusion wherever he looked. But it did not matter. He loved Germany. To him, it was the home of the strongest people on earth. Any change in plans would be only a minor diversion in the grand conquest he believed would eventually take place. He was happy to be a spy for them and now for the Japanese.

He had flown in from a Nazi airfield in southern France, near the town of Mont-de-Marsan, about 100 kilometers from the Spanish border. His first stop had been Abwehr headquarters to see old friends and receive instructions. His chief had then sent him to meet with a high-ranking officer at the Japanese Embassy.

Since the Russo-Japanese War of 1904–05 Japan had been intensifying its espionage efforts. By 1935 it had the most extensive spy network in the world. At its core were patriotic organizations, societies such as the Black Dragon, White Wolf, and the East Asia One-Culture Society. These groups were extensions of the Meiji era edict that every Japanese should be an agent of the homeland. As such, members worked with religious zeal. Pearl Harbor had been their crowning achievement.

But with the exception of Latin America, where a sizable number of Japanese agents had infiltrated, the espionage was concentrated in Asia and the Pacific. The Japanese had difficulty setting up effective networks in the West. Europe and America had Japanese agents, but they were in small, conspicuous groups, clustered around embassies, consulates, and "Japanese clubs," such as those in California and Oregon. Right after Pearl Harbor, large numbers of West Coast

Japanese were arrested and put in detention camps. The already limited operations were severely crippled. The Japanese officer, therefore, was most eager to receive Alcázar de Velasco. He needed the Spanish spy.

Alcázar de Velasco claimed not to remember the man's name but thought he was a general, responsible for all Japanese intelligence gathered on the United States and Britain in Europe.

The only general at the Japanese Embassy at that time appears to have been Baron Hiroshi Oshima, the ambassador. A lieutenant general, Oshima was pro-German and had been instrumental in getting signed the Tripartite Pact—the 1940 agreement that allied Japan to Germany and Italy. When the war started, one of his top priorities had been to set up an intelligence network. In years to come the plan was to backfire. Because of Magic, the United States was able to listen in on almost everything he sent back to Tokyo by radio. Much of the information used by the Allies to plan the Normandy invasion was gathered from Oshima's communications. He had toured the defenses and dutifully reported everything he saw. He was also involved in negotiations with the Germans to send uranium to Japan. After the war he was tried and convicted as a war criminal in Tokyo.

"We joked," Alcázar de Velasco said. "He poked my belly laughingly, saying I would not have enough stomach to commit hara-kiri if we lost the war." As a token of his appreciation the general gave him a gold pen which wrote in invisible ink. "It's just a present," he says the general told him. "Don't use it in your activities. It will call attention."

Then the uniformed host produced a questionnaire, which he said detailed what the Japanese wanted from him. They were interested in war factories, troop and supply bases, ships, convoys, airplanes, defenses, and future military actions; America's internal political situation; and English-language newspapers, including the *Wall Street Journal,* technical, scientific, and military journals, and such periodicals as *Time* and *Newsweek.*

Alcázar de Velasco could not or would not produce the questionnaire. (He told me he wants to include it in one of his own books.) But recently declassified U.S. documents include one said to have been surreptitiously obtained from one of his agents. It confirms Alcázar de Velasco's recollection: "In general, we are interested in any information or data concerning the United States referring to the following points. Location of factories devoted to the production of war materials. . . . Bases and ports of concentration for embarkation of troops and war material. . . . destination of . . . convoys, losses of units . . . debarkations. . . . Projects . . . foreseen for possible future action by the United States," and so on.

The officer was especially interested in scientific and technological developments. Alcázar de Velasco said one of the first pieces of valuable information he provided the Germans was that the Liberty ships which the United States was sending across the Atlantic to help Britain during the Battle of Britain, were badly made and would sometimes "split" and sink of their own accord, although America claimed they were being torpedoed.

They discussed the ships, he says, and then the officer made specific mention of one item on the list: information concerning U.S. work on "atomic fission."

Alcázar de Velasco said he had heard of atomic fission before that. The Germans had asked him to find out what progress Britain was making on it when he had first gone to London. He had not found out much, but he did not think it odd that the Japanese asked. "Everybody knew that Germany and England were working on it, so I thought in all probability, America was working on it, too." Furthermore, the Japanese told him that should he need help, they had a scientist contact in Chicago. They were, he stressed, very interested in America's progress.

Alcázar de Velasco did not know it at the time, but America had just committed itself to the most expensive atomic bomb program of all the countries entering the field. On December 6, 1941, one day before Pearl Harbor, President Roosevelt authorized funds for the creation of the Manhattan Project. Its primary research site would be Chicago, where Fermi would be trying to create a controlled nuclear reaction.

U.S. interest had begun in earnest in January 1939, when Niels Bohr, Nishina's good friend, arrived in America with news of the discovery of fission. U.S. scientists, many of them European refugees, immediately saw the possibility of the bomb and got Arakatsu's teacher, Albert Einstein, to write Roosevelt a warning that the Germans were probably ahead of America. The U.S. uranium embargo and journal censorship followed, as did the setting up of the Chicago lab.

"Where are you going to put your agents?" Alcázar de Velasco told me the general asked him.

"The big cities—the big centers of information."

He could have a "suicide squad" if he needed it, he says the general told him. "Just let us know when and where." The squad was to be used for sabotage.

"And we would appreciate it if you didn't give your information to anyone else, including the Germans."

"I'll have to give it to SIM."

"All right, but no one else."

As they were concluding the meeting, he said, the general asked him, "What shall we call the ring?"

According to Alcázar de Velasco, he looked at the door in front of him and said, "Why not 'Door—door to the West'?"

"TO," said the officer smilingly.

As soon as he could, Alcázar de Velasco left for London to formulate his plans. Back in his office in the Spanish Embassy, he took out his maps. "I drew circles around the cities I wanted to concentrate on." They included Los Angeles, San Francisco, Detroit, Houston, Philadelphia, New York, and Washington, D.C. He drew a heavy circle around Detroit. "I had information they were making some interesting machines there."

In his first act for the ring, he said, he dispatched several agents, including "a man from the Canary Islands" who was working for him in London. The agents proceeded to Central America by Spanish ship and then slipped into California by crossing over the Mexican border. When he received more money, he would send more agents, mainly Spaniards posing as journalists and diplomats, although he felt he eventually could buy a wide assortment.

Intelligence would be forwarded by shortwave either to Spanish ships off the coast of the United States or down to Chile, where, he said, the Japanese told him they wanted him to use the relay service of an Argentine military attaché named Juan Perón. He did not know the South American fascist who was to become Argentina's dictator in 1946 and would have preferred to use someone of his own choosing. But he went along.

From Chile or the Atlantic, the intelligence would be relayed to Madrid. If less urgent, it could be forwarded directly by mail, by telegram, or in the Spanish diplomatic pouch. The advantage of the pouch was that international law forbade its being opened by other countries. But he knew the pouches were oftentimes surreptitiously opened, so all intelligence would still have to be coded or written in invisible ink, or both. In England he used every technique of communication, including special courier when the information was vital.

His rabbit farm on the edge of Madrid's Barajas Airport or his apartment in the middle of the city would be the collection point for the relayed intelligence. Some of the cages at the farm concealed transmitters and receivers. The intelligence would be taken first to SIM, possibly to the Germans, and then to the Japanese, who would send it on to Tokyo. He had several addresses, including his own, Conde Xiquena 4, for the mail and telegrams. Information sent by the diplomatic pouch could be handled directly by SIM. The key to his codes would be his Madrid telephone number, 29824. Franco, he says, was to be kept abreast of everything.

He was engrossed in this planning when he received an emergency message from Madrid: "They've broken into your apartment. Get out while you can."

The British had suspected him of spying since his 1940 intelligence coup about their losses at Dunkirk. He had eluded their probing so far. Now, in an effort to confirm their suspicions, British agents had broken into his home and found proof. Luckily for him, Spanish intelligence had found out in time. He fled for his life. "They were checking all the seashores for me," he wrote in 1962.

Safe in Calais, he met again with the Japanese. This time it was with a new officer, he said, and the man gave him a code name, X27Z —a change from Guillermo, which was what the Abwehr called him. The officer told him he had to take the plans back to Berlin for approval. Alcázar de Velasco took the opportunity to enjoy some French night life with the Germans. In three days the officer returned.

"They liked them," the officer informed him. But Alcázar de Velasco remembered being told "not to worry too much about the Northeast—concentrate on the West." Find out about the U.S. atomic project, his superiors reiterated, but also find out about everything else. "In intelligence you must report everything, even what you don't understand." He had left his London ring in the hands of a colleague. He promised the new officer the Japanese would receive intelligence from London, too.

Going back to Madrid, which was for the time being his headquarters, he got word that one of the agents he sent to California had been injured in a car wreck and would be hospitalized for ten days. "It was a good sign," he commented. "In the past, when things had started out well, they usually had ended badly."

What he did not know was that in discovering him, the British had infiltrated the German ring he had left in London. Confidently, then, he began planning his next major move: a secret trip to the United States.

PART

⊡

TWO

7

Whatever Nishina's attitude had been before Pearl Harbor, he quickly decided afterward to back his country's gamble to the hilt. "We are in it now, and it can't be helped," he told his new secretary, Sumi Yokoyama. "If we work hard and fight hard, who can say what might happen? In any case, however we may feel, we must all do our best for our country." He may have been a scientist with many friends outside Japan and inclined more toward peace than war, but as one of his sons said decades later, he was also a "Meiji-man," one of those brought up in the era when every Japanese was taught that it was his sacred duty to serve his country—even to die for it, if need be. Personal feelings and desires were secondary to such men.

But being a Meiji-man did not prevent Nishina from venturing an expert opinion. Several times during the first months of the war, when, because of nonstop Japanese victories, there was little pressure on him to produce the bomb, he is said to have questioned military leaders on the use of money for development of atomic energy— essentially a gamble—when the money might be put to better and more immediate use by helping troops in the field. He was assured that even if it wasn't ready for the current war, it would be needed in the future.

However, by the fall of 1942 Japan had been stopped at the Coral Sea and defeated at Midway and Guadalcanal. Although the Japanese people at large were given no hint of the turnaround, their leaders began talking in secret about a longer war than they had expected. The idea of using an atomic bomb in the nearer future grew. Accordingly they began to pressure Nishina to step up his efforts.

In August 1942, about the time the situation at Guadalcanal was worsening, Nishina, according to reports received by General Douglas MacArthur after the war, was informed that his project was being taken over by the army air force headquarters. General Yasuda had moved there and been promoted to air force chief. In conjunction, Nishina was to be given an additional large sum of money to increase his efforts—500,000 yen, or about $125,000. Although he'd already been keeping the army project secret from the navy (by then he was chairing deliberations of its committee of experts), the army project was now officially to become top secret. Whereas before, he had been loosely affiliated with the Sixth Army Technical Lab, a chemical lab, now he was to get priority assistance from the Eighth Army Technical Lab, which was strictly munitions and therefore more pertinent. In addition, Nishina was to pick ten young men from the universities to bolster the staff already working on the project. Each young man was to be given a deferment—additional evidence of the project's growing importance.

Nishina did not like the secrecy. Once the war had begun, he became a leader in trying to organize Japanese science for the war effort. He chaired several committees involving scientists and government and military leaders. Their purpose was to promote coordination for the war effort. But none of them would ever break through the military obstinance. The competition between the services was intense, occasionally violent. Sometimes the scientists conferred with each other despite the difficulties. But ultimately there was no way of telling what efforts were being duplicated or how much important information was lost to a project because the head of a similar one would, or could, not share.

One of Nishina's first new recruits under the deferment allotment was Kunihiko Kigoshi, a twenty-three-year-old chemist. (He later became a world-recognized scientist holding a chemistry chair at Tokyo's Gakushuin University.) In October 1942 his chief recommendations were good grades and a graduate thesis on the then new and exciting topic of the products of uranium fission.

Because Kigoshi wanted to pursue chemistry, he really didn't want to join physicist Nishina. But Nishina told him he needed somebody to produce the uranium gas that would be required for the separation work. Kigoshi had already received his induction papers, had reported to the induction center, and was eating dinner in the mess hall when he was told he was going back to Tokyo as a Rikken chemist. By that time, noting the harsh military life he was about to enter, he was glad Nishina had "requisitioned" him, he said.

Another man who joined the project at this time was Masa Takeuchi, who was thirty-two and had worked with Nishina since 1931, when he had been graduated with a degree in chemistry from what today is Tokyo Engineering College. Nishina and Takeuchi had worked on X ray and cosmic ray experiments, and Nishina, who at that time had just returned from Europe and was building his staff, had grown to depend on Takeuchi. While tracking cosmic rays with the Rikken's new cloud chamber, Takeuchi had been the first to get a photograph of Yukawa's elusive but predicted atomic particle, the meson. As such, he had gained a measure of distinction. But he was surprised to be asked by Nishina to join the project. His job was to head the important effort of separating the U-235 isotope from natural uranium. He had never done that kind of work before.

In 1980 as a professor at Yokohama University, Takeuchi wrote of his participation in the project. He said he had no idea Nishina was working on an atomic bomb until December 8, 1942, when the physicist called him and several others in for a meeting and laid out the situation. Nishina told them they had a job to do for their country and the project was part of it. "I was surprised," he said, but "excited." He recalled that just the day before, the first anniversary of the attack on Pearl Harbor, Nishina had called on everyone in the lab to do his "patriotic duty." This now would be the way Takeuchi would do his. His only reservation was that he felt he had got the job by a process of elimination. Others, he noted, were not as keen to participate, asking to be excused so they could continue with their own projects. Nishina had excused those who seemed to have valid work under way which they could not leave. He didn't seem to care if the project was war-related, said Kigoshi, who also attended the meeting, just that it was important.

But Takeuchi didn't dwell on what he observed. "I was young and happy to be participating." He and Kigoshi were to be among the most important researchers in the project, which included, or soon would include, the following others: Tamaki, who was close to finishing, or had already finished, his report; Yazaki, who headed Nishina's cyclotron group; and some of those under him, including Fumio Yamazaki, Asao Sugimoto, and Eizo Tajima, a neutron specialist. Kigoshi's teacher, Kenjiro Kimura, and another Kimura

(Motoharu), also a neutron specialist, were to play key parts. So would Toshio Amaki, who worked on the critical mass, and Shinichiro Tomonaga, who, after the war, became the second Japanese in history (after Yukawa) to win the Nobel Prize. These men, when Nishina was dead, became the scientific leaders of their country. Backing them up were to be twenty or thirty others and anyone else in Japan whom they saw fit to consult.

They were lagging behind America. No question about that. America by this time had thousands working on the project, and only six days prior to the first meeting Takeuchi attended, Fermi had created the first atomic reaction at Chicago. With that successful experiment, the United States became ready to move from theory to execution.

But Nishina's project was moving ahead too. By the first of the new year, 1943, Takeuchi had been told to come up with a method of separation. Kigoshi was starting to work on the uranium gas and on making pure uranium metal out of the gas, which was the form the eventual critical mass would have to take. Tajima had begun planning a reactor, just as Fermi had done for America across the ocean.

Tamaki was put in charge of the theory group. It would be doing the numerous calculations that would crop up. The project had yet to establish exactly what the size of the critical mass would be. For one thing, it would depend on the amount of separation or enrichment Takeuchi could make. Takeuchi was now center stage.

8

Separation of atomic isotopes was in its infancy when Takeuchi was assigned to head Nishina's effort to separate U-235. Isotopes—atomic nuclei chemically the same as their hosts, but atomically different—had been discovered only half a century before. Not much practical use for them had been found. Takeuchi, therefore, did not have a great deal of information with which to start.

But he had Nishina's library: the American *Physical Review* and the main physics and chemistry publications from Britain, Germany, and France. The lab subscribed to approximately ten such foreign publications. And although because of the war, they had stopped arriving through regular channels, Nishina still received them from his government, which was getting them directly from Germany and indirectly from its spies in the West.

The journals contained much pertinent information. For instance, they reported the American success in 1939 at separating small quantities of U-235. There was, therefore, no question that the job could be done. But how? Out of the methods so far developed, which would be the best? It had already been decided that because the Japanese researchers lacked extensive facilities and resources, they would attempt to develop only one. Theirs was only a pilot program.

By the first of the new year Takeuchi was deep in research of the problem. The journals had been his starting point, but he also had help at home. Isotope separation was being conducted in Japan for the making of heavy water. But that was made by electrolyzing water, and uranium was a metal, not a liquid. Thus the separation was going to have to be effected, Takeuchi learned, by changing the metal into a gas, as had been done in America. It could then be manipulated.

Most of the isotope separation methods using gas so far depended on the differences in atomic weight between the isotopes and the ordinary atoms in the host. Atomic weight was determined by the number of particles in the nucleus. Uranium 238 had 238 particles in its nucleus and therefore was heavier than U-235, which had 235. This difference in weight would make the atoms act differently in various situations, most of which (such as vaporizations) could be created in the laboratory.

For instance, the American separation success in 1939 had been by mass spectograph. This method employed a large apparatus in which uranium gas, shooting out in a jet stream, was electrified until it became highly charged, or ionized. The enclosed beam of ionized particles was directed into an electromagnetic field. Since the heavier U-238 atoms contained, by definition, more charged particles than the lighter U-235 atoms, and since greater charge meant greater attraction, the U-238 atoms would break off from the beam, forming a separate beam closer to the magnet. This, in turn, would leave the U-235 atoms by themselves in the original beam.

This was a good method, and Takeuchi was attracted to it. But another Japanese physicist, Goro Miyamoto, an affiliate at the Rikken who was working for Sagane at Tokyo University, had already begun experimenting with it. Takeuchi decided that he had best leave it to Miyamoto, not only because he had already initiated the project but also because he felt there might be major difficulties in making and sustaining the ion source, which he felt would be an extremely difficult part of the apparatus to construct.

The Rikken could convert its cyclotron into a mass spectrograph. America had already done that with one of its cyclotrons. Sagane's teacher Lawrence was already producing about a tenth of an ounce of U-235 per day with his cyclotron at Berkeley. This may have been why Miyamoto, under the tutelage of Sagane, had decided to pursue the method. But the Rikken had only one operational cyclotron and another on the way. It needed both for other purposes, including many of the experiments having to do with atomic energy. After a conference at Nishina's house on January 4, Nishina and Takeuchi decided not to make the conversion.

They also considered separation by centrifuge and gaseous diffusion. America eventually used both of these methods too. But both seemed too complicated for Takeuchi, who felt they would require too much time, effort, and money. The centrifuge process required the construction of a huge, covered rotor that spun the uranium gas so fast that the heavier atoms separated to the outside. Gaseous diffusion employed a porous barrier at the top of the separator. It had holes so tiny that more of the smaller U-235 atoms, spurred by pressure from below, would pass through than would the larger U-238 atoms.

But uranium gas, a foul green substance that can eat through almost any metal, was so corrosive, and the differences in the relative sizes of the two atoms were so small, that inevitably, after only a little bit of separation, the tiny pores in the barrier would corrode and widen enough for the larger U-238 atoms to start coming through. That meant that one had to switch what little enriched gas had accumulated to a new separator, pump in new unenriched gas, and start over again. That, in turn, meant lots of separators—acres and acres of them. The required operation, called cascades, would be too large for their pilot project.

What the Nishina group finally did settle on was a process called thermal diffusion. This had been one of the first isotope separation processes devised. But until it was perfected by two German scientists, Klaus Clusius and Gerhard Dickel, in 1938, it had not been practical. Stated simply, thermal diffusion relied on the fact that light gas moves toward heat. Clusius and Dickel constructed a simple device consisting chiefly of two metal tubes placed one inside the other. The inner tube was heated; the outer tube was cooled. When the apparatus was turned on, the lighter U-235 moved to the heat wall; the U-238, to the cold wall. Convex currents created by this movement sent the U-235 upward; the U-238, downward. The result was something like a heated house in winter: hot air rising; cold air staying at the bottom. At a certain point the U-235 at the top could be collected, and new gas pumped in. It was a simple and rapid way to get relatively large concentrations of U-235.

Not only had this method been developed in Germany, meaning easy access to detailed information about it, but it was also being used by an assistant of Kikuchi's at Osaka University. This meant that Takeuchi could probably get some firsthand knowledge of the process. Eiichi Takeda, an isotope specialist, had been using thermal diffusion to separate isotopes in chlorine and other elements—not uranium, however. But he had built a Clusius tube and coauthored two papers on the process which had been published in the August 1941 *Proceedings of the Physico-Mathematical Society of Japan.* Takeda said he would help Takeuchi in any way he could.

In mid-March the Nishina project members formally ratified

Takeuchi's choice. By the next month two events had thrown the project into a higher gear. First, Tamaki's long-awaited report was forwarded to General Yasuda. It said, according to Suzuki and others, that production of an atomic weapon was indeed possible, that an explosion of 1 kilogram (2.2 pounds) of pure U-235 would equal that made by 18,000 tons of gunpowder, and that thermal diffusion was a viable method for the army project to use for separation.

The report could not have come at a more opportune time. Yasuda's planes were being shot out of the skies on almost all battle-fronts. Before, Yasuda had only *wanted* an atomic bomb; now he *needed* it.

The other development, according to General Toranosuke Kawashima, later called the General Groves of the Japanese project (after General Leslie Groves, who headed the Manhattan Project), was that Premier Tojo himself received word of the enemy's atomic bomb advancement and ordered Japan to keep pace.

"I think it was the beginning of '43," Kawashima recalled for the writers of *The Emperor in the Showa Era*. "Tojo suddenly called me. I went to his office in the Army department [Tojo served also as minister of war]. He said, 'The atomic bomb projects of the U.S. and Germany are progressing. If we are behind, we will lose the war. You start to make it.' This was the first I ever heard of an atomic bomb. But I was just a colonel at the time, so I said yes and went to talk with Yasuda."

Exactly what Tojo had learned, or from whom, is not known. But at the time he was telling Kawashima to upgrade Japan's program, an officer in another army department was asking if uranium could "explode" underwater, presumably because new incoming information had posed the strange question. According to a document marked "Top Secret" and published in *The Comprehensive History of Japanese Science and Technology*, a 1970 multivolume work by the Japan History of Science Academy, Yuzuru Chikamatsu, chief of the Eighth Army Technical Lab, answered a query from Lieutenant Colonel Niimi of the Army Weapons Administration Headquarters, to the effect that uranium would not "explode" if put in "cold water." The document is dated April 17, 1943.

General Yasuda's aide Lieutenant Colonel Suzuki said that he heard after the war that the War Ministry had received information that "America was planning 'to make an epochal weapon from uranium and water." Puzzled by the "water" reference, the ministry went to the Eighth Army Technical Lab and was told "uranium and water would only make uranium oxide." Niimi, wrote Suzuki, then dropped the matter. Suzuki concluded: "However, the information was in fact very crucial, implying that a nuclear reactor could be made from uranium and heavy water. . . . At that time, the study of the production of an atomic bomb was already under way at the army air headquarters, and thus, had the information been conveyed to the army air headquarters, instead of the weapons administration headquarters, it would have been extremely useful."

Nishina was well aware of the use of water as a moderator. He had already discarded it for the much better heavy water. The fact that he was not consulted was perhaps one of the first crucial mistakes that the Japanese leaders made in their program. Nevertheless, Tojo's order was enough to stir things up again. Even though he had never heard of the atomic bomb before, Kawashima, after being briefed by Yasuda, went directly to the Rikken to see Nishina.

He brought with him important news: As of that date, the project was being further upgraded. Whereas Nishina had been given 500,000 yen the previous year, he was now to be given 700,000, with even more to be allocated later. His project was also now to get a letter designation: NI. The letters meant "Nishina—Large Bomb," and receiving them meant the project had moved to the top echelon of priorities. Seven young army officers were to be assigned to the lab to help him. They would be especially useful in cutting red tape. An entire new building to house the project was to be erected at the Rikken. It would be ready in several months and was to be called Building 49.

The most important new development, however, Kawashima told Nishina, was that unlike all other scientific projects initiated by the army air force, which were always administered through army labs, NI was to be controlled directly by air force headquarters. He and Hatsuzo Taniguchi, another high-ranking air force officer, were going to take charge of it personally. Pointing out the significance of the moves, Suzuki later wrote that "this was the only direct research of the Air Force during the war." Kawashima said they were proceeding in this unusual way to assure the project's secrecy and speed.

As direct liaison between Nishina and air force headquarters Kawashima appointed Colonel Mitsuo Arimura, head of the air force's technical section. Helping Arimura would be Lieutenant Colonel Kenji Koyama, also of the technical section. Koyama would actually visit Nishina on a day-to-day basis, seeing that everything he wanted was taken care of.

Nishina, as far as accounts now available suggest, had only two notable responses to Kawashima's news: He was not sure which would come first: atomic power or the bomb. And he told the general, "Get me more uranium!"

9

Since he had begun the army project, Nishina had been getting uranium. How much, and from where, are not clear. Before the war he had obtained 1 kilogram (2.2 pounds) of the fissionable material from either England or Germany. This would have been enough for his early experiments. But it would not have been enough to carry out the work projected for 1943. For that he would have had to have found much larger amounts. To get these larger amounts, he first went to Satoyasu Iimori, the Rikken's chief geologist.

Iimori was a long shot. Prior to the war, uranium was not a common commodity. There simply was very little use for it. Asian potters sometimes used it to get rich yellows and blacks in their ceramics, as we have already noted, and physicists used tiny amounts in experiments. It was also sometimes used in film emulsion. But these uses promised little profit for suppliers, and consequently, very little prospecting for it had been conducted.

But Iimori had a surprise. In the 1920s and 1930s, wanting to continue the studies in radiochemistry he had begun at Oxford, he spent many years looking for deposits of radium-containing ores. Uranium was one of those. He therefore told Nishina, according to an interview I had with him in 1980, that he had several possible source locations, the first of which was, happily, not more than 100 miles east of Tokyo.

While prospecting in 1936 in Fukushima Prefecture, he had found a mine that was full of "heavy elements." It was near the town of Ishikawa. The year before, 1935, he had also brought back from Korea some fifty tons of black sands, an ore which contained small amounts of uranium. It had already been refined.

In addition, he told Nishina, in Malaya, which had fallen in the first days of the war, there was a large amount of tin-ore residue, called *aman* by the natives. It contained uranium-bearing monazite and zircon. The British had left it. The *aman* was being shipped to Japan, and he had been promised some.

Nishina would have preferred that Iimori knew of veins of pitchblende and uraninite, which were "primary" sources of uranium, sometimes yielding up to 85 percent of the fissionable element. But he was well aware of the scarcity of such veins. Only three or four were commonly known to exist in the world. The Americans had access to some at Great Bear Lake, Canada. Perhaps the richest veins were in the Belgian Congo. And the Germans now had the so-called Curie stocks, named for Madame Curie, who had first used them at Joachimsthal (Jáchymor), Czechoslovakia.

By the beginning of 1943 approximately 5,000 tons of the *aman* reached Tokyo from Malaya by tanker, and Iimori, with the help of the Rikken's refinery, had produced from it, and from the other ores he had there, between 2 and 25 pounds of uranium oxide shaped into little disks. (He can't remember the exact quantity; various amounts are cited in the sources.) The disks were called yellow cake. They looked like "Japanese rice crackers," he recalls. They were put in bottles and eventually delivered to Kigoshi, who was responsible for making the uranium gas for Takeuchi's separator. That done, Nishina went to Fukushima to begin work on the Ishikawite ores. There he ran into problems.

What these were is not clear. Much later, according to documents, the Ishikawite mines were still being counted on to provide ores with up to 20 percent uranium content. Perhaps the excavation bogged down. Perhaps there just was not a lot of this medium-grade ore. Whatever the reason, Nishina gave up on it and then the Malayan ores stopped arriving. The tankers carrying them could not get through the growing net of American submarines south of Japan. The ore was ending up on the bottom of the Pacific.

At about this time, early 1943, Kawashima from army air force headquarters came to the Rikken with news that the project, on Tojo's orders, had been given higher priority. "I didn't know much about uranium or its bomb," the officer was quoted as saying in *Showa* in reaction to Nishina's request to find him more of the element. "So I thought it would be easy."

He soon found out differently.

Nishina told him the Ishikawite ores were "sparse" and of low quality. Checks in Japanese factories turned up little uranium. Then

Nishina told him that Iimori believed there was a lot of it in Korea and that he himself knew that uranium is often associated with gold, and there were many gold mines in Korea. One mine in particular was mentioned: Kikune. It was near Seoul, in the middle of the peninsula. Kawashima, several of his officer aides, and Otokichi Nagashima, Iimori's chief assistant, left for Korea immediately.

The mine, located near the thirty-eighth parallel (not a political distinction at that time), was closed when the party arrived. Kawashima went to the general in charge, Junjiro Ihara, who balked at opening the mine. Kawashima then took a chance. Even though NI was top secret, he told Ihara why they needed the mine open. Ihara said he would still have to get clearance from Korea's governor-general, Kuniaki Koiso. Kawashima went with him. They did not tell Koiso about NI, Kawashima said in *Showa*. But the mine was opened.

It was in the middle of a rice field, Kawashima recalls. He quickly organized some workers. They dug out a sizable sample and washed it. When he saw how small the emerging pieces of uranium were, he says, "I wanted to cry." The main uranium ore in the mine was fergusonite, a brownish black mineral that has about 8 percent uranium content. But the mine's production returned only about 4 to 5 percent fergusonite. That meant it was going to take a lot of digging to get what they needed: a minimum two tons of uranium, Nishina had told Kawashima before he had left. The headquarters officer decided he had better find alternative sources.

Nagashima was left in Korea to supervise Kikune and continue to search the peninsula for more productive mines. Kawashima went back to Tokyo. As soon as he could, he issued an order to all commanders in the empire. It was short: "Find uranium!" For a while the response seemed promising. A message from Manchuria said it had a "uranium mine" and already had "3 to 5 tons" of "unrefined" ore ready to ship. He radioed back, "Send it right away." But nothing came, says Kawashima.

Kawashima next went to General Reikichi Tada, chairman of the Board of Technology, one of the major government organizations supervising scientific research for the war. Among Tada's specialties were minerals. He had been the officer through whom Iimori had received the tin ores from Malaya. In conjunction with the government's project to develop radar, he had already been searching the empire for rare elements needed in vacuum tubes. He told Kawashima he would put uranium on his list. Search parties went out.

The quest was considered so important that Kawashima was given his own private airplane, a large Mitsubishi transport. Where he went is not known. But documents indicate search parties of one kind or another were seen in Korea and throughout Southeast Asia, including Burma. During this time Kawashima heard at the Rikken that the Czechoslovakian Curie stocks were in Nazi hands. He decided to take a bold and dangerous step.

For at least six months, because the sea-lanes had become so treacherous for the Axis, Tokyo and Berlin had been talking about sending courier flights, possibly with cargo, between Germany and Japan. The air route was to extend across the underbelly of Asia, roughly on the southern borders of China and the Soviet Union, originating or ending in Berlin or Singapore. Most of that territory skirted enemy-held land. Since Kawashima was in air force headquarters, he knew of the plan and decided to make use of it. He would ask the Germans to send them some uranium, but without telling them its purpose.

Not only was this risky from a security standpoint, but Kawashima should have had reservations about whether it was practical. Although Germany and Japan were allies, racial differences and feelings of superiority on both sides hampered cooperation. In comparison with the close relationship that Britain and the United States enjoyed (although not without its own prejudices), contact between the Axis partners was often stiff and formal.

Nevertheless, on July 7, 1943, using the army's secret wire, Kawashima radioed Ambassador Oshima in Berlin: "Please make an immediate investigation of the possibilities of exporting to Japan pitchblende from Czechoslovakia." Recently released Magic interceptions of this wire by the U.S. National Security Agency are garbled. But the message ended: "Please send this information and as large an amount of samples as you can on the plane."

The air courier plan, however, was abandoned. Test flights were failures. Air attacks, antiaircraft guns, and treacherous weather, caused mainly by mountains along the route, sabotaged them. A month and a half later, however, on August 24, Kawashima again radioed Berlin. "It is urgent that we get some pitchblende for research purposes. If you can't get the ore, get some of the leavings from the refining of radium. Start negotiations for this again." He now planned to use submarines.

Concurrent with the air route scheme there existed a rather more realistic plan to send submarines fitted for cargo between the two countries. Japan had been using cargo submarines in the Pacific since 1942. They were safer than tankers in enemy-controlled waters. Soon the Germans endorsed the idea. Both countries needed commodities the other had. Germany wanted rubber, tin, tungsten, copper, opium, coconut oil, and gold from the Japanese. The Japanese wanted German aluminum, mercury, machine tools, ball bearings, and precision instruments. Previously they had used raiders, stripped-down and souped-up surface vessels. But growing Allied control of the world's airspace and oceans was making that breed impractical.

The sub route was also dangerous, but at least it was hidden. It began in the North Sea, usually Kiel, a major German naval base. The boats sneaked through the English Channel into the Atlantic, headed south past Spain and Africa, and made the turn east south of the Cape of Good Hope. British sub-killing airplanes were thick in the skies off eastern Africa, but if the submarines made it into the interior of the Indian Ocean, they were probably safe. A base to receive them at the lower edge of the Pacific had been set up at Penang, Malaya. Crews of German U-boat administrative officers and maintenance specialists had been sent there to man it.

Ironically, the officer to whom Oshima detailed the job of getting the pitchblende from the Germans was Major Yascazo Kigoshi. His brother, Kunihiko Kigoshi, was the chemist Nishina had saved from the draft to make the uranium gas. It was Kunihiko who would first have need of uranium. But because of the security surrounding the project, neither brother knew the other was involved until after the war.

Yascazo Kigoshi, a technical specialist with the Japanese contingent in Berlin, was a metallurgist. In a 1980 interview, he told me that at first the German Ministry of Economics was uncooperative. "When I met the bureau chief, he asked me for what purpose was the ore to be used. I didn't know." He cabled Tokyo for an answer.

When Kawashima received the wire, he was stumped. Not being a chemist, he had no idea what to tell the Germans. He gave the problem to Nishina, who gave it to Kunihiko Kigoshi. "We did not want to tell them we were working on an A-bomb, so it took me a long time to think of an answer," said the chemist, who also spoke with me in 1980. On November 15 the Berlin Embassy received the following secret wire: "Uranium oxide is used as a catalyst in the manufacture of butanol." The pitchblende was ostensibly to speed the chemical reactions involved in the making of industrial alcohol.

When Yascazo Kigoshi, unaware that the reply was a lie and that his own brother had made it up, presented the cable to the ministry chief, the German, he says, looked at him incredulously. "He said, 'In Germany we don't use it for that purpose.' I don't think he believed me."

The Germans, of course, were also working on nuclear energy. But a chief in the Economics Ministry may not have known that. The project, like America's and Japan's, was top secret. On the other hand, he may have known something of uranium's primary worth.

Kawashima reported that he eventually got back an answer that the Germans would not send the ore. "So because of my nature, I got very angry and I sent a telegram to the German government by myself. I told them, 'The reason we need pitchblende is for the development of atomic power. We are now under the Tripartite Pact [the Axis] and we are both fighting against America and England. So what is going on here that you don't want to cooperate?' Either my telegram was good or Oshima talked to Hitler directly. . . . They answered that they would give us two tons."

Yascazo Kigoshi told me that the ministry finally agreed to send two tons with the stipulation that if the pitchblende really were to be used as a catalyst, they would receive a report about it.

The first shipment, one ton of Joachimsthal pitchblende, was loaded aboard a submarine at Kiel and left sometime shortly thereafter, according to both Kawashima and Yascazo Kigoshi. Whether or not it made it to Japan is not known. Both men say they heard the submarine was sunk en route. But Yoichi Yamamoto, an army major involved in the project in its later stages, wrote—and told me in a 1980 interview—that portions arrived.

In any case, Nishina had enough uranium in 1944 and 1945 to continue his pilot experiments.

10

Ever since Kunihiko Kigoshi began work for Dr. Nishina in late 1942, he had been having trouble. It was no easy task making uranium hexafluoride.

The choice of U-hexafluoride for Takeuchi's separator was not the problem. It was a good choice: crystalline solid that, with a little heat, would easily convert into a gas, more easily than any other uranium solid. Moreover, the fluorine, the gas which was one-half the compound, had no isotopes; that meant it would not interfere with the separation process. (The United States had made the same choice for its separation operation.) But U-hexafluoride, like uranium itself, was so little used at that time that few had any experience making it. In fact, Kigoshi did not even know how to make fluorine, the most corrosive, reactive gas known.

Kigoshi could have gone to the army's poison gas laboratory and probably got some fluorine. But he decided against that for security reasons. Supply, which had been ordered to cooperate with NI, did not have any. He decided to make it himself. All he had were textbooks, which said plainly that one made fluorine by electrolyzing potassium fluoride. Potassium fluoride, a soldering aid, was available. Kigoshi and his newly assigned assistant, Takehiko Ishiwatari, who previously had been working with Yazaki and Nishina on uranium fission, built a special tank and began the process. But no fluorine emerged.

They read and reread the instructions. Each night they turned out the lights and locked up the lab, shaking their heads in frustration. Several weeks later Nishina called them in and scolded them for having failed to make progress.

Kigoshi finally decided he would have to do something rash. There were two professors at Tohoku University, Fusao Ishikawa and Eizo

Kanda, who he knew had made fluorine—the only such two in Japan. Because of security, he had not yet checked with them. Now he made the trip to Sendai.

By a lucky coincidence he arrived the morning after Ishikawa had made a batch of the gas and was lecturing his students on it. "He opened the lecture by stating that the only reason he had the fluorine this day was that he turned the switch on the night before. Suddenly I understood what I had done wrong. A very long time was required to generate the fluorine gas—24 hours." His mistake, Kigoshi realized, had been turning the electricity off at night when he went home.

Shortly after that he and Ishiwatari successfully made fluorine. Then things began backfiring.

There had been no problem in getting enough uranium for their present needs. Sumi Yokoyama, Nishina's young secretary, had delivered it to them: 100 pounds in small bottles. Where she got it, Kigoshi did not know. He was young, and it was not his place to ask. The problem was that it was uranium nitrate, a powdery salt. The books said that in order to get uranium hexafluoride, to react with the fluorine, it had to be a solid metal.

At first Kigoshi tried to make the powder into a solid metal. But he could not do it. He began to believe—wrongly, as it would turn out—he did not have the right lab equipment. He just had not come up with the right chemistry. But he became impatient.

"I thought, "OK, what the hell, I might be able to get the uranium hexafluoride from the powdered uranium anyway.'" He decided to try to combine the uncombinable two.

Fluorine is volatile if it reacts too quickly. Powdered uranium, itself chemically volatile, gives the fluorine too much surface to react with. Heat combustion built rapidly. BAM! The mixture exploded, hurling glass and chemicals through the lab. If one of his assistants had not called to him, Kigoshi would have been facing it and might have been blinded. Luckily he was just cut and burned a little and badly frightened.

Now it was Nishina's turn to explode. He called Kigoshi into his office. "Can you make it or not?" he demanded.

Kigoshi's morale was at its lowest. The near disaster had left him shaken. The security measures were hampering his progress. He felt he needed help. And even if he made the uranium gas, his talks with Takeuchi, now intensely involved in making the separator downstairs, had convinced him that it was still going to be very hard to get any U-235. "No, I can't," he blurted. He was surprised at his own candor.

Nishina's face turned red. He rose in anger and had others in the project brought to his office. He called in each one by one and asked the same question. "Do you think we can succeed?" He received the same negative answer.

"If that's your attitude!" he shouted. Then he stopped, checking himself. His voice lowered. "Just keep going." He sat back down and waved them all out.

"Dr. Nishina was convinced he could do it," Kigoshi told me. "He had a very firm conviction. We were not. . . . But he was very passionate. . . . He asked each one of us, 'Are you convinced we can do this—make the chain reaction?' . . . We did not think it could be done. He got very angry. He said we never could stop the work. He wanted to make it. . . ."

Following the admonishment from Nishina, Kigoshi seemed to find new purpose. He went back to the books. There were more failures, but eventually he learned how to make the uranium metal: heat the nitrate until it became a black, crystalline oxide, then combine it in a 1,500-degree oven with carbon, which he had gotten from burning sugar. The result was a dark, dull metallic bar. But to Kigoshi, it shone like gold.

It was late 1943 or early 1944 when he finally was ready to try to make the U-hexafluoride. Ishiwatari was with him. They placed the uranium metal in a quartz vessel with the solid fluoride. The vessel had a tubular head leading to another vessel to which they hoped their product would wash out and in which it would be deposited.

When heat was applied, the fluoride released fluorine. It crept over the uranium oxide, reacting with it, and the resultant gas traveled up through the tube and became a solid again in the cooler, second vessel. When they opened this vessel, there was cause to cheer. In the bottom was a tiny crystal. It was uranium hexafluoride.

It was a small victory. They now knew how to make the U-gas, and mass production could at last begin. The two were so happy that despite the bitter-cold night, they joined hands and danced and whirled for joy through the deserted lab.

This was in Building 49, which the army had built especially for the project. Next door was Building 29, which housed Nishina's office. Although they had not finished with the successful experiment until near midnight, and it was getting colder by the hour, the two researchers decided not to go home. They were so excited over their success that they waited until morning to be able to present it to Dr. Nishina when he first walked in.

"I went over, and I told him, 'I've finally made it!' " recalled Kigoshi. "He said, 'That's good.' He was excited."

It had been nine to twelve months since Kigoshi had begun his task. On the other side of the ocean, the United States, which had several universities, many more researchers, and much more money devoted to the problem, had produced the gas in something like a month. But they knew nothing of that progress, according to Kigoshi, other than what he had heard at the beginning of the war that an American uranium mine was "very active."

Downstairs Takeuchi had his problems.

He was not an engineer, and he had gone through four drawings before Nishina had approved his design for the thermal diffusion apparatus. It was a large machine, looking something like a sixteen-foot-high water heater. Its heart was a midsection made of two thin pipes, one to be placed inside the other. The inside pipe would have a heat coil on its inner wall. The outside pipe would be surrounded by cooling water. In between, in a 2-millimeter space, would flow the gas. The U-235 would move upward along the hot wall, to be collected in a receptacle at the separator's top. The heavier parts would descend along the water-cooled wall.

The first problem had been making the pipes. Because the hexafluoride was so corrosive, they could not be made out of ordinary metal. It would have destroyed them. Gold or platinum would have been best. But for reasons unspecified (which might have been a lack of the precious metals or Takeuchi's timidity to press for them), he decided on copper, which was not nearly as strong.

He had farmed out the job of making the pipes to the Furukawa Engineering Company in Nikko, about a four-hour drive from Tokyo. He had been very specific about how straight and level he wanted them. When they were assembled, the distance between them, the 2-millimeter space, had to be uniform throughout. Otherwise, the gas convection would be interrupted. He did not want more than an 0.1-millimeter variation.

But the pipes had been delivered bent. The roads between Tokyo and Nikko were bad, and the pipes had been damaged during the truck ride. It took him more than a month to straighten them; he had to forge them in a Rikken industrial oven. To keep the 2-millimeter space between the pipes uniform, he silver-soldered three small pegs at equal distances down the pipe assembly. Following vacuum tests, designed to make sure the space would be airtight, the pipes were ready to be placed in the body of the separator. But he had not yet built the body, and he was to experience considerable difficulty doing so.

His main problem would be supplies. He needed many different materials for the separator: cement for its base, more copper for other parts that would come in contact with the U-hexafluoride, raw gum and asbestos for sealing and insulation, a motorized pump and cooler for the water, lots of steel, a thermostat, and a heater. Although air force headquarters had assured him he could have anything he wanted, it was not that simple.

Supply was set up in an exasperating way. Coupons were needed for everything. Materials were hard—sometimes impossible—to obtain. Rather than simply issue him a motorized pump, supply required that he first collect all the parts of the pump and give them to the pump supply officer. Then the branch could give him an assembled pump. He therefore had to study a motor and learn all its parts. Each part was obtained at a different place, from a different officer. In one instance, he had to fill out thirty-two forms to get one part. One part he needed was patented by Mitsubishi, and he was told he would have to get permission to use it from the company, as he finally did. At no point was he allowed to reveal the high-level priority of the project.

Takeuchi simply accepted the hardships and tried to do his best under the circumstances. The war was clearly going badly for Japan by this time, and he could see hardship all over. Furthermore, the fact that he was not wearing a uniform did not help. More than once he was told that the military had priority over civilians. When he invoked NI, he was told that frontline requests had precedent. He did not argue.

Not until he went to Major Koyama, air force headquarters liaison with the project, it appears, did the logjam begin to break. "I had no idea that the Nishina lab people were having such a hard time getting materials," Koyama said in *Showa.* "By that time, it was hard even to get materials for the front lines. . . . Also the Army and Navy were fighting over materials. . . ."

By October 1943 Takeuchi finally had all the parts he needed. Also by that time he and Kigoshi, along with some of the other members of the project, had moved into Building 49. It had two floors, each approximately 700 square feet and divided into various rooms. Kigo-shi's second-story room was right above Takeuchi's. Since the separator was going to be taller than Takeuchi's ceiling, a large hole was cut out of Kigoshi's floor to allow its top to protrude. A spiral stairway through the hole was built so Takeuchi would not have to take the long way up. Because of this accommodation, Takeuchi and Kigoshi began more extensive collaboration. A friendship grew. When he finally made the tiny uranium hexafluoride crystal, Kigoshi left the gas's large-scale production to his assistants and joined Takeuchi.

By November, with the help of the Rikken's engineering department, the separator was assembled and ready for testing. The first test was a measure of its heating capabilities. It failed. The heat produced in the inner pipe's copper wall was not uniform. This was a major setback. The entire machine had to be disassembled, and the pipe redesigned. It was too thick. In order to heat uniformly, it had to be thinner.

By now Takeuchi was experienced. He had the Rikken do the job. He advised the workers daily. The pipe was back within a month. Reassembled, the separator passed the heat test. There were other adjustments—many of them. The compartment where the U-hex-afluoride was placed did not fit. The water-cooling system leaked. The thermostat was erratic. The new year came and went. Finally, on March 12, 1944, the separator was ready.

"I was very happy," Takeuchi recalled in *Showa*. He had done most of the work himself. "So the pleasure [of completion] was all mine. Of course, I didn't really do it all myself. I always had lunch with people from the theory group. I talked to Tamaki very often and the Rikken's engineer had helped." Toward the end Nishina, too, had tested the machine.

The gas and the separator were now part of the project. The next step was separation.

11

News of NI's progress had considerable impact when it reached air force headquarters. Japan by this time was suffering serious defeats in almost all parts of the Pacific. It had been turned back at Guadalcanal and Midway, lost most of its southern ocean possessions, and was staring at an almost certain Allied invasion of the central Marianas Islands. If taken, the Marianas would provide the Allies with a land base for the wholesale bombing of Japan itself. That would be the beginning of the end—and the Japanese leaders knew it. They desperately needed new weapons with which to fight the advancing Americans. The news that the separator was on the verge of producing fissionable uranium seemed a godsend.

General Yasuda ordered another NI upgrading, probably after consultations with Premier Tojo, and possibly even the emperor's younger brothers, Princes Mikasa and Takamatsu, both military officers, who several sources say were now actively interested in the project.

Officer scientists were sent to the Rikken to help Nishina's already bolstered staff of 100. The Rikken itself shifted into high gear and began a new project policy. Rather than ship unrefined uranium ores home for processing—a cumbersome and increasingly unsafe method—it opened a separating plant in Korea and began processing and stockpiling the ores there. When Nishina was successful, the processed ores would be ready for shipping.

The Eighth Army Technical Lab was put entirely at Nishina's disposal. Yoichi Yamamoto, an engineer, was one of its officers. He says in his 1976 book *True Story of the Japanese Atomic Bomb* that Nishina ultimately was given a budget of 20 million yen (approximately $35 million in today's currency) as a result of the upgrading.

This is the highest budgetary figure the project is as yet said to have been given. It conflicts with other, lower figures, but a possible explanation is that the lower figures do not count support budgets, such as the Eighth's, or the search for and processing of uranium.

In order to increase the production of uranium hexafluoride, sugar, a luxury virtually nonexistent in Tokyo except on the tables of notables, was flown in from Formosa and burned to provide carbon. Kigoshi said with a smile that the lab became a gathering place for security-cleared scientists and higher-ups hoping to go away with "leftovers." But pilfering ended quickly since further experimentation soon showed that starch, far more abundant and easier to get, would carbonize just as easily as sugar.

On May 27, Lieutenant Colonel Suzuki arrived at Building 49. After doing the spadework on the uranium bomb project for General Yasuda, he had gone on to a similar job for a project to develop bulletproof steel. But with the worsening war situation and NI's further upgrading, he was ordered back to the project.

"Since I had not been there for a while, I knew it was going to be hard for me," he said in his memoir. "But the war situation was getting worse by the day. We needed an epochal weapon to break the impasse. I joined the Nishina lab firmly determined to do my best as a physicist to develop the atomic bomb"—and fast. The lab workers recalled his telling them upon his arrival that the army needed the bomb "as soon as possible."

Nishina seemed to catch the fever, the result of optimism at having reached another plateau and his realizing the seriousness of the situation. He gathered the new officer scientists together upon their arrival and gave them a pep talk. "He told us we were going to make an atomic bomb," one of the new officers, Masao Sabaru, is quoted as recalling in Showa. Any vacillation he might have had about the project appears to have disappeared, at least for the moment. However, he had just been appointed chief of the newly established Electronics Bureau of the Transportation and Communications Ministry, a post in the government's latest attempt to organize science for the war effort. So he had other things to do as well. It appears he left day-to-day operation of the project to Suzuki.

When Suzuki arrived, Takeuchi and his assistants were in the midst of attempts to separate isotopes in argon gas, a preliminary test they thought would be a good warm-up to U-235 separation. But when the tests were analyzed, they turned out to be failures. Takeuchi wrote that he was "disappointed" but hoped the reason was that the machine was designed for uranium hexafluoride, not for argon. Suzuki told him they could not wait for further argon experiments. Saipan had been invaded on June 15, and according to Yamamoto, some of the generals had hopes of dropping an atomic bomb on that island if it fell. If the Americans got control of Saipan, as it seemed they would, they would finally be within range for nonstop bombing raids on Japan proper.

The experiments began on July 14, 1944. Kigoshi brought in a 170-gram crystal of uranium hexafluoride in a pound-capacity glass beaker. The crystal was light green. Takeuchi attached the beaker to the bottom of the separator and turned on the heat to change the crystal into a green gas. With a vacuum, the towering machine sucked the gas into its thin separation channel.

Now the heat in the inner copper tube was turned on. The water in the outer steel tube cooled. Because, after a while, the researchers could see a noticeable decrease in the amount of U-hexafluoride in the beaker, they assumed the convection had started. But there was no increase in gas pressure. In fact, after several days there was a decrease. But pressure had to build in order for the process to work.

At first Takeuchi and his assistants just added more uranium hexafluoride. Their work was agonizingly slow. They did not know much about the gas. How long did it take to heat up? What was its convection temperature? The pressure continued to fall. Had the gas turned back into a solid inside? Was it leaking out?

It was suspected that the vacuum was the problem. They checked it and found a possible problem in the outer structure. They rebuilt it. By the time it was back in order the end of August had come. Saipan had indeed fallen. Tojo had resigned. Daily bombings had started.

The scientists began to suspect that maybe the separation chamber itself was not right. It was so thin—just 2 millimeters thick—and kept that way by only a few small pegs spaced at intervals. But if that were the case, they could not do anything about it. Only a completely new design could change that.

Then they suspected that the problem might be no more than a faulty gauge. They had taken so many precautions to make it resistant to the corrosive gas; perhaps the extra metal coatings had affected its ability to work. But adjustments did not help. The pressure continued to show a decrease. When Takeuchi tried to remove the machine's upper receptacle to determine if any of the gas had been enriched, the receptacle broke and the noxious green gas spewed out all over the lab.

Although they were coughing and fending with their hands, at least now they knew that *something* was being deposited in the receptacle. But it took another month to fix the damage. And when they were finally able, through cooling, to examine what that something was, it looked no different from what they were putting in at the other end. It was hard to believe there had been any enrichment.

There was a test for enrichment, of course. But they did not think that they had yet reached the testing stage. Things were not working smoothly enough. And there was another problem. They all knew that one separator would not be enough. It would take acres of separators and perhaps, by one estimate, one-tenth of the electricity available in Japan to enrich enough uranium to make a bomb.

Where would they get that kind of concentrated power, that kind of industrial might? they wondered. Certainly not in Japan. They had not had it before the siege. Where would it come from now?

Doubts mounted. These underlings were not privileged to know the military's schemes. Often they worked on isolated aspects of the project, not knowing what had preceded their task and what would follow. Their doubts threatened to undermine the project.

Nishina finally called a meeting which Lieutenant Colonel Suzuki attended. The younger and newer men kept their opinions to themselves. But those who had been with Nishina a long time spoke up.

Asao Sugimoto, a member of the project's calculations section and one of those who had helped build the small cyclotron before the war, wanted to end the project. Suzuki argued against him; the fate of Japan rested in their hands, he told the scientists. Nishina did not hesitate: He was with Suzuki. He "insisted we continue rather strongly," recalled Sugimoto. He "believed he could make an atomic bomb."

Surely the military, at least the men at the top, knew that they needed more power than was available in Japan. Suzuki and Nishina did not seem bothered by this problem. They were pushing harder than ever. The Japanese military, like the American military, was probably keeping its vital plans secret.

To Takeuchi's technical problems, according to The Day Man Lost, Nishina said, "Don't worry. Just keep going. Just keep giving [the separator] more gas."

The doubts eased or at least were no longer spoken. Most, if not all, of the project members appeared to abide by what Nishina and Suzuki said. Even if they did not understand how the actual bomb would be made, they would do their part to see the project successfully completed. They also knew that if they folded the project, most of them would be shipped to the front.

By the end of 1944 Takeuchi's problems seemed to be disappearing. The pressure in the separation chamber was finally rising. On November 10 he was able to take his first sample from its top.

The job was not easy. The gas in the top receptacle first had to be changed to an oxide. As a gas it was too reactive. The scientists changed it by adding liquid ammonia and then burning the liquid off. The result was a solid crystal again.

Takeuchi decided it was finally time to analyze the substance. His outlook was brightening. Nishina, he began to believe, had been right.

Suzuki had different feelings. Standing in the wings observing NI's agonizingly slow advance, the army officer had begun to have nagging doubts, especially after witnessing the episode of poor morale at the special meeting. Even before the meeting he had begun to worry about the increasing bombings of Tokyo. He did not feel comfortable with only one pilot separator. What if it was destroyed?

One separator was simply not enough. It was constantly breaking down. Delays had been costly. Japan did not have much time left.

One solution would have been to remove the separator to a safe place. Nishina, by late 1944, had already sent Kigoshi and his assistants north to the mountains so they could mass-produce uranium hexafluoride safely. But moving the separator presented major problems. It was big, complex, cemented into Building 49. Since the Rikken was outside the main target area, they decided to stay there. But Suzuki still felt another separator was needed.

After he had become familiar with the separator's design, it worried him as well. He did not like the inner copper cylinder. Copper was known to soften with heat. Even Nishina constantly told him that. Maybe that was the cause of some of the machine's problems, he reasoned. Softened, the tube could bend toward the cooling cylinder and close the tiny convection gap. Bending could also affect heat distribution and thus convection. Heat would not spread evenly on a "wrinkled" tube.

Considering these problems, Suzuki hit on a solution: build more and better separators before they *had* to. Now that NI had the highest priority, they could do so—and much faster than before.

The army agreed with him, as did Nishina, when maps showing the Rikken targeted for bombings were found in late 1944 in the wreckage of an American B-29. (The United States knew only that the Rikken was an important research center.) It was decided to establish an NI extension in Osaka University.

Osaka was already well prepared for a uranium bomb project. It had a giant separator built by Eiichi Takeda, the isotope separation specialist who had helped Takeuchi. The head of its atomic physics lab was Seishi Kikuchi, the scientist who had participated in the early atomic bomb deliberations and was currently a leading figure in the navy's development of the "death ray," another priority "win-the-war" weapon. Osaka also had a mass spectrometer, key to one of the three other known methods for isotope separation—the spectrograph—and perhaps the only mass spectrometer in Japan at the time.

Kikuchi and his assistants began knocking out floors in one of Osaka's largest buildings in order to house the five separators Suzuki planned to build. They were to be huge. "If we were going to succeed, we were going to need a lot of U-235," wrote Suzuki. Whereas Takeuchi's separator was five meters high, Suzuki's were twenty meters, or sixty-one feet, high. The Osaka lab had to remove the second through the fourth floors to prepare for them.

This time Suzuki lined the inside of the cylinder (the side containing the heating coils) with steel. The lining would be thick. It would absorb the heat initially, then distribute it evenly throughout the copper, which faced the corrosive gas. Nishina did not agree that the new design would work. But Suzuki told him, "We don't know until we try." Nishina reluctantly agreed.

The small space for the gas between the cylinders in the new units was narrowed from Takeuchi's 2 millimeters to an even smaller 1.5 millimeters. "The smaller the space, the higher the separation efficiency," Suzuki wrote. "I [also] made a window so we could see the convection [as Takeuchi could not]."

To construct the new improved separators, Suzuki went to Sumitomo, one of Japan's largest industrial companies. Its plant in Amagasaki, right outside Osaka, had all the materials needed. General Yasuda, backed by an order from the Ministry of Munitions, the main government organization deciding war manufacturing priorities, had them assembled in a matter of months—an incredibly short time, considering the year and a half it had taken Takeuchi and the worsening supply situation in Japan at that time.

Suzuki encountered resistance to his plan. Various factions were bent on seeing their particular solutions for victory supported at the expense of the others. One wanted the army to drop NI altogether. Another wanted to expand it to include separator prototypes for gaseous diffusion, mass spectrograph, and centrifuge. But backed by Yasuda, thus by the air force, the plan had been implemented.

As 1945 approached, NI had expanded out of the Rikken and Nishina's exclusive charge.

12

By spring 1943, as the navy head-quarters' committee of experts was concluding that an atomic bomb project would be fruitless, the fleet was beginning to want to hear the opposite. Its leader, Isoroku Yamamoto, who had conceived the attack on Pearl Harbor, had just been killed by American pilots (who, with information gleaned from Magic, had been able to set up an aerial ambush of his touring plane). The battles at the Coral Sea and Midway had cost the admirals most of their carriers. Like the generals, they were now looking for decisive weapons with which to regain the initiative. In addition, the committee had concluded that the United States could build a bomb if anyone could.

Accordingly the admirals had politely thanked the "experts" and, in May 1943, given their secret atomic bomb researcher, Bunsaku Arakatsu, half of a newly promised 600,000-yen grant (approximately $150,000) with which to step up his efforts. The project was designated the "official" navy uranium bomb project and given a priority code name, F-go (F probably stood for "fission," although some accounts say it meant "fluoride," as in uranium hexafluoride, which it would use). Other accounts say the project was called Nichi, a Japanese word for "sun."

Speaking to Japanese interviewers in the hospital before his death in 1974, Arakatsu recalled, "The war situation had worsened. The navy began to talk about atomic bombs." He was told to change his emphasis from theory to development—and to be quick about it.

Like Nishina's, Arakatsu's first major task was selection of a separation method. He knew Nishina was using thermal diffusion. In fact, he went to see the separator, and Nishina himself let him inspect it. It is not clear whether Nishina knew Arakatsu had his own project. But because Nishina was using thermal diffusion, Arakatsu determined early that he would pursue one of the other methods.

According to Kiichi Kimura, a physicist at Kyoto whom Arakatsu put in charge of the project's uranium ore gathering, F-go did not succeed in finishing a large cyclotron, the kind needed for the electromagnetic (mass spectrograph) method. (It had only a Cockcroft-Walton type of particle accelerator.) Mass spectrographs were the largest type of separator and would therefore present the largest mass production problems if F-go's program ever proceeded to the production stage. In addition, none of the researchers had any experience with the porous barriers needed for the gaseous diffusion method.

What remained of their choices then was the ultracentrifuge method: an enclosed, whirling rotor, similar to, but not as intricate or big as, a cyclotron, which used a force similar to gravity to spin heavier U-238 to the outside wall, leaving the lighter U-235 to collect around an inner surface. What F-go liked about this method, said Kimura, was that it involved only the differences in isotope weight. Since there was no need to design filters or complicated ion sources, the centrifuge was relatively simple, at least in principle.

Sakae Shimizu, the Kyoto physicist in charge of designing the unit, has said that the group picked centrifuge separation because it seemed to have the best chance of succeeding, considering Japan's lack of uranium, construction materials, and electrical power. Because it was the most direct method, less uranium was needed. But Arakatsu himself recalled, "Since I was a child, I had always liked rotating bodies. Maybe that is really why I chose centrifuge. My favorite research [throughout my career] was on rotating bodies."

The ultracentrifuge may have been the simplest in theory, but the actual design was probably the most difficult. For one thing, it demanded fantastic rotating speeds. F-go determined that its machine would have to make between 100,000 and 150,000 revolutions per minute. Such centrifuges had been built before, but to work properly, they had to be built with incredible craftsmanship. In fact, the United States, while recognizing the simplicity and merits of the separation operation, had already decided to forgo large-scale production of U-235 by ultracentrifuge because of the engineering problems involved.

But the next generation of Japanese would usurp America's claim to world technological superiority, and scientific engineers, such as those in F-go, were the precursors of that advance. Arakatsu, Shimizu, and the others threw themselves into the design. *Showa* has a picture of one of their early drawings. It shows a complicated and intricate mass of chambers, pipes, disks, and thin axles. It looks not unlike the engine for some streamlined jet car and was probably as big as, if not much bigger than, Takeuchi's multistory thermal diffusion unit.

At its heart was a huge rotor, fitted into a chamber. The rotor, shaped like a giant saucer, had fins. Down its middle was a thin shaft centering it in the chamber. (The shaft had to be thin because the scientists wanted as little friction as possible. It would slow the rotor, hindering separation.)

The most unusual aspect of the ultracentrifuge, its most complicated design and production aspect, was that the rotor, except for the shaft, "floated" in the chamber. An extremely powerful stream of air shot from beneath it, "cushioning" the huge rotor, striking the fins, which were at a slight angle, and initiating the furious spin. A strong magnetic field around the chamber then combined to "pull" the rotor to fantastic speeds. Once it was spinning at the desired rate, it was to be a relatively simple matter to introduce the uranium hexafluoride into the chamber and gather the U-235, which would be funneled off.

In order to use the centrifuge, of course, F-go needed uranium. At the beginning of the project the navy, like the army, thought finding uranium would be relatively easy. For one thing, there was early talk about the China fleet's having some. It was supposed to be in Shanghai, probably procured from stocks used as pigment for ceramic art.

Whether or not those stocks ever arrived in Kyoto is not clear. But the navy very soon found out about the scarcity. And by the time Arakatsu's program was stepped up it had been forced to purchase all the uranium oxide in Kyoto ceramic shops, giving F-go about 100 pounds of uranium oxide in glass bottles, and to launch a search of its own.

During the deliberations of the committee of experts, Hantaro Nagaoka, the senior physicist at that meeting, had speculated that since uranium was one of the heaviest elements, they might find it in Burma, which had lots of hills, depressions, and cracks into which heavy elements might fall and gather. It is said that the Japanese were poised to go into Burma to look for uranium as soon as their armies had taken the country, but they never did.

"We decided we needed one and a half tons of uranium oxide in order to separate enough U-235 to make a bomb," said Mitsui. After aiding the project's start in 1943, Captain Ito had left, and Mitsui had taken over as navy liaison with Arakatsu. Besides China and Kyoto, he said, the only other place the navy went looking for uranium was in Korea.

The navy lacked the resources to go looking throughout the empire. And in October 1944 matters got even worse. What remained of the fleet was annihilated in the Battle of Leyte Gulf off the Philippines. The navy had no more offensive forces—only planes, a few submarines, which long ago had been converted into supply carriers (perhaps a fatal mistake by the admirals in view of the success of Allied submarines used offensively), and some support ships. This finally put the navy in a desperate situation. The uranium bomb project was stepped up even further and was given a priority behind only suicide squadrons, jet planes, and perhaps defensive radar and probably equal to or greater than the "death ray," lethal gases, and germ weapons.

Along with this further upgrading, Arakatsu was given all, or at least a large chunk, of the balance due him under the project grant. Scientists from navy labs and elsewhere were dispatched to aid him. And Lieutenant Commander Tetsuzo Kitagawa, a top officer scientist from the navy's chemical warfare section, was sent to Kyoto to be a full-time liaison with F-go, to work in conjunction with or to supersede Mitsui, who had other duties as well. In addition, the navy and the army began, by necessity, to discuss cooperation. Accordingly official lines were opened between NI and F-go. The navy, however, seemed to take more than it gave.

To make F-go's uranium gas, Arakatsu had commissioned Kyoto Professor Koji Sasaki, a chemist specializing in radioactive elements. Because of the newly instituted collaboration, Sasaki, unlike Kigoshi, his counterpart at NI, did not have to learn by trial and error how to make the uranium hexafluoride. He went to the Rikken, and Kigoshi recalled, "He stayed at our lab about an hour. He said he had to make uranium hexafluoride [and remarked on the importance of the work]. That's how I found out about the Kyoto project."

Working with Sasaki was Kyoto University engineer and electrochemist Shinzo Okada, a specialist in metals. Okada's job was to produce the uranium metal, essential to making the U-gas. Prior to joining F-go in the late 1944 upgrading, he had been developing for the navy a dry-cell battery using manganese oxide. Before that he had become expert at purifying tungsten and steel-strengthening vanadium.

Arakatsu's theoretical section was strong. It included Yukawa, the future Nobel Prizewinner. One of the men doing calculations was Minoru Kobayashi, a theorist who worked for Yukawa. In *Showa*, Kobayashi explained that they drew on Arakatsu's earlier work, indicating approximately 2.6 neutrons were emitted per fission, when they calculated the critical mass. "I used a hand calculator. It took me one or two nights to get the answer. It would take an amount of pure U-235 with a diameter of between 10–20 centimeters [barely 5 to 10 inches] to get the explosion. Break that up and keep them apart until you want the explosion. Put them together and they will explode."

It is at least possible today to get an explosion with 10 to 20 centimeters of U-235 if it is enriched sufficiently. But F-go might not have aimed at producing a highly enriched mass of U-235. In a document on the navy effort contained in the Atomic Bomb Mission report, Lieutenant Commander Miroshi Ishiwatari, of the navy's weapons development, says F-go "thought . . . that if U-235 could be concentrated at 10 percent or above, bomb or power possibilities would be likely." Other accounts indicate the same.

However, F-go, late in 1944, still did not have enough uranium to make either the small critical mass of highly enriched U-235 or the larger, easier to acquire mass that 10 percent enrichment would have demanded. And Kobayashi had no idea where they were going to get it. "We were going to need a lot of uranium ore . . . and a big factory in which to separate the U-235. . . . I asked Dr. Arakatsu about this and he said, 'Don't worry about it. There is a lot of uranium ore in Korea.' "

In 1944 Arakatsu's uranium metal producer, Okada, came to Iimori at NI and inquired about Korean black sands. Furthermore, the Atomic Bomb Mission cited Takuichi Ikumi, manager of the Rikken's Korean office, as telling them that a scientist who seems to have been Arakatsu secretly visited Korea in September 1944, just about the time the navy upgraded the project for the second time.

F-go, therefore, was undoubtedly looking to Korea for its uranium, and there is evidence to suggest it might also have been dealing with the Noguchi interests at Konan, Korea. The Atomic Bomb Mission reported that Kyoto's head geologist, Professor Jitsutaro Takubo, who was searching for uranium in Korea and therefore must have been working with Arakatsu, was also working for Noguchi's Konan interests. Also, the mission said that Arakatsu was getting "20 grams" per month of heavy water from "Haber process ammonia plants" in Korea and in Kyushu, the southernmost Japanese island.

Noguchi, the sole producer of heavy water in Japan at the time, appears also to have been the only person in Korea making ammonia. He was doing so at Konan and with the German-invented Haber process. He also had an ammonia plant on Kyushu.

As soon as he could, Arakatsu decided to commission several agencies to design and make centrifuges for F-go—this in spite of the fact that the project was working on its own design. Two Tokyo companies were assigned to do this: Hokushine Electric, a specialist in ship gyros (which, since they have "floating rotors," are similar in design to centrifuges), and Tokyo Keiki, a huge electric company, officials of which were friends of Arakatsu's. The designs were variations on F-go's design, finished by the end of the year. Actual construction was farmed out to Sumitomo, the powerful industrial combine.

13

And what had Alcázar de Velasco been doing during this time?

If he had picked up information on the U.S. atomic bomb program in 1943, had he received any more?

No, he told me in Spain. The Japanese had told him to get more, but he had not been able to. He did not at the time fully understand the significance of the atomic bomb information, he said regretfully. So he did not press. It was a big mistake of his, he said, and of the Japanese, too. As the war dragged on, he said, they became mainly concerned with getting information on troop and ship movements in the Pacific—to defend themselves against the growing Allied "island hopping" toward their homeland.

As 1943 approached, the United States and TO were playing a game of cat and mouse. America knew of TO's existence, but few names or details had been revealed in the intercepted communications. The organization appeared to be fairly large and to operate extensively in the States. Alcázar de Velasco claims TO aided in the sinking of perhaps eight hundred Allied ships.

He was using Spanish intelligence from Washington, as well as the Spanish diplomatic pouch. While he was reluctant, and in most cases refused, to name his agents, many of them, he said, were attached to Spanish embassies and consulates.

In August 1942 two important TO reports were forwarded to Tokyo. On August 9 Suma cabled that "whispers circulating among [New York] military [personnel]" indicate that "American forces are going to land in the Aleutians." The U.S. invasion of the Aleutians did not take place until early 1943, but the information correctly discerned U.S. intentions.

On August 20 Suma radioed another TO dispatch from New

York: "Rumors are being circulated to the effect that if the American troops which landed in the Solomon Islands can hold on there for another month, they will then be supported by powerful reinforcements."

The Solomon Islands were America's first ground objective in the Pacific. Taking them was the beginning of the offensive which America's leaders felt would end at Tokyo. Marines had landed on August 7 and met little resistance. But in September the Japanese began pouring in reinforcements.

The bloodiest fighting in the earliest part of the Pacific island war was on the Solomons. It is possible that TO's information helped forge Japanese determination to hold them.

In February 1943 Suma cabled Tokyo with one of the many TO reports about new weapons being developed in the United States. It was datelined Washington: "According to a secret report, [U.S.] Army Ordnance has approved the manufacture of a new powder which is 50 percent more powerful than any other known powder. Its formula is very secret, but it has a basis of ammonium nitrate. It will be used principally in aerial bombardments."

Attached to the intercept was a note from Magic decoders: "Army Ordnance advises that about a year ago the formula for a new high explosive was obtained from the British and its manufacture in large quantities was commenced. The explosive is known as 'RDX' and, by ballistic mortar tests, it is 50 percent more powerful than TNT. Ordnance regards RDX as a closely held secret. . . ."

It was right around this time, Alcázar de Velasco said, that he also received the information on the Manhattan Project.

Although, at times, voicing displeasure with certain TO information which they regarded "too fantastic to be true," the Japanese were satisfied enough to send Suma large sums of money to keep TO in operation. According to Magic intercepts, Tokyo sent Suma 400,000 yen (approximately $100,000) in August 1942 for TO operations, and 500,000 yen (approximately $125,000) in December. The money was deposited for conversion in the Berlin branch of the Yokohama Specie Bank. Wild schemes to fund the intelligence gathering were also put into operation. For instance, pearls to be converted to cash were twice sent from Tokyo by a German blockade-runner and twice mysteriously disappeared en route.

In addition, $500,000 secretly left in the abandoned Japanese Embassy in Washington were to be used to pay TO agents, according to Magic. As a "neutral" Spain was given responsibility for Japanese interests in the United States and had charge of the abandoned embassy. America could have moved in and confiscated the money, but War Department officials were afraid its cabled disclosure might be a trap to see if they were listening in. Magic was worth fifty such nets, the United States knew. The $500,000 was allowed to go to TO.

In his book *Memories of a Secret Agent,* Alcázar de Velasco wrote of this period: "I began to receive enormous sums of money for our North American operation."

But American detective work had already begun to pay off. From the beginning of 1942 not only was Magic monitoring bits and pieces of TO's operations, but the FBI, too, was getting its independent glimpses.

Right after Pearl Harbor the British, who had finally infiltrated Alcázar de Velasco's English spy network, alerted FBI Director J. Edgar Hoover that they had information that he might be coming to the United States. Hoover's inquiries to the War Department about Alcázar de Velasco produced only negative responses. Nobody there had ever heard of him.

But as TO intercepts began piling up in the Magic code rooms, those whose job it was to coordinate information in both agencies began putting the parts together. The State Department called the ring TO. The FBI called it Span-Nip, the *Span* standing, obviously, for "Spanish" and the *Nip* for "Nippon." Everybody knew it was the same ring.

On March 10, 1942, according to a State Department memo, a Washington meeting of the Joint Intelligence Committee, which included chiefs of the navy and army and OSS director Colonel William ("Wild Bill") Donovan, decided on the basis of the growing evidence to put the "closest possible watch" on Spaniards using the diplomatic pouch. Not having many names, the FBI was forced to meet ships which, intercepted dispatches indicated, might be carrying TO agents as passengers. This led, according to FBI reports, to the close tailing, for instance, of a jittery Chilean statesman named Rafael Moreno, whom Alcázar de Velasco had sent to the United States specifically to check on shipbuilding, labor conditions, presidential politics, and new antimine devices. But Moreno quickly spotted his tails and dropped the mission.

Similarly, another TO dispatch disclosed that agents had been arrested in Baltimore. They turned out to be the captain and several crew members of the Spanish ship *Motomar,* which regularly sailed the strategically important Atlantic waters between Spain and the American Northeast, where Allied convoys made their secret voyages to theaters of war and supply. A quick dispatch from a passing liner trying to spot the convoys could—and did—get many of them quickly attacked. The *Motomar,* in fact, had been stopped previously by American naval vessels seeking such spy ships and ordered to leave the strategic area. But the October 1942 arrests in Baltimore produced only charges of illegal smuggling against the Spanish sailors. Apparently the FBI could not prove anything else.

An early 1943 watch for a "telegraphic expert" who, according to Magic intercepts, would also serve as TO's "paymaster" brought FBI agents to U.S. docks to meet the SS *Magallanes,* a Spanish liner which had previously been suspected of bringing agents as well as smugglers. But the spy, if he existed, eluded them.

America still could not move against the ring without jeopardizing Magic. Then, in mid-October 1942, Magic intercepted a message from Suma which said TO was getting ready to send a Spanish diplomat, Fernando de Kobbe Chinchilla, to Vancouver, British Columbia. Kobbe, according to the dispatch, was going to report on the important Pacific sea-lanes passing Vancouver. Spain was cooperating fully, creating a new consulate in the Canadian city expressly for the espionage work. Suma wanted to know if Tokyo had any specific instructions.

Almost simultaneously, another spy whom Alcázar de Velasco had recruited for TO walked into the American Embassy in Madrid and told a surprised U.S. Ambassador Carlton J. H. Hayes that he wished to be a double agent for America. José María Aladrén, a Spaniard whose TO cover was to be an assignment as U.S. correspondent for the Madrid periodical *Alcázar,* explained that he was tired of Axis influence in Spain and wanted to help end it.

Hayes was skeptical. But Aladrén brought with him secret codes, invisible inks, and detailed instructions he said he had got from Alcázar de Velasco and the Japanese. "He said he had dinner last night with Alcázar de Velasco," Hayes cabled back to Secretary of State Cordell Hull, "and the two of them were joined briefly by Mr. Fumio Miura, a secretary of the Japanese Legation, who wished him all kinds of success in his new enterprise."

Included in Aladrén's instructions were orders to gather intelligence on "war factories," bases, and convoys. But his major disclosure, it appears, was the fact that he identified Kobbe as one of the spies who would be traveling with him. U.S. War Department officials now had direct confirmation of Alcázar de Velasco's participation and a compromisable source in Aladrén.

What happened to Aladrén is not clear from available sources. But since Kobbe was going to Canada, the Canadian government was advised of what he had told Hayes.

Canada would now do what the United States would not.

14

The plan to put Kobbe in Vancouver had been hatched back in July 1942. According to documents, including Magic intercepts, the Germans and especially the Japanese wanted intelligence from the northern Pacific. Spain willingly complied with the request. Not only Alcázar de Velasco but SIM was involved in putting the operation together. Suma conducted a personal investigation of Kobbe, he said in his intercepted messages, and he was impressed. Kobbe had spied for Franco during the Civil War.

Alcázar de Velasco did not like Kobbe. "Suma said he was a good man," he wrote in *Memories of a Secret Agent,* "but I had met him before. . . . I felt he was effeminate."

Nevertheless, Kobbe got the job. He was to be paid 50,000 pesetas up front, more as he turned in information. Several days before he left, Alcázar de Velasco arranged a meeting with Kobbe and Suma at a Madrid café, Bar Cristales, which had booths with curtains that could be drawn for privacy.

Alcázar de Velasco wrote: "Kobbe came in with a girlfriend. She wore black glasses so no one would recognize her. It was stupid. Nobody cared about us. Kobbe was nervous. He wanted to know if we thought any enemy agents were around. He had a trim mustache and was well dressed. It was a contradiction. He was not inconspicuous."

Kobbe was given his instructions. In reply to Suma's earlier inquiry, Tokyo had cabled back: "Kobbe is to investigate the following items: (1) airfields and naval establishments in the Alaska and Aleutian regions; (2) concentrations and increases in the Army, Navy—including transport and merchant ships—and Air Force (especially heavy bombers); (3) air communication facilities between America and Russia; (4) the number of roads between America proper and

Alaska, their quality and the situation with respect to transportation of material. . . ."

Alcázar de Velasco wrote: "I told him that he was to maintain telegraph communication with us and that his information was probably going to be more interesting to the Japanese than the Germans. I told him how delicate and dangerous his mission was and if he committed treason he would have to answer to us."

Meanwhile, in response to discreet inquiries to various branches that might know something about him, the War Department was receiving memorandums such as the following (addressed to a Commander Wharton):

Kobbe is at present on duty in the European Section of the Spanish Foreign Office with rank of First Class Consul and First Secretary of Embassy. He has applied for diplomatic transit visas for himself and daughter, Beatriz, in order to proceed to Vancouver. While Kobbe belongs to a group which formerly believed in German victory, he has later showed surface friendliness, and the British believe he is not pro-German. He has been entangled with a Spanish woman named Ametua, who has a bad reputation as a blackmailer, and some Spaniards state that she is in German pay. The British think Kobbe is trying to break away from her and so they are in favor of his getting a visa.

Because of Magic, the Americans could not tell the Canadians—or the British, for that matter—all they knew about Kobbe. Consequently, Assistant Secretary of State A. A. Berle, Jr., who was handling the matter for Hull, got back a reply from the Canadians stating that since Britain wished it, they were going to recognize Kobbe's appointment. "You will, of course, appreciate that as Spain is in charge of Japanese interests in Canada, it would not have been easy to refuse [Spain's request to establish the new consulate in order to look out for Japanese interests]—especially as the Japanese are congregated largely on the Pacific Coast—unless we had good reasons for such refusal," said the note.

In November more information on Kobbe came in. Hayes forwarded some of his codes, which the ambassador said he had received from Aladrén. The codes, said the secret cable, "will consist of Japanese names." He enclosed four of them: AKIYAMA, OJANO, IKEDA, ICHIKAWA. The words probably stood for important intelligence targets, such as "convoy" and "troops." Enclosed with a seemingly innocuous communication from one of the Japanese he was charged to aid, they would alert Suma to something Kobbe had learned.

When Kobbe left, wrote Alcázar de Velasco, "he was pleased with everything except the money." He wanted more. "I told [Suma] that his daughter is the weak link. Suma showed concern, but said, 'We'll keep a tight rein on him—and the money will enable us to do that.' . . . I was also worried because our methods were no longer the latest."

On November 28, a certain Gordon at the Department of State got a "foreign activity correlation" stating that Kobbe and his twenty-one-year-old daughter, who had been born in London, were on board the SS *Marqués de Comillas*, a Spanish liner often suspected of carrying spies to New Orleans.

"Before he left Spain," said the memo, "Kobbe is said to have been intimately associated with a Nazi agent, whose influence over him will wane, it is hoped [by the British] in proportion to the distance he is away from her." A telegram from the woman was waiting for him at New Orleans, "thanking him for a check, and professing undying affection." He would be under surveillance while passing through the United States, and "the Canadian authorities are supposed to be on the watch for him."

While Canada, with Britain's urging, had decided to accredit Kobbe, it also, because of the American warnings, decided to watch him closely. The FBI was to be alerted should he make trips to the United States, as he did. After Kobbe and his daughter had arrived in New Orleans in December, FBI agents followed them to New York, where they spent Christmas 1942, and then watched as their counterparts in the Royal Canadian Mounted Police took over when the pair crossed into Montreal on the twenty-ninth.

It was not long, according to Alcázar de Velasco, before Kobbe began sending back "very good intelligence, especially for the Japanese." This consisted of information on "ships, their cargoes, weapons, and how frogmen were trying to get information on electronic devices in a Japanese submarine that was sunk in the Bering Straits. . . . After that, Kobbe sent us four very valuable pieces of information." But he did not elaborate.

The first intercepts from Vancouver logged by Magic were sent out in March 1943 and tell of a force of Allied ships, carrying weapons and soldiers, heading for the Aleutian Islands. A month later the U.S. Seventh Infantry Division landed on Attu in the Aleutians and began battling to retake it. Prior to the March messages, Attu had a garrison of 1,000 Japanese troops. But by the time the Seventh landed the garrison had been increased to 2,400, who had been dispersed into "excellent terrain," according to military records. It is possible that Kobbe's information alerted, or helped alert, the Japanese to the impending attack.

The alert, if it came, did no good. By May 29 the battle was over, except for some mopping up. Almost the entire Japanese force was wiped out. Kiska, the other important Aleutian island, was then evacuated by the Japanese without a fight.

Faced perhaps with knowledge of Kobbe's effectiveness, the United States and Canada increased surveillance of him. What happened next is not clear. According to a December 1978 article in the Spanish magazine *Historia,* a Mountie disguised as a civilian courted Kobbe's daughter and thus, perhaps unknown to the spy, was able to catch Kobbe as he prepared and sent a secret intelligence by radio to Madrid via Argentina. But around September 1, 1943, according to Canadian documents, an intercepted letter was found to contain codes "to be used in reporting ship and troop movements, defense installations, etc.," $1,000 in payment for spy services, "formulae for manufacturing secret ink," and instructions from Alcázar de Velasco and the Marques de Rialp, head of the Spanish Foreign Ministry's press and information office.

The last bit of evidence was crucial. It meant that the Spanish Foreign Ministry itself was involved. And since Franco was known to keep a tight rein on it, he must have known—an allegation that Alcázar de Velasco often made in telling of his involvement with TO.

The United States, of course, was pleased with all this. Now Magic would not have to be compromised. It cooperated in the resultant investigation, forwarding what it could to Canada and making recommendations.

By September 11, 1943, the case had reached the office of Prime Minister William Lyon Mackenzie King. He personally was reviewing the facts and deciding what to do about Kobbe—and not without some relish. Catching him gave the Allies a fist with which to deal a blow to pro-Axis activities by supposedly neutral Spain.

"This is a very important matter," N. A. Robertson, secretary of state for external affairs, wrote the prime minister in a "Most Secret" memorandum, which continued:

It raises serious questions of policy, both for us and the United States and United Kingdom governments. The evidence of Kobbe's complicity is complete and, what rarely happens in espionage cases, the evidence against him is of a character that could be produced in court if it were thought in the public interest to prosecute him.

The case confirms what a good many people have suspected—that Spanish diplomatic and consular facilities are being used in the interests of the Axis powers. . . . I am inclined to think the best thing to do is to inform the United Kingdom Government of the facts . . . and allow them to use this information to put the screw on Franco. In the present phase of the European political situation, the threat of exposure of Spanish collusion with the Axis may be a very useful lever in securing further concessions from Spain, or, if this course seems more desirable, could be used to discredit the present dictatorial regime completely.

The Canadian prime minister wrote on the memo: "I agree with suggested procedure," and initialed it. The United States concurred. When the war ended, we would want bases in Spain. British Ambassador Hoare, whom Alcázar de Velasco said he had tricked in order to get to Britain at the beginning of the war, was given the job of presenting the evidence to the Spanish.

According to a secret coded message sent to the Canadian ambassador in Washington, Hoare handed photostatic copies of the evidence to the new Spanish foreign secretary, Francisco Jordana, on Sunday, January 16, 1944. He told Jordana that unless the Spanish took certain steps, not specifically spelled out in the documents available so far, a public trial, which would be embarrassing to Spain, would be held. "The Foreign Minister was greatly shocked and promised a most rigid enquiry, adding that he would keep it in his personal control," reported Hoare.

Almost immediately Jordana ordered Kobbe home. Within days of Hoare's ultimatum, Canadian Mounted Police officials arrived at Kobbe's residence and informed him and his daughter that they were under arrest and being expelled from Canada. Their residence was searched, and they were not allowed to leave until everything was ready for a clandestine journey.

Around February 1, 1944, according to the Canadian documents, they were "unobtrusively" escorted to the border, where FBI agents, at the request of Canada, took over and escorted them to New Orleans. There, on February 6, they boarded the SS *Magallanes,* the Spanish liner suspected during the earlier "telegrapher" search, and headed home.

At their destination there was panic.

Alcázar de Velasco wrote: "Our liaison agent sent me a note. 'Urgent we see each other. "K" has been discovered. He has had to leave his position. But the worst thing is that they have all our codes and inks.' "

Kobbe had also given the Allies the names of many of their agents, Alcázar de Velasco said later. These included Spanish journalists and diplomats, who by that time constituted the last line of Axis informers there. "It was the coup de grâce to the Abwehr [in the United States] as well as the Japanese service," wrote Alcázar de Velasco. "Kobbe confessed everything. He answered all questions. He even talked more than he should have."

Shortly after the beginning of 1944 Franco, aware that the momentum of the war was shifting strongly in the favor of the Allies, began curbing Axis activity in and from Spain. One of the last "Most Secret" memos from the Canadian foreign secretary to Prime Minister King said: "This Kobbe case has been an annoying and troublesome one. I feel, however, that its political importance in helping to bring Spain into line and in forcing a general clean-up of her foreign service will be such as to make it well worth the bother and expense."

As for Alcázar de Velasco, he suddenly found himself on the run. "From then on I was accused of being the leader of spies everywhere. Now they had a dossier about me. That gave them the material with which to attack me even in Spain."

The remnants of TO, a few remaining diplomats who had not yet been found out, were transferred to Juan Perón's ring in Argentina. "Perón had been giving good service to the Japanese and had been getting a lot of money for it"—money which helped him gain power after the war.

But the decimated ring produced nothing thereafter.

At the beginning of the summer of 1944, Alcázar de Velasco said, he received unexpected visitors: a group of Allied agents—an American, a Briton, and a Canadian—who wanted him to become a double agent. He refused. They threatened. "The Canadian was especially offensive for what had happened in Canada." Finally, he says, they gave up, but with a warning: Stop spying for the Axis or "we'll kill you."

On July 4 he left for Germany. The few FBI documents about him released so far to me under a Freedom of Information request say he might have served in the Blue Division, the unit of Spanish troops that fought beside Germany on the Russian front. In 1960 he wrote a book in which he said that shortly after the war he had escorted

Martin Bormann, the hunted Nazi, to Argentina in a submarine. In his book *Aftermath,* about the search for Bormann, the late intelligence expert Ladislas Farago wrote that he believes this last story.

˙ So as 1945 approached, Alcázar de Velasco and TO were effectively out of the picture, and Japan was probably not receiving any intelligence about the later stages of the Manhattan Project and American development of the atomic bomb.

PART

THREE

15

Fumio Yamazaki, who had helped build Nishina's large cyclotron (which was now in operation), was selected to analyze the product Takeuchi took out of his separator. Although he was officially listed on the NI chart as a member of the "measurement of separation" section, he was not in Building 49. He was working with the cyclotrons, which were elsewhere on the complex. Nishina thought it would be better for the testing to be done by someone outside the separation operation.

Because NI was now using the large cyclotron for theoretical experiments, Yamazaki had to use the small cyclotron. Four samples from the separator's receptacle were brought in: small green-black specimens sealed in paraffin bags. His plan was to put each in the cyclotron, fire neutrons at it, thus causing tiny fissions, and measure the beta rays that resulted. He knew the amount of radioactivity uranium hexafluoride emitted. If the samples released more, then they were enriched. The degree of their enrichment could also be calculated.

Beginning in February and possibly stretching into March 1945, Yamazaki tested the specimens. One by one, he got the same result. In his opinion, he told Nishina, there had been no enrichment. The material from the receptacle was measuring almost the same radioactivity as the uranium hexafluoride. "I remember that I reported to Dr. Nishina that it was possible that it had been enriched in very small amounts," he recalled, "but it would have to be under one percent."

Nishina, it seems, was devastated by this news. Right after the war Dr. Hideji Yagi, president of the Board of Technology, the major civilian agency helping administer war projects, told American investigators that in February Nishina had told him he "was not making very good progress with thermal diffusion of uranium and expressed the thought that there might be a limit to the concentration of U-235 which could be obtained."

But Nishina apparently did not convey this to Takeuchi, for in Takeuchi's words, he himself did not "despair" upon receiving the test results from Yamazaki. On the contrary. The young assistant writes in his diary that he continued as if nothing had happened. "Many times experiments don't go right the first time," he said. "I decided just to go back and do it again."

Yamazaki suggested that maybe the uranium hexafluoride was not pure enough. It was supposed to be clear, he understood. Yet it seemed cloudy to him. Perhaps it needed to be made in a different way.

Takeuchi had his own ideas. The problem might be "turbulence of gas in the tube," he said in his diary of the experiment. He began trying to refigure the amounts of uranium hexafluoride and temperatures he was using. Perhaps the problem lay there.

By this time he had the able help of Mitsuo Taketani, a brilliant young theorist who, unfortunately, was also in jail.

Taketani was as promising as any up-and-coming physicist in Japan at the time. He had aided Yukawa and Sakata in the refining of the meson theory that later won Yukawa the Nobel. At the time he came to the project, he was working for Shinichiro Tomonaga, who would also win a Nobel. But in 1938 Taketani had been in trouble with the government thought police for being a Marxist and been imprisoned. He had been released in 1939, but hysteria over Russia's possible entry into the war late in 1944 had led to his rearrest. His Marxist leanings were recalled, and the fact that he had a Russian wife did not help.

Nevertheless, Nishina, mindful of Taketani's exceptional skills, had been able to arrange special privileges for him: a private office-cell at the prison, materials with which to work out his calculations, and a regular pickup for what he produced.

Taketani told Takeuchi that since uranium was a heavy element, its molecules, including those of its isotopes, had a particularly intricate structure, and therefore, the transfer of energy between colliding molecules might not be as unimpeded as was imagined. Convection would be interfered with.

Whatever the problem, Takeuchi appears to have felt he had made progress in solving it, for by April, despite increasing air raids, he had another batch ready to analyze.

16

Lieutenant Johann Heinrich Fehler moved his submarine, *U-234,* slowly out to the Baltic. Behind him this March 25, 1945, and on all sides of the widening Kiel Fjord, were the remnants of a great Nazi naval base: splintered shipyards; blasted-out marine and armament factories; humbled warships seeking refuge from enemy attacks, especially in the open waters ahead. They loomed in the blacked-out darkness like jagged, cowering shells. In the following month, nearly a third of the surrounding city, one of the prides of historic Schleswig-Holstein, would be destroyed by Allied bombing.

Fehler, thirty-five, a former officer on the infamous German raider *Atlantis,* had been given command of the *U-234,* a converted minelayer, at its commissioning, March 3, 1944. He had been training with it for this day ever since. He knew this was probably his last action for Germany. The *U-234* was one of the largest Nazi U-boats afloat: 294 feet long; 22,000 tons fully loaded. It had been converted into an undersea transport. With Germany crumbling all around, it had been given one of the last desperate missions of the Reich: Get to Japan with secret weapons that would help carry on the war.

Packed in metal containers in most of the torpedo tubes and in entire compartments converted for cargo—even in the ballast compartments—were approximately 240 tons of documents and war matériels. These included mercury and lead for keel ballast; the latest proximity bomb fuses; new armor-piercing antiaircraft shells; the newest German high-altitude pilot's chamber; blueprints and parts for jet planes and rockets; and several items so secret they were only listed on the manifest as "confidential," and in ten individual containers destined for the "Japanese Army" were 1,120 pounds of uranium oxide—enough uranium by modern standards to make two atomic bombs.

Traveling with the cargo was a special contingent of passengers: monocled and arrogant Luftwaffe Lieutenant General Ulrich Kessler, one of Germany's top air experts and former commander of special bombing and attack wings based in Norway; Luftwaffe Colonels Fritz Sandrat and Earl Neishling, also from the Norway commands. Assigned specific responsibility for the cargo were two Imperial Japanese Navy officers, Lieutenant Commander Hideo Tomonaga, a leading Japanese submarine designer, and Lieutenant Commander Genzo Shoji, an aircraft expert. Both had come over earlier on submarines to study German weaponry. There were also civilian German jet and rocket engineers from Messerschmitt and Peenemünde; perhaps even German physicists.

The submarine's crew was young but experienced. They were survivors of Germany's decimated but still proud U-boat corps. Fehler himself had graduated from naval school only in 1935, as had his first officer, Lieutenant Richard Bulla, who had served with Fehler on the *Atlantis*.

While the wolf packs had attacked convoys almost at will during those early years of the war, Fehler and Bulla, as officers on the *Atlantis,* had played the sometimes much more dangerous game of surface deception with the enemy's shipping: The *Atlantis* would disguise itself as a friendly vessel and lure unsuspecting ships to within range of its camouflaged guns, torpedoes, and deck attack planes. Fehler was then nicknamed "Dynamite" for his job of scuttling captured vessels. He was a munitions expert.

The *Atlantis* had been the most successful of the raiders. Operating in the Atlantic, Indian, and Pacific oceans, it had sunk or captured twenty-two Allied ships; 145,697 tons of enemy cargo. That was more even than the larger pocket battleships had managed. But as the war had turned on the U-boats, the *Atlantis* became a supplier for the submarines, rendezvousing with them in dangerous, daylong fuel hookups. The two ships had to entwine themselves in fuel lines and stay as inactive as possible. Both U-boat and raider were then extremely vulnerable. On November 22, 1941, the *Atlantis* and *U-126* had been caught in just such a hookup.

U-126 had dived and escaped the onrushing British cruiser *Devonshire*. But the *Atlantis* had been sunk. Fehler and Bulla were among the 100 survivors later picked up by *U-216*. But because there was little room for them on the one submarine and because the

German U-boat chief Karl Doenitz had valued so highly the *Atlantis*'s contribution and its crew's courage, he had eventually dispatched two U-boats to bring them back safely. The U-boats put the men in rafts attached to the outside of their hulls. The rafts were to float away in case the submarines had to dive suddenly. And slowly, proceeding on the surface, the U-boats had brought the survivors all the way back to France. The operation had become known, even among the Allies, as one of the greatest sea rescues of the war.

So Fehler and Bulla had known extreme danger as well as heroics. They were not novices. And Fehler's experience in the eastern oceans, as well as in dodging and tricking the enemy as a raider, was also certainly among the reasons he had been selected to command *U-234*. In view of the almost total dominance of the air and seas that the enemy now had, he would have to be every bit as cunning as any raider commander just to get by England. For the Germans, there were no more silent passages.

The other *U-234* crew members were the second officer, Lieutenant Karl Ernst Pfaff, a boyish-looking Berliner who later settled in Canada; First Lieutenant Günter Pagenstecher, a 1939 graduate of the German naval school; the ship's doctor, Medical Officer Walter Franz; and about fifty submariners.

Because of its size and relative submerged cruising speed—seven knots per hour—*U-234* had been specially groomed for this final mission. There had been numerous trials in the Baltic. It had passed them all. It had the new *Schnorchel,* the air gatherer, which would enable it to cruise for long periods without surfacing.

At least two other large submarines had been designated by the high command to take additional cargo. But it is not clear from available data whether they ever left. If they did, it appears they went before Fehler.

A special Nazi commission, known as the Marine Sonder Dienst Auslands, had convened in December 1944 to determine exactly what cargo the U-boats going to Japan would carry. Presumably the mission was the result of negotiations with Ambassador Oshima in Berlin. The Japanese had been getting such shipments in trickles. But with the end nearing, Hitler had decided that if he himself could not continue the war, at least the Japanese could.

In addition to its military cargo, *U-234* carried fuel and provisions for a six- to nine-month trip. Its route would be the same used by the earlier submerged transports: out to the North Sea, down the Channel past England, into the Atlantic, south around Africa, into the Indian Ocean, and then the Pacific. It used to be that if a U-boat was lucky enough to make it into the Pacific, it was relatively safe. But safety no longer existed anywhere along the route. There was now a saying among submariners: A trip to Tokyo was a ticket to the grave. Fehler knew this. He stoically told his officers that he was convinced they would not make it.

This was a strange way for a commander to talk. But events soon to unfold shed light on the reason for such fatalism.

Although *U-234* had orders not to engage the enemy, it was armed with seven torpedoes (two ready for the forward tubes), and deck guns, including a 37-millimeter cannon. Heavy railroad ties were welded to its bow for icebreaking or ramming.

That night the boat moved through the Baltic near Denmark and two days later, March 27, arrived at Horten, Norway, in the Oslofjord. There it underwent *Schnorchel* trials for eight days. By mistake, it was rammed by a smaller submarine and sustained minor damage.

Repairs were made at Kristiansand, and on the evening of April 15, *U-234* moved by a hastily erected sign above the Kristiansand pens which said, "The enemy shall find nothing but rats and mice in Germany—we will never capitulate—better death than slavery." It submerged and began its desperate voyage.

17

The most important year in the Japanese atomic bomb efforts was 1945. They would succeed or fail in that year. But the Japanese were now under siege. They were acting in factional, disjointed ways.

Suzuki's five separators were ready early in the new year. But according to his memoir, delivery was delayed by increased bombings by the Americans, who, late in February, captured Iwo Jima and were thus only three hours by air from Tokyo. Then, on March 12, an air raid over Osaka knocked out all the electricity and water to the area at Osaka University being readied for the separators. A new place for them had to be found.

The separators were now in a huge, hangarlike building at Sumitomo's Amagasaki plant, right outside Osaka. Dr. Toshio Ikejima, a Sumitomo scientist, was in charge of them. Suzuki spoke with him, and he agreed to let the army experiment right there.

Suzuki quickly began preliminary testing. "First we heated the inner cylinder to see how it reacted to temperature increases," he stated in his memoir. "The differences in the expansion coefficients of copper and iron caused no problem. The system worked quite well."

Next, Suzuki and his team actually separated isotopes in nitrogen and in carbon dioxide. Unlike Takeuchi, Suzuki thus had a proven machine. "We were able to have confidence that we would succeed in uranium isotope separation."

All he now needed was the uranium hexafluoride. It was at the Rikken.

But then the inevitable occurred. On the night of August 12 the worst firebombing of Tokyo to that time commenced. By the time it was over even the Rikken was ablaze. Takeuchi and the others, who had endured the raid in shelters nearby, ran back to find Building 49 safe but surrounded by burning buildings.

They worked most of the night helping extinguish the nearby blazes and left just before dawn to get some sleep. That was a mistake. An unseen smoldering cinder somehow got to the building, and as the sun came up, NI headquarters burst into flames. By the time Takeuchi returned all that remained was his diary, which someone had saved. Nishina's lone separator and the entire stock of uranium hexafluoride at the Rikken were destroyed.

The Rikken fire should not have been so disastrous. The previous fall, worried about such an occurrence, Nishina had sent Kigoshi and Kigoshi's assistants to Yamagata, a small town in the north near Sendai. They were to continue making their uranium gas. But nothing was coming from them. Since shipments of uranium-bearing ores from Korea had been halted back in 1944, their production had dwindled. Eventually their only source of uranium was what Iimori could process for them in the two separation plants at the Rikken. And these plants, too, were destroyed in the April 12 raid.

So Suzuki had five apparently good separators, but no uranium gas to separate. He says he waited for Nishina.

Nishina, it would seem, should have been defeated by the raid. His entire project was wiped out. But he ordered his scientists to relocate and continue.

Iimori was ordered to Ishikawa Prefecture, Japan's only possible mainland source of uranium. He was told to set up a new separation operation as soon as possible. According to Yamamoto, digging there had already begun. (The Atomic Bomb Mission report said Iimori was given 10,000 yen at this time to develop the Ishikawa ores.)

The capital of Ishikawa is a large city called Kanazawa, which is almost directly across the thin width of Honshu from Tokyo. It faces Korea, with only the Sea of Japan between them. Nishina told Takeuchi and the rest of NI to go to Kanazawa and rebuild the separator.

Why he picked Kanazawa is not known. But one of the NI members, Masao Sabaru, a low-ranking army scientist who had joined the project in the 1944 upgrade, thought the order so strange that he broke custom and questioned his superior. "I asked Dr. Nishina, 'Why don't we go to Yamagata to continue? That's where Kigoshi is.' But for some reason Dr. Nishina insisted we go to Kanazawa. So we went."

One reason for the move could have been its proximity to Korea. Things were now so bad in the home islands, both because of the B-29 attacks, which were now coming two and three times daily, and because of raw material shortages, that many industries were being relocated there. "On January 18, 1945," said OSS Report No. 116461, dated February 9, 1945, "the garrison commanders of Northern, Eastern, Central and Western Japan were ordered by the High Command to maintain a state of siege. . . . Industries that cannot be moved will go underground; those that can be moved will be moved to Korea."

The result included the movement of entire factories, according to Jerome Cohen's *Japan's Economy in War and Reconstruction,* one of the few available sources about Japan's industry at the end of the war. "The most important single move," wrote Cohen, "was that of the Osaka plant of the Japan Iron Manufacturing Company at Seishin [Japanese name for Chongjin], Korea. The plant was completely dismantled in the spring of 1945—part of the equipment reached Seishin, some was sunk, and at the end of the war some remained in crates at the old site waiting to be shipped."

It is interesting that this one factory—this "most important" move by the Japanese at this time—originated in Osaka, where there were at least eight separators (three at Osaka University and five with Suzuki at Amagasaki) and concluded in Seishin, which was one of Noguchi's big centers along the complex extending north from Konan. Perhaps the huge separators (or some of them) could have been moved there in the guise of being parts of the factory.

The extent to which Korea was by this time becoming a stage and supply area for the expected last great battle—the defense of the homeland—is summed up in OSS Report No. 130787 (dated May 2, 1945): "Korea has been turned into an enormous supply base for the Japanese Army. At the end of 1944, there were 3800 units [involved in] war production. [These factories] are making guns, rifles, aircraft, ships, vehicles and clothing. Output is 30–40 percent of Japan proper. War production is entirely under the control of Mitsubishi . . . Mitsui . . . and Noguchi. . . . Korea's hydroelectric production is 3½ million Kilowatts, more than that of Japan. . . . Even schools were closed down in June 1944 and converted into arsenals and the students compelled to work in them. . . ."

We were finally becoming aware of Konan. The report goes on to say that it is the center of Korea's industrial activity. But what we still did not know was that it was also the center of at least one top-priority secret war project: the all-out effort to manufacture special fuel for Japan's jet planes.

With the jet planes from Germany, of course, had come the formula for the fuel that would power them. The fuel had three main ingredients: hydrogen peroxide, hydrazine hydrate, and sodium permanganate. Crucial to production of these ingredients were industrial salts and acids, ammonia, and nitrogen, all of which, because of the availability of raw materials nearby were being produced in quantity at Konan. According to interrogations conducted by USSBS officials, although there were approximately seventeen plants, most in Japan, charged with producing the jet fuel, Noguchi's main plant at Konan alone was responsible for nearly half of the approximately 12,000 metric tons per month the Japanese were expecting to make. Because of its safety and capacity, it was the only plant they were really counting on.

It seems likely that the secret atomic bomb program was relocated to Konan as well. It was certainly the logical place. Nowhere else were there the raw materials, production capacity, freedom from attack, and available electrical power. Perhaps the plans were to put Nishina as near to Korea as possible.

Still, with the destruction of Building 49, NI went into decline. Not so F-go.

Its ascendancy appears to have started in late 1944. At that time, faced with the inevitability of Japan's swift defeat unless they cooperated, the army and navy had been forced to put aside differences and consolidate efforts. Previous relations had been so bad, according to one naval officer (interrogated by USSBS), that the fact that the two services used different-size aircraft ammunition meant that planes of one service, out of ammunition, couldn't use what was available at nearby bases of the other service.

Suzuki recalls that "in the beginning of 1945" the navy's technical people came to air force headquarters and said that "they wanted to concentrate on making atomic bombs . . . [and] it would be a waste of time to start from the beginning [so] they asked us for the data we had from the Nishina lab. I believe at that time the Navy had lost more than half of their ships so they needed something to change the situation. We decided to give it to them."

What those data were can only be speculated upon. As Spencer Weart noted in the November 1977 issue of the *American Journal of Physics,* all nuclear work done outside the United States during the war, including Japan's, was "done hastily, written up incompletely in reports that were not widely circulated, and discussed in meetings that produced no documents at all." Nevertheless, says Suzuki in his memoir, "The army's study on the characteristics of uranium . . . was well under way, thus necessary data for the Navy's study was provided by the Army."

NI was at least working on the calculations to create the slow chain reaction, or what is today commonly called a reactor. This was the logical way to go about making an atomic bomb. It was how the United States, with Fermi's pile, had gone about it, as had Germany, according to David Irving's *The German Atomic Bomb,* the only book in English devoted entirely to the subject. Indeed, members of NI today freely admit that a reactor *was* one of the things they were working on.

A reactor would have given the Japanese the "controlled" reaction from which they could learn crucial information (as Fermi had) about how to make the "fast," or bomb type of, chain reaction. In fact, they may have constructed a reactor. Professor Eizo Tajima, a member of NI's physics group, which was mainly working with Nishina's large cyclotron, has said he built a "miniature" of a "nuclear reactor" for NI.

The project, according to Takeuchi's early notes, appears to have begun its attempts to produce a slow reaction by using French physicist Francis Perrin's early 1940s calculations about the size of the critical mass when water was the moderator. Nishina's basic plan for the project's progress, formulated sometime in 1943 and reprinted in 1970 in *The Comprehensive History of Japanese Science and Technology,* stated that "chain reaction experiments" were to be conducted *simultaneously* with the separation work.

Furthermore, wrote Philip Morrison, "under insistent questioning" from the top U.S. scientist attached to the Atomic Bomb Mission, Nishina "finally" admitted that NI had "worked on the problems of the chain reaction. He said they considered the slow reaction more important, intending someday to use it as an energy source for all purposes. The fast reaction seemed remote to him, he claims, and he did not believe it very realistic to expect an explosively fast reaction for use as a bomb:

"Dr. Amaki had earlier calculated the critical mass of a slow reactor, using pure 235 and water, with various reflectors. Nishina felt that under a kilo of U-235 might go, and even implied that unenriched material might go if properly moderated. To the end of improving the constants needed for Amaki's calculation, they undertook to measure the thermal capture cross-section of U-238 and the number of neutrons emitted per absorbed neutron in the normal mixture. The methods they employed were standard, but done only moderately well. . . ."

Another mission report stated:

Nishina's calculations [about the Hiroshima bomb] made very clear the level of his knowledge on the fission bomb. He had mapped the induced activity in phosphorus and sulphur to estimate the total neutron flux. He knew only vaguely of the fission fragments and of the prompt gamma rays, which he did not try to use as an estimating means. He made no correction for neutron diffusion or absorption in the air, but used simple inverse-square law. The parameter left free to fit the resulting mapping was the height of the burst. Nishina believed it to be 500 meters, which fitted rather well with his curve, but he was very anxious for me [Morrison] to confirm it, which I did not do. From this calculation, he estimated 10^{25} neutrons, and, taking 2 or 3 neutrons per fission, he concludes that there was burned between one and two kilos of U235. From the blast damage, he estimated 10,000 tons of HE [a code word], or about one kilo of U235. These estimates are, of course, quite good. . . .

But Nishina, it turned out, was lying to the mission. He was trying to conceal what he had done. He may have had much more knowledge than he displayed. The mission noted: "It is interesting that Nishina depended for many details upon Yamasaki [Fumio Yamazaki] and the other younger men"; basic knowledge was dispersed throughout the project. NI went further than he led the mission to believe.

Unfortunately it is Arakatsu's project, especially from January 1945 on, about which there is the least information. Accounts by Mitsui, Kitagawa, and Arakatsu himself are contradictory. While agreeing on the importance of the project to the navy and the sense of urgency with which its members were imbued, they tell little about its later stages, implying that not much occurred. But a lot did occur.

The Day Man Lost noted that "trying to reestablish itself through [this] new and decisive weapon," the navy, by this time, had ordered "Arakatsu and the scientists who worked under him . . . to carry out research around the clock." And there is evidence that the army gave the navy unprecedented cooperation. In April 1945, according to an occupation document I found at Suitland, Yukawa of F-go and

Yamamoto and Iimori of NI were working together on the Ishikawa uranium ores. Also in April, according to a Japanese fleet report I found at Suitland, the navy itself was taking wide stock of all the uranium available to it and counting heavily on ores at the Rikken and in Manchuria and Korea.

Some interesting details in the five-page fleet report—prepared at the direction of an Admiral Sasagawa, later identified for me by Mitsui as the navy's chief of material, and dated April 1, 1945—are those under the heading "Technical Matters and Reagents," referring to those required to extract uranium from the ores. It says that a "special technique is not required." What is needed is just certain chemicals: "soda ash . . . in large amounts, also oxalic acid and hydrogen peroxide. . . . In addition ammonium sulphate. . . ." While these, by this time, were in very short supply or nonexistent in the home islands, they were plentiful at Konan. In fact, Konan, because of the jet fuel project, had one of the few plants in the empire manufacturing hydrogen peroxide. And that plant was making much more than any other plant.

Just as the navy took the lead in the project, uranium processing on the Asian mainland was stepped up. Akimasa Kamio, a Kyoto geologist, told in *Showa* how, in January 1945, he was summoned to the Japanese Embassy in northern China and told by an army major, "Don't ask any questions. Just start sending one ton of monazite every month." Monazite, which usually has only about 1 percent uranium content, was one of the ores listed on the April fleet report as a possible source of the navy's uranium.

Kamio continued: "At the same time, I remember that northern Korea and Manchuria were ordered to send one ton per month." None of the ore ever reached the home islands. Kamio had trouble with Chinese bandits. The monazite was under the beaches of the Shantung Peninsula, a remote plat of land jutting out into the Yellow Sea across from upper Korea. The bandits presented a problem that the Japanese, retreating by that time, could not handle. But they did have control of Inner Mongolia, Manchuria, and Korea. And in 1945, according to many documents I found at Suitland, the Japanese did increase their uranium mining in these areas.

As early as February 1944, according to formerly secret intelligence reports I found at Suitland, uranium-containing pegmatites were being mined and stockpiled in hill country near Heichisen, Inner Mongolia. The deposits, associated with mica, also contained beryllium, a frequent source of neutrons in fission experiments.

Fermi, for instance, used beryllium to start his 1942 chain reaction in Chicago.

Sometime probably in late 1944, according to the formerly secret reports, an expedition led by General Tada, who had gotten the Malayan uranium ores for Iimori and was heading the Japanese search for strategic minerals throughout the empire, visited the Heichisen mines. In February 1945 a larger expedition, led by Japanese engineers from Ryojun (Japanese name for Port Arthur), Manchuria, arrived and began large-scale excavation. By the following month "300 Chinese coolies" were working in the mines. Another report said that in nearby Pau T'ou "uranium was being experimented with."

In Manchuria most of the activity was in the Mukden-Dairen area, no more than 200 miles from the northern Korean border. Numerous reports said that the Kwangtung Army, which controlled the area, was mining pegmatite, a crystalline rock with uranium ores in it, in the Anshan area, just south of Mukden. According to one report, "1,000 men" working in the Anshan mines had excavated "300,000 tons of the uranium ore" before the war's end. Another report said that at Haicheng, south of Anshan, "five tons" of what appears to have been euxenite, containing "about 8 percent uranium oxide," had been "obtained by handpicking from 25,000 tons of ore." Samples of these ores were supposedly sent back to Tokyo "for atomic bomb experiments."

There was even a pitchblende deposit reported in Wan-Ch'ing, Manchuria, by the Korean-Russian border. The report said the Japanese "assayed the ore, and finding it rich in uranium immediately launched a project to develop the mine—however, the end of the war halted the program."

However, in the intelligence reports I found by far the highest concentration of uranium mining was carried out in Korea.

In the Seoul-Inchon area, just below the thirty-eighth parallel, at least three tons of fergusonite with a "four to five percent" uranium content was reported stockpiled when the war ended. The Atomic Bomb Mission confirmed this, as it did the uranium ore-bearing pegmatite in Manchuria. The mission's information was that both stockpiles were to be used for atomic bomb experiments. Stockpiled alongside the Korean fergusonite, according to other reports, were approximately 1,000 tons of black sands, which also had a uranium content, albeit small.

But most of the Korean ore activity was reported to have occurred in the North. There was the Chuul-Chongjin area north of Konan. Before the war, according to geological records, Iimori had found thorium and other heavy elements there. Documents at Suitland indicated that in 1947 American intelligence was still trying to determine if the Chuul mines, by then guarded by Russian soldiers, contained uranium. But they could not get reliable agents in.

In 1946, acting on "a letter received from Washington," a special contingent of geological experts led by Major R. R. Entwhistle descended on Seoul to get "confirmation of pitchblende deposits" in Korea. It is not clear yet whether the pitchblende was believed to be in the North or the South, but indications are it was in the North. It could have been the Chuul deposits since they were reported in 1946. The mission also could have been organized in response to the reports about the Konan atomic bomb project, which were coming in at this time. It was through trying to find out more about this 1946 mission that I ran across the fact that "Plants for the refining of . . . rare element minerals did not exist [in Korea] except for the isolated case of Nippon Magnesite Chemical Industrial Company," a Noguchi plant near Konan.

Elsewhere in the North, in interrogation by the Atomic Bomb Mission, Kyoto University geologist Takubo said he found uranium at the "Tamyoku Mine" near Pyongyang, which was in the center of Korea, just above the thirty-eighth parallel (the Japanese called it Heijo and it is now the capital of North Korea). Also just above the thirty-eighth parallel, but closer to the western shore of the peninsula, was a mine near Kaesong (which the Japanese knew as Kaijo), owned by the Manchurian Mining Company. It was supposed to be furnishing ore, possibly fergusonite, for atomic bomb experiments that ended when the war did.

There were still more reports of North Korean deposits, for instance, at Haeju (which the Japanese called Kaishu), just above Inchon, below Chinnampo, on the coast. Chinnampo itself was supposed to have black sands stockpiled. "The Japanese did absolutely incredible things," Bill Overstreet of the U.S. Geological Survey told me. He had gone to Korea to take stock shortly after the war. Of course, he had not been able to go into North Korea. But in the South, he said, "We were in fluorite mines where they excavated veins so narrow that they had to use children seven and eight years old to get into the openings. At their big tungsten mine at Sangdong their extraction procedures were so poor that they had five thousand coolies panning downstream to recover what they were losing."

But they were using "state of the art" exploration methods, he added. In hunting for nickel and cobalt, for instance, they employed "emission spectrographic analysis," a system whereby potential metal beds were located by the taking of surface samples of an area at regular intervals. The Japanese drilled in the areas where the highest readings occurred. "Sort of like drilling in the yolk of the egg," said Overstreet; "the white part can be discarded." This had been pioneered by the Russians and the Swedes in the 1930s, he said. "We began using it during the war, too. It's now standard procedure."

In relation to the Japanese mining for uranium, however, Overstreet said: "We never got a whisper of that while we were in South Korea. We had good relationships with the Korean geologists who were working with us and access to most of their documents. But we did know that before the director of the Japanese [geological] survey was repatriated, and before American troops came to Inchon, the Japanese officers of the geological survey spent two or three days burning files. That's a fact. . . . If they had been searching for uranium, they burned it.

"And there's an entirely different aspect—the South Manchurian Railroad Company." This was the Japanese company entrusted with developing Manchuria. Its headquarters were in Dairen, close to the northern Korean border. Dairen was a staging and receiving area for the Anshan–Haicheng mines, and was connected to northern and southern Korea, including Konan, by extensive and well-developed and guarded railways. The Atomic Bomb Mission said workers at the company's central laboratory at Dairen had "done a good deal with the Clusius tube." The Clusius tube was the kind of separator Takeuchi had built. Was this still another aspect of the project?

"The railroad company had its own geologists," said Overstreet, "and they were working all over Manchuria. I don't know where on God's earth you can get records on what they did. I did have a man who was part of it working with me in Japan. But I'm sure he's dead now."

18

U-*234* proceeded submerged for the first sixteen days. A large enemy steamer almost rammed it at a point in the English Channel where fog and its shallow depth rendered it particularly vulnerable. But the steamer did not see it, and it got through the Channel undetected.

"From then on," according to a formerly classified U.S. Navy report, "she usually ran two hours on the surface at night and spent the balance of the time submerged to depths between 40–100 meters [120–300 feet]"—deep for a World War II submarine. Bad weather, which would hinder the operation of the *Schnorchel*, sometimes forced it to surface more often.

Inside, the trip was the usual cramped boredom mixed with moments of intense fear, especially when the steamer almost hit them. The presence of cargo packed in every available space was an added discomfort. But the Japanese, at least, appear to have been jovial. They gave a samurai sword to Fehler, as well as a "sizeable sum in Swiss francs." Gifts were also given to the other officers and passengers, two of whom may have been Messerschmitt engineers, Dr. Schauerns and Dr. von Chilingensberg, both laboratory heads.

Tomonaga and Shoji shared a forward berth compartment surrounded on its outside by the ship's large batteries, thirty-three in all. That meant it was one of the warmest compartments, even in the severe North Atlantic cold. It had four bunks. Kessler, who had led fighter groups against Poland in his combat days, spent a lot of the time reading.

"The first ominous sign," says the report, was when the submarine stopped receiving radio signals from Nauen, a headquarters near Berlin. (Berlin fell to the Russians on May 2.) Fehler had expected such trouble from the outset. He submerged and proceeded for several days without radio contact. He had no specific information about what had happened. He switched to shortwave. "On the 4th of May," the boat "got a fragmentary report from English and American stations about Doenitz's elevation to supreme command in Germany." *U-234* was now well out in the North Atlantic but had not made its turn south. Fehler decided to surface "in order to receive complete signals."

Hitler's death was confirmed. So was Doenitz's move north from Berlin. Then, on May 10, they picked up Doenitz's order to surrender: "My U-boat men! Six years of war lie behind us. You have fought like lions. An overwhelming material superiority has driven us into a tight corner, from which it is no longer possible to continue the war. Unbeaten and unblemished, you lay down your arms after a heroic fight without parallel. We proudly remember our fallen comrades. . . . Long live Germany!"

The order was followed by another giving more specific instructions: U-boats were to surface and, displaying a large black or dark blue flag, make for the nearest Allied port.

Those on board, perhaps with the exception of Fehler, were stunned. *U-234* "was at the intersecting point of two lines dividing the Atlantic into four zones for U-boat surrenders," Second Officer Pfaff told an American newspaper reporter years later. It could go to Britain, Gibraltar, Canada, or the United States.

Fehler was a "very democratic skipper, having served in the Merchant Marine," according to Pfaff. He put the decision to the crew. "Considerable discussion arose among the officers and passengers as to what course they should follow," says the report. Argentina was first proposed. The U-boat had harbor plans for several South American ports, and the largest number of crew members—those without families, according to Pfaff—favored Buenos Aires. Fehler took everything under advisement and proceeded south, surfacing at night and submerging during the daytime. As he did, he heard other U-boats surrendering. He finally decided to report his position to the enemy. He was going to make course for the United States.

But it was not so easy. Apparently everybody wanted the prize. The boat's first orders came from Britain on May 12 at 8:00 A.M. Britain wanted the boat to surrender in one of its ports. Fehler disregarded the order and continued westerly, toward the United States. Canada, which thought it was going to get the boat, began sending orders on how to proceed. So did the United States. Fehler told Canada it was coming and that its speed was eight miles per hour. But he actually took a more westerly direction at between twelve and fifteen miles per hour. Apparently he was trying to race to the United States, where other accounts say most in the crew felt they would be best received.

"When it became apparent to the Japanese officers that Fehler intended to obey surrender orders," said the navy report, "they informed him of their resolve to commit suicide. Fehler made some attempt to dissuade them from this, particularly by citing the surrender of [General Oshima and his staff in Berlin] as an example. But the pair requested that they be allowed to remain undisturbed in their cabin, which was granted. . . . A guard was placed outside their compartment, and the two took an overdose of Luminol [a barbiturate which sedates and induces sleep]. They were still alive some 36 hours later, much to the disgust of the crew, and efforts on the part of ship's doctor to revive them failed."

Tomonaga and Shoji were buried at sea on May 11, according to the navy report, and Fehler disregarded a request they left that Japan be notified. A U.S. patrol plane finally caught sight of the sub, and the discrepancy in its reported and actual speed was noted. Taking no chances, the United States dispatched the *Sutton,* a destroyer, and at 11:30 P.M., on May 14, 500 miles from Cape Race, Newfoundland, *U-234* was boarded by an American prize crew. It was decided to take it to the Portsmouth, New Hampshire, naval yard, a base which was specially equipped to handle submarines and had a naval prison.

Three other U-boats—*U-805, U-873,* and *U-1228*—had surrendered earlier to the United States. But *U-234,* by far the largest and carrying its important cargo and passengers, was the big story. Top secret security was instituted almost immediately. But news of the surrender quickly got out. One of the first wire service bulletins, according to *Surrender at Sea,* a compilation of stories broadcast over WHEB radio, Portsmouth, said:

A German submarine which was headed for Japan with three high Luftwaffe generals aboard has surrendered. . . . Admiral Jonas Ingram, commander-in-chief of the Atlantic Fleet, reveals . . . [that] two dead Japs aboard . . . committed *hari-kari,* probably to avoid capture by the Americans. There are no details at this hour on [their] identity . . . or what they were doing aboard. . . . Neither is there any clue to the strange drama which must have been enacted aboard . . . when it learned that Germany had surrendered and when it decided to give up rather than continue the long trip to Japan. Admiral Ingram says charts and aviation equipment of the German Air Force were found on the Japan-bound U-boat. This indicates that the German officers may have planned to carry on their air war against the Allies from Japan.

The dispatch had errors, but it produced a gang of reporters at the docks when *U-234* came in May 19. Interviews were not allowed, but the reporters wrote what they observed.

Charlie Grey, author of most of the stories in *Surrender at Sea,* reported, "If anyone ever saw a typical Hollywood version of a German general, Kessler was it. As he strutted off the gangplank he casually looked around, saluted [Rear Admiral Thomas] Withers as he passed, and swaggered to a waiting bus. He wore a long leather greatcoat which reached to his ankles, highly polished leather boots and an Iron Cross which hung tightly about his neck. He posed for newsreel cameramen and seemed to be enjoying the publicity he was receiving."

The *New York Times* ran two pictures with its story: tugboats escorting the large U-boat and Kessler, monocle in eye, reading an English-language book, *After the War What? Times* man William M. Blair wrote:

Whether any prize Nazis were among the passengers is not known. [A] civilian . . . in a wrinkled gray suit covered by a soiled gabardine raincoat of the military style, was reported to be an engineer. As he strode hatless from a Coast Guard vessel, he lugged a bulging cardboard suitcase. . . . The officers and members of the submarine crew were in sharp contrast to the smartly clad general. . . . [They] wore nondescript apparel of all shapes and sizes. Several had the traditional gray rubberized suits covering turtleneck sweaters. Others had blue fatigue clothes and the caps made famous by the German Afrika Corps. . . .

One incident highlighted the spectacle. . . . As the U-boat commander, Kapitaenleutnant Johann Heinrich Fehler, . . . prepared to leave the ship, he protested to [Coast Guard] Lieut. Charles Winslow. . . . Winslow had heard that the Nazi officers had been complaining below decks and asked him what troubled him. Fehler, tall, round-faced, talked rapidly in German, saying that he and his men had been forced to sit with their hands folded across their chests. He shouted: "Your men treated us like gangsters!" An interpreter relayed the words. . . . The American officer's eyes flashed. . . "That's just what you are! Get off!" The German officer, carrying a stuffed brief case and a couple of paper packages, strode quickly to the dock. . . . He appeared angry and close to tears.

It was a good show, fitting for the victors. But the most important events concerning *U-234* were conducted in secret. Uranium was not a household word in May 1945. The first atomic bomb was not to be exploded until the coming August. Few people, other than scientists and military men, were even aware of uranium's significance to weaponry. It's extremely doubtful that any of the reporters knew it was on board, and if so, none mentioned it.

But War Department officials were aware and, it appears, feverish to find out all they could. Within hours of *U-234*'s docking, most of its crew had been taken to Portsmouth's naval prison, while Kessler, some of the sub's officers, and all its other passengers were put aboard a navy bomber and flown to Washington, along with eighteen metal cargo cylinders. Second Officer Pfaff, who visited the *Portsmouth Herald* in 1954 to look at the newspaper's clippings on the surrender, recalled for reporter Bob Norling that there was much anxiety in Washington on the part of officials who were preparing to open the cylinders with acetylene torches and feared they might be booby-trapped.

They were not. The cargo was revealed. A translation of the sub's manifest I got from the Naval Historical Center's Operational Archives, Washington, shows that in it were "560" kilograms of "uranium oxide," listed between "2.5" kilograms of "cable" and "620" kilograms of "stock parts for percussion caps." The uranium was in "10 cases" and destined for the "Jap Army." Similarly Pfaff told Norling that "uranium oxide mined in Germany" was among the "top secret" cargo on board. Norling quoted Pfaff to that effect in his story of the former submariner's return to Portsmouth. The story appeared in the *Herald* on July 9, 1954.

What happened to the uranium? I have not been able to find out. Inquiries to government agencies have produced nothing. It's as if the incident had never occurred, as if *U-234*, its important passengers and cargo had never arrived. My guess is that the uranium was taken over by the War Department and that the secret disposition of *U-234* and its cargo was the beginning of a top secret burial, in the interests of security, of everything concerned with the Japanese atomic bomb program. *U-234*'s capture and cargo alerted U.S. officials to the fact that the Japanese had been exerting serious efforts to make an atomic bomb. From that time on, the Manhattan Project and the War Department determined to find out just how far Japan had gotten. The War Department began to wonder about the Japanese's atomic potential just as it had worried about the Germans'. Almost certainly the fact that Japan might be building an atomic bomb would have been presented to President Truman when he considered dropping the first atomic bomb on Hiroshima.

Bruce Scott Old, a naval officer who had been on the Alsos mission to Germany to determine what progress the Nazis had made in atomic physics and returned to be a naval liaison with the Manhattan Project, remembers a representative from General Groves's office coming into his to discuss what Olds believes was probably *U-234*. "Groves almost had apoplexy when the Germans launched a submarine called *U-235*," he said. But he added it was probably *U-234*. "The thing that disturbed Groves was that the intelligence report indicated the submarine was headed for Argentina. His intelligence guy came to me to find out what to do about it."

It might have been in reaction to the implications of *U-234*'s uranium that the idea of sending the Atomic Bomb Mission to Japan was born. Even as Pfaff, Fehler, Kessler and the others were being sent back to Portsmouth and elsewhere, the navy, army, and the Office of Scientific Research and Development (OSRD), the civilian board aiding the War Department in scientific mobilization, began compiling lists of Japanese physicists who would be interrogated once the Japanese had surrendered. I saw such a list among documents retrieved for me by the Navy and Old Army Branch of the National Archives. Arakatsu was listed as a potential "target." It had been compiled under the auspices of Alsos. *Combat Scientists,* by L. Thiesmayer and John E. Burchard, a 1947 book about the OSRD, says, "Long before the Japanese surrender, plans were made for [Alsos-like] investigations in Japan. . . ."

Back at Portsmouth, *U-234* was dry-docked, cordoned off by marine guards, and taken apart piece by piece. "It was the first German submarine they did that to," recalled Lee A. White, who was working in the yard at the time. "Apparently, they were looking for other things." Discovery of the mercury used as ballast made a major splash in the local newspapers. "The sensational discovery . . . was hidden between the inner and outer hulls on either side of the keel," broadcast Charlie Grey on WHEB.

19

One of the reasons Nishina's project continued after Rikken's destruction was that General Yoshijiro Umezu, who had succeeded his old friend Premier Tojo as head of the army, refused to cancel it. Colonel Mitsuo Arimura, who, after General Kawashima had been transferred to a suicide unit's command structure, had become the top army technical officer with direct responsibility for the project, had recommended cancellation. But Umezu was bitterly opposed to surrender to the very end and was, by April, deeply involved in the planning for the defense of the home islands.

The defense of the homeland, Japan's last effort to turn the tide, was, to put it mildly, fanatical. The main weapon was to be suicide: waves and waves of suicide units in the air, on and under the sea, and swarming over the land. Newly developed weapons would bolster these units. Jet planes, guided missiles, possibly lethal gas, the "death ray," and the "fission" bomb were among the weapons being planned.

The Japanese rightly expected the Allied invasion to begin in October or November. By that time they planned to be dug into caves, mountains, and underground fortresses. The attack would commence when the Allied invasion armada appeared off Japan's shores. "The [combined army and navy] air force plan was to attack the Allied Fleet by Kamikaze planes, and for that purpose the full air force, led by the Commanding General, was made ready to destroy the Allied ships near the shore," Lieutenant General Noburu Tazoe, one of the planners, told USSBS interrogators. "We expected annihilation of our entire air force, but we felt that it was our duty. The Army and Navy each had 4,000 to 5,000 planes for this purpose. Of that force, waves of 300 to 400 planes at the rate of one wave per hour for each the Army and the Navy would have been used to oppose a landing on Kyushu (the southernmost of the four main Japanese islands.)"

The kamikazes were to aim first at the troop transports, then at the landing craft. Their third priority was the warships. In other words, American soldiers were their priority target. In addition to the suicide planes, suicide midget submarines and small surface craft were to be part of the attack. Finally, there was the Baka bomb, a guided missile, sometimes with a suicide soldier inside, to hurl at the invaders. It would be very fast and thus very hard to shoot down. American intelligence officers gave it the name Baka, Japanese for "fool."

If the jet planes, death ray, and fission bomb could be developed in time, they, too, would be thrown into the initial phase of the defense. Japanese commanders thought they might be able to get the jet plane ready. They were less optimistic about the death ray or fission bombs.

In essence, the death ray was a huge microwave shooter. It is probably part of the arsenals of today's major powers. According to a report by the occupation's Technical Intelligence Detachment, which I found at Suitland, the Japanese learned about it in a newspaper article that told of the Germans trying to make one during World War I. When war with America began, they started work on it in earnest.

The death ray program paralleled work on the fission bomb. Several labs were involved. By 1945 appropriations on the order of 1 million yen were being given to the work. Its heart was a huge machine which generated the electrical ray. By 1944, said one document, it had killed monkeys "the size of a dog." Death resulted from brain and lung damage. Death ray lab workers complained of headaches and loss of appetite. Other experiments showed that the ray could stop aircraft engines, but only when they were uncovered. Planners of the homeland defense were hoping that the ray could be perfected for use against B-29 crews and engines. One researcher, Dr. Shunichi Yoshida, was trying to produce an electrical "thunderbolt" for disabling planes. He had already produced a "small one in his lab," says the report.

The fission bomb held the most promise. One bomb-bearing suicide plane could destroy entire formations of B-29s or fleets of troop-carrying ships. The Japanese had successfully used kamikazes against ships in the Battle of the Philippines in 1944 and at Okinawa in April 1945. The kamikaze had become its most feared weapon. Suicide planes, in smaller numbers, had also attacked and destroyed B-29s. One suicide pilot in the Philippine campaign had been found with his feet tied to the plane pedals. The suicide pilots were not going to back down.

It also appears that the Japanese were at least considering the use of poison gas. Magic reveals that by 1944 they had a strong interest in American intentions to use gas. (Interestingly a secret 1943 report by British Ministry of Economic Warfare, which I found in the OSS files at the National Archives, said that poison gas was being produced at a Noguchi-controlled plant on the extreme northern coast of Korea at Rashin [Najin in Korean].) By March 1945, according to Magic dispatches, the Japanese were convinced America would use poison gas. In fact, American losses had been so heavy in earlier island invasions the United States *was* considering it. This means that in addition to all the other horrors planned, the invasion sites very well could have been covered with choking, searing, blinding fogs of floating death.

If America decided not to invade but, instead, relied exclusively on B-29 bombardment, which was exacting a devastating toll on Japanese life and industry, to make Japan surrender, then the new weapons being developed became even more important. Premier Kantaro Suzuki, the Japanese prime minister at the time of the surrender, told USSBS interrogators: "If the United States had not landed in Japan and had just continued bombing Japan, I believe the Supreme War Council intended to fight America in the air with planes. At that time Japan was on the point of finishing the development of a superior-type plane and various other weapons such as rocket planes with which we hoped to offset the advantage given you by the B-29s, so that I believe the alternative plan was that, if you did not land, we would fight it out with you in the air with the new equipment which we hoped to have available very shortly."

U.S. intelligence estimated that several million American and Japanese would die in the invasion of Japan. And it was into this caldron of planning for resistance against the Allied invasion, of intrigues and conflicting schemes that the last months of the Japanese atomic bomb program were played out.

Nishina is variously said to have both admitted defeat and actually separated U-235. According to the Eighth Army Research Lab's Yamamoto, Nishina handed a report to the army on June 28 that said making an atomic bomb was not possible. The stockpiling of ore for him in Korea was halted, and all emphasis was shifted to the navy program. But in a report ordered by the occupation in 1948, the former NI liaison Major Kenji Koyama, Colonel Arimura's aide, said, "Dr. Nishina's laboratory was completely destroied [sic] and separation of U-235 was not completed till May 1945." This was probably a mistake; Koyama may have been trying to say that NI definitely ended in May 1945. But we cannot be sure now. The fact that reports were ordered by the occupation as late as 1948 indicates that the Allies still were not sure about what had occurred.

But there is no confusion about F-go in May 1945. Members of Arakatsu's project were making a frantic, last-minute effort to produce the bomb. Kyoto had been spared the B-29 bombings that were destroying so many other Japanese cities. A Kyoto University scholar told his sister "that Japan would soon be in possession of . . . a uranium bomb." In Arakatsu's lab "work was going on both day and night. . . ."

The exact nature of the work at this late date can only be speculated upon. But various sources give these glimpses: *Showa* said there were meetings, which involved at least Yukawa, Okada, and Sasaki. The 1948 occupation-ordered report on the navy project, which accompanied Koyama's (and was written by Captain Mitsui), said, "The cyclotron in Dr. Arakatsu's laboratory was completed just before the end of the war," and this agrees with other accounts. Arakatsu said he had hoped to get a new cyclotron out of the navy program, but the roster of F-go participants and duties in *The Comprehensive History of Japanese Science and Technology* lists both the project's "basic measurement" machine and "isotope separation" machine as cyclotrons. Both used magnets, so Mitsui's sentence could refer to a centrifuge.

The centrifuge, of course, was the more important. Kyoto already had a cyclotron, as did some of the other labs that were working with F-go. And Arakatsu was in the midst of constructing a large (in those days) thirty-nine-incher, according to the Atomic Bomb Mission report. This new cyclotron would have aided the project on some of its theoretical problems. But a working centrifuge, capable of the crucial separation they were seeking, would have meant more. It would have been a milestone.

Whether or not F-go ever produced a centrifuge, and what happened to it if it did, are still debatable. F-go members interviewed in *Showa* indicated that no machine was ever built. They say that the Hokushine Electric factory was bombed and that no machines materialized from Sumitomo's or Tokyo Keiki's efforts. But Lieutenant Commander Kitagawa, the navy liaison equivalent to NI's Colonel Suzuki, suggests the unit at Hokushine *was* completed. His memoir says it was destroyed at a railroad station *en route* to Kyoto University. All published sources agree that the centrifuge's design was completed. So the possibility exists that either a design or a completed unit could have reached Korea.

On July 21, 1945, an important F-go meeting occurred. For the first time, say most sources, the admirals convened with F-go members to discuss progress. The meeting was held at Lake Biwa, just north of Kyoto, the largest lake in Japan and one of the most beautiful.

In attendance were all the important Kyoto researchers, most notably Arakatsu, theoreticians Yukawa and Kobayashi, centrifuge designer Shimizu, and radiochemists Sasaki and Okada. Representing the navy, in addition to Kitagawa, were Rear Admiral Kuroda, Kitagawa's boss at the Naval Technical Research Lab; Rear Admiral Shigearu Nitta, who was working with Tokyo Keiki on the centrifuge, about which he was an expert; and Captain Mitsui. Shoichi Sakata, the Nagoya University theorist who worked closely with Yukawa, was there; F-go's roster shows him as the project's neutron theorist. Kitagawa said that at least one NI member, possibly the Rikken's Toshikazu Kimura, a neutron specialist, was present. There are also indications that several scientists from Osaka University were there.

Osaka's participation in the Japanese atomic bomb program is obscure. Takeda, working at Osaka, had helped Takeuchi in the beginning of NI's separation efforts, and Colonel Suzuki had turned first to Osaka and its head physicist Kikuchi when he and the army had decided to enlarge NI. Even after the air raid which damaged Osaka University and caused Suzuki to abandon it as an NI enlargement site, Osaka is said by several sources to have ended the war with three thermal diffusion separators and one of the only mass spectrometers in Japan. What happened to the mass spectrometer is a mystery. Takeda told the Atomic Bomb Mission that it "was moved to an evacuation research center situated at Okayama [300 kilometers west of Kyoto]. . . ."

Accounts of the Lake Biwa meeting are slim. But the following is generally agreed upon: Arakatsu opened with a discussion of where the project was (unfortunately he does not elaborate). Rear Admiral Nitta, using a bamboo pointer to refer to blackboard illustrations, explained the centrifuge. Kobayashi spoke on critical mass, and reports on pertinent cross sections and how to make uranium metal were circulated among those present.

In his memoir, Arakatsu said he doesn't remember much about the Biwa conference: "Some were serious about the project, and some were not. I remember we had a good dinner and there was a thorium factory in Niihama on Shikoku [one of the Japanese islands], and some said couldn't we do anything with the thorium?"

This was not the first time the possibility of using thorium, which can be converted into fissionable material, had been brought up. Iimori says that when the big push to find uranium was launched in 1943, he and the other geologists were told to find thorium as well. Thorium decays, when bombarded by neutrons, into fissionable uranium 233. The United States was aware of this and was working on using it in its atomic program. While uranium was scarce in the Japanese Empire, thorium was relatively plentiful. One of the best sources of thorium, for instance, is monazite, which, as we have noted, was in abundance in Korea.

The meeting ended, said Arakatsu, with few prospects for the future. According to *Showa,* F-go was dissolved. But Kitagawa said the meeting was convened for the express purpose of finding out "how to make the bomb." And when questioned by the Scientific Intelligence Survey, a group of scientists sent in by the U.S. Army to assess what Japanese science had done to help the war effort (with the exception of nuclear progress, which was to be handled exclusively by the Atomic Bomb Mission), Dr. Hideji Yagi, one of the top scientific coordinators for the imperial war effort, said that a navy official told him on August 15, 1945, that "Arakatsu had been working for the Navy right along on atomic problems, and that this had been kept secret from both the Army and the Board of Technology," the top scientific-military coordinating board.

Magic revealed that in response to the atomic bombings of Hiroshima and Nagasaki, the Japanese high command sent out a message that "F-operations are to be alerted along with Operation Homeland." There do not appear to have been any "F" operations other than F-go. Arakatsu said in his memoir that by August 15 "my lab finished the research about the atomic bomb in outline." This, too, indicates he continued working right to the end.

How far had Arakatsu progressed? Spencer Weart wrote in his 1977 article in the *American Journal of Physics* that Arakatsu seemed to have deduced three of "four factors" needed to make a chain reaction. "So far as I can tell from the evidence I have seen, the Japanese closely approached the four-factor formula but never quite reached it." But Weart was working predominantly from Arakatsu's memoir, which is short on specifics.

If, as Arakatsu implied, he had finished all the theory by the end of the war, then what really was left by this stage was an engineering problem: industrial application of the theoretical physics that had been worked out.

20

Spurred by fears that Germany was developing an atomic bomb, the United States had exerted maximum effort in its project. Nothing had been held back. Whereas Germany and Japan, buoyed by battle successes and belief in their invincibility, started slowly, the United States had gone to the other extreme. As a September 17, 1945, article in the *New Republic* noted, "A bold step had to be taken. Instead of setting up a small pilot plant to test . . . manufacturing procedures [much as the Japanese had done], it was necessary to jump at once into large-scale production. 'In peacetime,' wrote [H. D.] Smyth [in the official postwar U.S. Army report on the atomic bomb], 'no engineer or scientist in his right mind would consider making such a magnification in a single step.' But there was no alternative. The Nazis were known to be working on an atomic bomb."

So following Fermi's chain reaction, not just the most promising atom bomb-connected projects but every project with *any* chance of success were funded to the hilt. The entire length and breadth of the United States became a secret, humming, sometimes roaring bomb research and development facility. At Berkeley, California, under the leadership of Sagane's mentor, Ernest Lawrence, a cyclotron, converted into a large new mass spectrograph, eventually began separating a tenth of an ounce of U-235 a day. Across the country at Oak Ridge, Tennessee, after development at Columbia University, acres of gaseous diffusion barriers were erected and began enriching uranium hexafluoride gas. The mighty Tennessee River provided the power.

Back West, the Columbia River at Hanford, Washington, was supplying the energy and coolant for a reactor, modeled after Fermi's. It was making plutonium, another fissionable element, which was a decay product of the uranium pile. Neither Japan nor Germany appears to have been aware of its possibilities for the making of a fission bomb. But work at Berkeley focused on it as promising because it could be chemically separated from the reactor decay products. This was easier than isotope separation.

Down in Los Alamos, New Mexico, General Groves set up his bomb design and assembly plant. With the theory worked out and the fissionable material at hand, the last step was bomb design. The Los Alamos scientists were directed to find out how small a mass the fissionable material could be and how to trigger it. Elsewhere, mostly in the industrial heartland around the Great Lakes, were various other projects, among them production of more plutonium near Chicago, porous barriers at Decatur, Illinois, and uranium hexafluoride in Nebraska.

By 1944 General Groves, who reported directly to the War Department, had spent more than $1 billion. No expense was too high. The original estimate of completion had been mid-1944, but problems with the various separation methods and plutonium production pushed that back to mid-1945. The target changed from Germany to Japan. The main problem relating to triggering the bomb was this: It would explode when two subcritical masses of fissionable material were suddenly forced together to form a supercritical mass. But how did one get the two together quickly enough to avoid starting the reaction prematurely and thus having the bomb fizzle? The speed needed was on the order of a thousandth of a second.

At first, firing one lump into another in a gun type of assembly was favored, but calculations showed that this method might not be fast enough. Then the idea of implosion occurred: A lump would be surrounded by explosives, which, when set off simultaneously, would instantaneously compress it into a supercritical mass. This was the quickest way and had the added advantage of needing less fissionable material.

By summer 1945 there was enough plutonium for a bomb. The capture of the Marianas Islands put B-29s, modified to carry the large projectile, within delivery range. At dawn on July 16 a test was conducted at Alamogordo, south of Los Alamos. It was successful.

President Truman's decision was reached by July 25. Truman was not an indecisive man, and most sources indicate he made a quick decision. On the one hand were arguments that the weapon wasn't needed, that Japan was already near collapse, and the morally repugnant step of using such a horrifying bomb could be avoided. On the other were intelligence estimates that the Japanese were going to fight to the last man, and unless the bomb were dropped, an invasion would cost the lives of millions on both sides. Now that Germany had been defeated, some of the American scientists involved in making the bomb submitted a petition that at least a test for the enemy be conducted. But intelligence belief in the probable need of an invasion was strong, and if a test failed, said the estimates, it might have the opposite effect of strengthening Japanese resolve. In any case, argued some of Truman's advisers, wartime was not the place to talk of moral obligations. The stakes were too high.

That, in brief, is publicly what is said to have transpired. No doubt it did, and the above arguments were the primary ones. But what else was said? Was the possibility that Japan might have some nuclear capability of its own brought up? So far I've found no written evidence of it. But almost certainly this was discussed at the time of Truman's deliberations.

In addition to the convincing hard intelligence Truman had about *U-234*, numerous rumors were circulating late in the war. In February 1945 there was an OSS report about "stories" of "an atomic discharge to be used against [Allied] aircraft." Then a few months later Alsos mission headquarters ran into a report about a scientist getting up before the Japanese House of Peers and announcing that "he is succeeding in his research for a thing so powerful that it would require very little potential energy to destroy an enemy fleet within a few moments." The reference was clearly to an atomic bomb, according to the sheet I found at the National Archives' Navy and Old Army Branch. Alsos, which, of course, was created to determine what progress the Germans had made on a bomb, had headed it "Quite a Coincidence."

21

Commander Mitsui was at his desk at the Kure Naval Base, ten miles down the coast from Hiroshima. It was approximately 8:15 A.M. on August 6. Since leaving the Kyoto uranium bomb project, he had been concentrating on jet fuel in his work for the special chemical section of the navy's Munitions Bureau.

Suddenly he became aware of a flash. He looked up. His first thought was that an electrical substation nearby had shorted. He got up to go to the window and take a look. There was a loud explosion. He rushed to the sill. The substation appeared fine. He now suspected that the noise had come from the direction of Hiroshima, beyond the mountains blocking his view.

His office was actually on the side of a hill, which was half surrounded by mountains. The semicircle broke where the sloping ground met the bay, where ships were anchored. He ran outside the office, meeting subordinates who had seen and heard what he had, and all of them ran to the top of the hill. A huge gray cloud was mushrooming above Hiroshima. "My first thought was that maybe a train carrying explosives had been bombed. But then I saw the width. It was the same size as the city." He also saw "red flame or smoke" snaking within the mushroom cloud.

Strontium 90 is the most deadly fallout product of a nuclear explosion. The crimson isotope is long-lasting. If absorbed into the body, it emits electrons which destroy tissue. The host dies slowly. It was strontium 90, Mitsui decided, that he was seeing within the cloud.

His work with Arakatsu and others came rushing back. "They did it!" he said out loud. The Americans had made an atomic bomb.

The man next to him had a camera. He ordered a picture taken.

It was one of the first photographs made of the cloud, taken approximately three minutes after the explosion. It has been seen by millions around the world.

Mitsui knew he could not make a hasty judgment. "Only a chemist could say for sure." Coming down the hill, he ordered five men to go to Hiroshima as soon as they could. "I told them to look for craters. If there were craters, then it would have been ordinary bombs."

The five men returned at around 10:00 P.M. Their story was incredible. The entire city was destroyed. Almost everyone in Hiroshima was either dead or injured. There was no crater. But there was fire and pain everywhere.

"They were very excited. The area of destruction was so big." They could not agree on what might have caused the blast. While they had gone, Mitsui told them, he had monitored an Allied broadcast calling the bomb "atomic." It said many more would be "rained" on Japan. "By the end of the meeting everyone agreed it was an atomic bomb."

By this time naval headquarters had ordered a full investigation. He was to lead the teams that would go into Hiroshima the next morning. Physicists, including Arakatsu, would be arriving. "I was going to look for radioactivity." That would be confirmation.

The army was organizing its own investigation. "On the morning of 7 August 1945, Army officers came to my laboratory," Dr. Nishina wrote in the formerly secret document later released by USSBS. Mrs. Yokoyama remembers the visit "clearly." The officers wanted Nishina to accompany them to Hiroshima to see what kind of bomb it was.

As they were leaving, wrote Nishina, a Domei news reporter arrived and asked him to comment on President Truman's statement that the Hiroshima bomb had the power of 20,000 tons of TNT. "When I heard this I felt that [it] might well be an atomic bomb because the above-mentioned figure exactly corresponded to the figure calculated at my laboratory by a student [Tamaki?] two or three years [before]."

They went to a briefing held at general staff headquarters. It was conducted by Colonel Seizo Arisue, chief of intelligence, who was in charge of investigating the devastation. Arisue explained what they knew and said two planes were waiting. He would leave in one; Nishina, in the other. Arisue proceeded to Hiroshima, but shortly after takeoff Nishina's plane was forced back by engine trouble. Mrs. Yokoyama was there when Nishina returned. He was "very gloomy. He did not say anything." He went into his office and "just stared." Finally, he asked her for a "physicist's tool." She didn't remember the name but thought it was a scale or ruler. He made some calculations. "Then he said it was an atomic bomb. He had not been there, but they had described it to him. He deduced that it must have been an atomic bomb."

Arisue confirmed this. The former general would not talk to me, said my interpreter, "because he does not like Westerners." But in a telephone conversation he told my interpreter, "Dr. Nishina knew it was an atomic bomb but had to investigate before he told the leaders." In my mind, Nishina was probably also hoping he was wrong. If he was right, he had failed. Only two weeks before, it appears, he had told the army that making a Japanese atomic bomb was impossible.

On the afternoon of August 8 he again left for Hiroshima. "In the meantime, I had received various reports concerning the serious damage . . . and I came to believe all the more that the bomb dropped there was the real atomic bomb."

He reached Hiroshima in the late afternoon. "We circled over the city and were shocked at the damage which lay below us. From the air I saw that the center of the city had been burned out and that the outskirts too were destroyed to a large extent." Upon landing he began making general observations. Roof tiles, which had bubbled and fused under the immense heat, "were torn from houses which had not collapsed. Corpses were seen on the streets. The city"—lying flattened and still beneath them—"assumed the aspect of death. Unlike cities damaged by fire bombs," houses outside the burned area were also destroyed. "This clearly indicated that the bomb . . . was not an ordinary bomb. I intuitively thought that it was an atomic bomb."

Soldiers who met him at the airport, a full five miles from the blast, had partially burned faces and hands. The scarred flesh had been facing the blast. "They told me that immediately after the flash, there was a great blast which caused houses and trees to collapse." Leaves on trees facing the blast were red on one side, as if roasted.

Arisue also met Nishina at the airport, and together they proceeded into the city. There were "corpses . . . everywhere . . . smoke rising from scattered fires where bodies were being cremated." The absence even of flies on the bodies attested to the utter destruction of life. He decided a film record had to be made. With his own camera he began taking pictures. Some of them appear in *Encounter with Disaster,* a 1970 book by Averell A. Liebow, one of the American physicians who came to Hiroshima shortly after the surrender. They show hopelessly burned patients lying hollow-eyed in rows.

Nishina also began making scientific calculations. He pinpointed the center of the blast by studying the direction in which trees had fallen. "Practically everything located between one and two kilometers from the center . . . was completely burned . . . [while] houses situated between two and four kilometers from the center were half destroyed; that is, they were damaged beyond repair." Reinforced concrete structures, he discovered, had withstood the blast. "But, of course, the insides of the buildings were burnt and the window frames were bent."

He was told that 30,000 people had been killed instantly, most of them incinerated in less than a second; more than 100,000 were injured. It was almost unfathomable, except that the evidence was all around him. "Persons, although they were not burned, lost their appetites, vomited and then died. All this caused an atmosphere of unrest among the people. Upon [the] making [of] some blood studies it was found that the number of white blood cells decreased gradually, [then] showed an astounding decrease right before the victim died." It was to become known as radiation sickness.

Two pieces of evidence cemented his conviction that the bomb had been atomic: Summoned to the Japanese Red Cross hospital within the city, he was shown sealed negative film plates that somehow had been exposed. "This showed that the bomb caused, or was accompanied by, radio-active rays, such as X-rays and Gamma rays," which had acted on the negatives. "The decisive evidence was that various materials on the ground became radio-active." Bones of corpses, sulfur on insulators, soil near the explosion's center—each gave an abnormally high reading when tested.

Furthermore, the radiation sickness itself was grim, living proof. "Experts know that when men's bodies are exposed to X-rays, Gamma rays, or neutrons, their white blood corpuscle count is decreased."

If he still had any doubts, they vanished in the midst of this new and mounting horror.

But he must have been very careful in what he was saying to his military companions, for it was not until Colonel Arisue reached over to touch one of the queer silhouettes of objects, like telephone poles, even human beings, caught as if by some mysterious camera at that black instant of detonation, that the officer comprehended what he was dealing with. "I felt it with my finger," Arisue told my translator over the phone, "and Dr. Nishina said I'd better wear gloves—that it was radioactive. It was at that moment that I realized it had been an atomic bomb."

Nishina sent back all manner of specimens to the Rikken. Mrs. Yokoyama remembered their arriving by army courier: tiles; burned pieces of houses; pipes. "We analyzed everything for radioactivity."

Arakatsu arrived on August 10, the day after the second atomic bomb, made of plutonium, had been detonated over Nagasaki. According to a formerly top secret report he made, which I found at Suitland, "On August 8, we received the information that an atomic bomb was dropped upon Hiroshima on August 6. Exploring parties were then organized and went to the destructed [sic] place."

He knew exactly what he was after. "Now, it may be expected that if the bomb is an uranium bomb, a great number of neutrons must be emitted at the instant of the explosion, and . . . substances . . . on the ground, such as copper, iron, aluminum, silver, sulphur, phosphorus, calcium, . . . may be [expected] to be radioactive. . . ."

He and his crews began taking samples. They had a Geiger-Müller counter. A normal count was about 18 blips per minute. Sand from the damaged area emitted 70 to 80 counts per minute; a bone of a horse emitted 529; an iron magnet, 364. There was no doubt about it. These were extraordinary levels of radioactivity.

By August 15, possibly earlier, he came to this conclusion: "By measuring the intensity of the activity and the maximum energy of beta-rays, as well as their half lives . . . we could affirm that the new bomb . . . was . . . atomic . . . [and was] accompanied by the emission of copious amount[s] of neutrons on explosion." This allowed him to estimate the amount of neutrons released, which could have been used to calculate the critical mass, had he wanted or needed to do so.

Unlike Nishina, Arakatsu put no emotion into his report. There were others from the navy surveying the damage. In addition to Mitsui and his group, Osaka's Professor Asada, who had first interested the navy in a uranium bomb and who was listed on Colonel Suzuki's Osaka project roster until that project had been canceled, was there. According to Lester Brooks in *Behind Japan's Surrender,* he had cabled Tokyo on the ninth: "The bomb dropped on Hiroshima unquestionably was an atomic bomb. We have determined this scientifically. . . ."

It is not certain when Nishina or Arakatsu reported their findings. On August 10 at a meeting in Hiroshima they both argued it was an atomic bomb. Nishina is even said to have gone before the emperor with his findings. Thereafter, both continued their studies. Nishina went on to calculate the size of the fireball (a diameter of 150 meters) and its temperature (approximately 9,000 degrees). Both he and Arakatsu noted that most of the neutrons released in the explosion were "slow"; this meant they had distinguished these from "fast" neutrons and thus knew this important key. Arakatsu pinpointed the approximate height and position at which the bomb had exploded and calculated that the duration of the flashes was between one-fifth and one-half second—all of which was highly classified information in America.

On August 13 Nishina flew to Nagasaki, where he stayed for half a day. "Nagasaki appeared similar to Hiroshima from the air," he wrote, but noticeable differences in the kinds of damage alerted him that the two bombs were different. The Nagasaki bomb, made of plutonium, was stronger. "For example, few chimneys fell in Hiroshima but in Nagasaki none were standing near the center of explosion. . . . Also, the fragments of houses and roof tiles in Nagasaki were smaller," indicating there had been a greater blast, and "the region where roof tiles melted reaches 1.7 times further from the explosion center than in Hiroshima." However, overall casualties and damage were less in Nagasaki. This was because Nagasaki was "a long town with hills on both sides"; the blast had reached a smaller area.

Brooks noted that "Japanese reaction to the bomb is a study in confusion, distraction, and obfuscation." Much the same could be said about Nishina's reaction. There is little doubt that he was a kind and compassionate man. He must have been deeply moved by what he saw. He had almost caused such misery himself. His burden was double because his own people had ended up the victims.

But the preface to his memoir begins: "The Atomic Bomb which led to the termination of the war was a magnificent product of pure physics. . . . [It] will remain in history as one of the greatest products of scientific research."

He clearly respected it as a scientific achievement. Members of the Atomic Bomb Mission detected this in their first interview with him and underscored it as a reason to keep him under observation. Tetsu

Hiroshige in *The History of Science in Japan* writes that right after Hiroshima, the "military office" revived its atomic bomb plans and asked Nishina if he could complete one in "six months." There is reason to believe that still a patriot, probably suffering deeply over his failure to produce what the enemy had, he might have tentatively agreed.

But probably not for long. Everything I've found indicates he finally returned to the Rikken convinced of the folly of carrying on the war and especially of the evil of atomic energy used as a weapon. As his son told me, he took a large part of the blame for the war on his own shoulders. His generation, he said, should have realized what was going to happen. His chemist Kigoshi told me that he had heard from Miss Yokoyama that Nishina considered suicide.

Whatever Nishina's reaction, the navy's was hard-line. Arakatsu was not heard from until months later, lending credence to Dr. Yagi's statement to occupation officials that he was secretly working on an atomic bomb right through Hiroshima and Nagasaki. According to both *Imperial Tragedy* and *Behind Japan's Surrender,* rather than make the admirals want to seek peace, the news from Hiroshima and Nagasaki made them immediately want "to isolate all Japanese physicists in the caves in Nagano Prefecture to have them produce atomic bombs."

Supporting this is the fact that on August 13 Magic decoders deciphered the following message sent on August 10 from the Kure Naval Base: "Researches into the atom, Uranium 235, are being (or possibly will be) conducted at the Tokyo Imperial University under Navy supervision. [Word missing] have not gone beyond the limits of theory. At [place missing], about five months ago, research was made into the [practical] application of Uranium 235, but no announcements have been made since then. However, it is believed that research into the [word missing] of the atom has since been completed and [word missing] research into this is considered to be of considerable value. It is believed that it is essential that this be completed immediately."

22

Right after the American atomic bomb had been dropped on Hiroshima, Robert Nininger, now one of the country's top uranium experts and at the time a lieutenant working for the Manhattan Project, was called into Groves's office and told by the general that he was being sent to Japan to help investigate what the Japanese had done in the field of nuclear physics. "We weren't Alsos, but we had elements of it," Nininger told me. Major Robert R. Furman, who had been with Alsos in Europe and was now on Tinian, where he had escorted the Hiroshima bomb, would be field commander. Overall command was in the hands of Groves's deputy, Brigadier General T. F. Farrell, also on Tinian. "I was picked because I was the only one in Groves's office who specialized in uranium," said Nininger.

By the day Nininger left California—August 14, V-J Day—Furman had already written his first report to General Farrell about the coming mission. It was to be split into two basic sections. One, headed by Furman and including Philip Morrison, one of the Los Alamos scientists at Tinian responsible for assembling the bombs, would investigate Japan's progress in physics. The other section, to be headed by Nininger, would look into its geological exploration; determine what fissionable elements it had found. Furman called the mission Group Three.

The mission had a third stated purpose: finding out what the Japanese knew about Russian progress in nuclear physics and, in particular, what sources of uranium they might have access to. Even before the surrender, elements of the U.S. military saw Russia as the next enemy. Japan had more information about Russia than nearly any other country.

Simultaneously with the organization of the Atomic Bomb Mission, as Group Three came to be called, another scientific investigation, broader in scope, was being readied. Called the Scientific Intelligence Survey, it was to include more civilians, explore Japanese advancement in many areas, and look only lightly into atomic physics. Its organizer, Dr. Karl T. Compton, instrumental in American war mobilization, said in *Combat Scientists:* "It was generally suspected that the Japanese were not as far advanced either in science or technology as were the Germans. Nevertheless, it was known that in a few fields their scientific men had done outstanding work in the prewar years. We wanted to know the extent to which Japanese science had been mobilized behind the war effort."

The two investigations were separate, although at times they ran into each other. Compton's group couldn't help picking up information on Japanese atomic bomb development. But the survey's reports indicate that it was instructed to leave the harder questions to the Atomic Bomb Mission.

Although Furman wrote, "If resistance is encountered we are prepared to make a formal demand for information, impounding documents and even individuals," it is clear that neither mission had the sense of urgency and do-or-die purpose that Alsos did. We wanted information, but we also wanted a friend to help us against the Russians.

Furman and his men read everything they could find on the targeted scientists: Nishina, Arakatsu, Sagane, Kikuchi, and many more. Navy and air force intelligence was used, as was interrogation of prisoners of war. "On the basis of pre-war information and the reports," Furman wrote, "we believe that Japanese scientists will be cooperative. It is therefore proposed to study the work in nuclear physics as far as possible by informal and friendly visits to the leading academic workers. A scientific approach will be used, with the authority of the occupation remaining in the background."

On September 7 the mission arrived in Tokyo: approximately a dozen men, five jeeps, hookup trailers, several command cars, weapons, typewriters, Geiger-Müller counters, special tools for breaking locks. "We got there ahead of MacArthur," Furman told me. "It's been a long time, and my memory's dim. But we had a great deal of intelligence and knew where to go."

The people were not hostile, but they were not friendly either. Mostly the Japanese kept out of sight. There was a real danger that some might not want to surrender and would carry on guerrilla activities.

Morrison had known Ryokichi Sagane in California. While on Tinian, he and the two other American scientists assembling the bomb had sent a plea to Sagane. It said in part, "We're sending this as a personal message to urge that you use your influence as a reputable nuclear physicist to convince the Japanese General Staff of the terrible consequences which will be suffered by your people if you continue in this war. . . . We assure you that unless Japan surrenders at once, this rain of atomic bombs will increase manyfold in fury." The letter was dropped from a B-29 between the Hiroshima and Nagasaki bombings. Sagane said the military kept it from him until September.

Sagane was the first to be interviewed by the mission. The interview took place on September 9, a Sunday, in his laboratory at Tokyo University. Nininger remembered Morrison and Sagane's talking about the letter. Then the two got down to business.

Sagane was guarded but somewhat cooperative. He told them that Nishina had done some pertinent work, but in general, "very little government or military interest had been shown in atomic bomb production." He told them how he himself had told the army and navy "if every available ton of uranium was mined, the amount would be negligible compared to the rich reserves at the command of the Allies." As a result, he said, he had worked on radar. Their examination of his nuclear physics laboratory, which they found "very small" with "old and hand-made" equipment, supported that contention. They noted the fact that since the lab had not been moved to a safe place out of town, the work there "was probably not sufficiently important to the immediate war effort."

The next day they met with Sagane again, apparently with the idea of catching him off guard. "Favorable contact was made by meeting Sagane by chance on the street—he felt obliged, it is true, to invite us in—but the lateness of the hour—4:30 P.M.—and the large number present [at his lab] were against us." The writer, probably Morrison, continued: "He knows about the chain reaction and the need for use of [a tamper, a neutron reflecting shield around the uranium core], but volunteered that at a [government] meeting, it was decided that, from want of [uranium] and from inferior resources compared to the U.S.A., no atomic bomb development should be carried on. I do not believe this story yet, but I am sure it is an agreed-upon story we will get from all these men, true or not. . . . He impresses me as still an enemy to the U.S.A., answering truthfully as his best present line. . . ."

At the Rikken there was more evidence that information was being withheld. Arriving at 8:00 A.M. on September 10, they found Matsuharo Kimura, one of Nishina's assistants, alone in his laboratory, examining bones from Hiroshima. Kimura, one of Nishina's neutron specialists, told them that the cyclotron "quote did work of some military importance unquote." But "in spite of [our] leading [him] through direct questions, he would not explain further what he meant," wrote Morrison. "I believe he did not want to give out the information without approval from his boss, Nishina." They noted he was sleeping in the lab and living on tea and potatoes grown outside in the ruins.

Nishina arrived at 11:00 A.M. He had come from the Ministry of Education, wrote Morrison, and probably had been working on a motion picture of Hiroshima. (Following his first visit there, he had decided that a motion-picture record of the devastation was needed. He had organized the project. At first the occupation went along with it. Then it stopped it, and finally it confiscated his film. Later Miss Yokoyama tried to get it back for the Nishina archives. The United States denied its existence. But with the help of Harry Kelly, who had been a high-ranking civilian in the Science and Technology Division of General MacArthur's army of occupation and had developed a close friendship with Nishina, the memorial library finally received it in 1967. Nishina was probably in the very beginning stages of organizing the film when he met with the mission.)

According to Morrison, Nishina wanted to discuss Hiroshima, "bringing with him maps, curves, papers, and having written an outline on his office blackboard. With him were Yamasaki—an able young man—and another quiet man whose name we lost. . . . He was utterly downcast when we carried through the story to which we were committed that we were not connected with the Hiroshima investigators, but soon warmed up as I talked to him about the physics of the situation."

They discussed Nishina's work. He said he had been more interested in the slow reaction than the fast. Morrison was impressed by his knowledge of the size of the critical mass used, the number of neutrons emitted, and the power of the blast. But he wrote: "It is clear that he was completely surprised by the bomb, and that only its main features had been thought of by him." He told them he had a small amount of heavy water—100 grams. Morrison concluded: "There is no evidence of much work in isotope separation, although they have studied two or three methods, not particularly applied to uranium. . . . There is no evidence of real government interest in the field before Hiroshima."

Furman's report on the same interview clearly indicates that Nishina concealed his atomic bomb involvement: "Nishina claimed that his staff had been diverted from nuclear physics research to the army and war work, and that very little support had been given his work by the government. The War and Navy Departments, he said, had no research project for atomic energy. He had been employed during the war assisting in the studies with the cyclotron for medical research." All his records had been destroyed in the bombings, he told Furman. A check of the Rikken's refinery revealed "no evidence of work with uranium-bearing ores."

On September 14 Furman wrote a field progress report to General Farrell and Brigadier General J. B. Newman, who was now at Tinian to relieve Farrell. "The following general conclusions have been reached: The government and the military gave no priority to research in the field of nuclear physics and had no program to produce a bomb." The principal nuclear physicists had been diverted to other work, such as medicine or work on radar. "Science in Japan was organized," but mainly to relieve shortages for industry. Labs were out of date and ill-equipped; they had not been evacuated, indicating their low priority.

"Government interest did develop after the Hiroshima bombing and physicists have been at work since that date . . . on the problem of how the bomb works and what mass of U-235 was employed." Furman sounded an alarm. "The Japanese would be able to organize a group of twenty first class scientists capable of initiating a project for the production of atomic energy. They have the theoretical background. They could progress rapidly to the point of production, especially if they were given the results of the work in America in any detail. They appear to have the interest necessary to form such a plan. Nishina would probably be the center of this activity."

The following day, September 15, the Americans went to Kyoto to see Arakatsu and Yukawa. "Our relations were most friendly," wrote Morrison, "and there was great exchange of gifts and courtesies." The Japanese guessed the mission's purpose, and Yukawa knew of Morrison's work. Morrison found him "retiring and scholarly." He "showed no interest in questions I asked on diffusion theory, in which he would certainly have been engaged if he were on project work to any large extent. The undamaged and almost normal character of Kyoto University and the very abstract interests of Yukawa himself are quite consistent with his having done little or no work in the theory of the project field."

He was also impressed with Arakatsu, calling him a "competent and very energetic experimental nuclear physicist," who "has built up a pretty good nuclear physics laboratory, with quite limited funds and resources. The high-tension set has been finished for about five years, and used somewhat as a neutron source. . . . It yields about 600 kev protons. . . . He had the first fission-chamber and linear amplifier set I have seen in Japan. It was somewhat amateur but very workable." He had "100 mg of Fatbe [code word] and has used it with a crude setup to measure the fission cross-section, the absorption and scattering cross-sections, and the number of neutrons per fission of uranium. All this was done for thermal neutrons and repeats the work of Nishina. . . ."

Arakatsu said he received heavy water from "electrolytic [ammonia] plants in Kyushu and Korea. He believed production was . . . about 20 grams per month. . . . Kyoto certainly never conducted any large-scale neutron diffusion work with any kind of moderator. . . . The general picture confirms the ideas gained earlier in Tokyo. . . . There is again no evidence of government support or unusual pressure for work in nuclear physics. There is no visible special material at Kyoto beyond the usual laboratory bottles of thorium and uranium compounds."

Furman took a more skeptical view. "Yukawa had been to Hiroshima," he noted, and "in my opinion he has probably been working on the probable construction of the atomic bomb since its use August 6." He said little about Arakatsu but found that the "number of courses being given in the university in the nuclear physics field shows an active interest in the subject. The building devoted to physics is modern in every respect."

He concluded, "A research center for all fields of study of interest to war industry had been set up near Kyoto in the district of Kugi and equipment and personnel had moved there to avoid bombing. However, nuclear physics work had not been moved, clearly indicating the disinterest of the government in this field."

Osaka University and Kikuchi were next on the list. The team arrived on a Sunday. Only a few students were there. "We freely inspected the buildings, apparatus and documents of the department," wrote Morrison. The building was badly bombed. "Windows are broken and boarded, as in Tokyo, people are living in some of the rooms, and even sick men are quartered in a few of the department's rooms."

Kikuchi's office, however, was "orderly." He had a "reprint file" which was active for Japanese documents through 1943. "It shows a general interest in fission, but no late work was discoverable." They found the "largest supply of uranium" they had yet seen in Japan. It wasn't much: "a fifteen-liter solution of uranyl nitrate . . . together with a small bottle of the crystals," indicating "that work has not been moved elsewhere."

A student's notebook found near one of Kikuchi's two cyclotrons contained some of the professor's "lectures on nuclear physics during the last school year. . . . A paragraph on fission discussed the energy release, the importance of the 235 isotope, the fission product activity, and the number of neutrons per neutron absorbed—2–3, as usual. All this was normal 1940 information. . . ."

Both Morrison and Furman noted the absence of the mass spectrograph said to have been there. It "was removed to the evacuation research center near Kyoto," wrote Furman, but "a check has shown that no nuclear research was being done at this evacuation point." It is not clear whether the separator was present or missing.

Morrison wrote that graduate instruction at both Osaka and Kyoto was "more solid . . . than at most universities in the United States." He warned that the United States might lose its lead in physics if it did not improve in this area. He concluded: "The overwhelming picture at Osaka is one of a shoestring effort being carried out during wartime. The fission problem was [one of] but many interesting problems which these people had the knowledge to attack but had not the resources to solve."

On the twentieth, the mission ran into Compton with the Scientific Intelligence Survey. Furman wrote in his report of the meeting: "Conversation was very informal and no attempt was made to discuss plans and operations, either his or ours." But Compton disclosed that he had told Nishina that the Nagasaki bomb was made of plutonium, a fact which Furman believed Nishina did not yet know. Compton defended his action by noting the information was part of the Smyth report, the government's report on the bomb which had been publicly released. "I informed him," wrote Furman, "that I had been told that the Smyth report had been recalled and security clamped down again." The meeting ended amicably with Furman offering the survey scientific papers he had collected "which were of no interest to this mission."

On the same day Morrison sat down and wrote out some recommendations. Although the group had found no evidence of any atomic bomb activity, he was worried that something unforeseen might happen. He pointed out that making atomic bombs was new, and the United States could not be certain that its production methods were the only methods. "Even now it is not theoretically impossible to make a fine bomb with only three tons of uranium as raw material, an easily-concealed amount, obtainable with some effort in any country."

He therefore proposed a watch be put on all Japanese physicists, especially those working with Nishina, Sagane, Yukawa, Arakatsu, and Kikuchi. "In each case there are from three to a dozen younger men involved, some of whom seem excellent, and training of students is going on at a high rate and with high standards. . . . The Japanese have . . . first-rate men in nuclear physics. They are handicapped by poor resources, and they seem several years out-of-date in technique as a result, but they know the fundamentals and they are capable of brilliant and original work."

Meanwhile, Nininger had been getting some idea of Japanese uranium mining, especially in Korea. For instance, Arakatsu's colleague Jitsutaro Takubo, Kyoto's head geologist, said that at the "request of Korean interests," he had made "two separate surveys of Korean and [Manchurian] minerals." He had found uranium-bearing ores, if not veins of uranium itself (the report is not clear). But to find out what use had been made of the discoveries, Takubo told him he would have to go to the Asian mainland and talk to some of the processors, such as Noguchi's Nitchitsu, "which handles all special elements in Korea."

After several such reports Nininger decided he had better go. By that time the Russians had sealed off everything north of central Korea, so visits to Nitchitsu headquarters at Konan or to Manchuria were out. He had to rely on what he could find out in South Korea. Dr. Iwao Tateiwa, director of the Korean Geological Survey, one of the Japanese geological agencies on the peninsula, told him of black sands, monazite, zircon, fergusonite, and other uranium-bearing ores' being available, but only in small quantities and little worked. Up in Manchuria there were some fairly good veins of uranium-bearing euxenite, capable of producing perhaps five tons of uranium per year, the director told him. Publications Nininger was given indicated the Japanese had been prospecting for uranium in Korea in 1944.

The next day, September 23, Nininger went to the Rikken's refinery near Seoul and was told that "three tons of fergusonite" had been mined and stored for "atom bomb experimentation." This appears to have been the first notice of such mining the mission received. He got a list of Japanese mines, many of them in North Korea. K. T. Kim, a Korean and the man at the Rikken refinery to whom Nininger talked, revealed that in the spring of 1944 word had come from the Tokyo Rikken to get the fergusonite ready. The three tons were accumulated over a period ending in July 1945. It never went to Tokyo, and Kim could not tell him why.

Startled by this information, Nininger wrote: "My feelings about this information are that it is inaccurate but bears check. The Koreans were not informed on company or institution affairs while under the Japanese. If the information on fergusonite is correct, it will appear more likely than ever that the Bureau of Mines of Korea [which apparently had told him there had been no uranium search] was uninformed or not completely informed as to uranium production in Korea." He determined to try to find out more.

Further investigation produced little. There had been a lot of activity on the part of the Rikken's outposts to gather uranium-bearing ores, but little could be verified. For instance, a return interview with Kim revealed that the "Rikken was ordered by the government of Japan to collect all black sands from other mining companies in Korea, separate it and send it back to Tokyo." But he could not determine for what purpose. Kim also told him, "Nitchitsu Mining Company was an exception to this. They shipped their own sands at Navy direction."

Nininger was continually running into Nitchitsu. It was the "primary company supplying rare metals to the Kogyo Sinkio," one of the main companies feeding them, in turn, to the Rikken. Most of the Korean monazite dug up in 1944—574 tons of it—was excavated by Nitchitsu, as was the columbite.

Nininger didn't remember Nitchitsu when I interviewed him, and he might not have worried much about it then. But by September 26 Furman, who had been receiving Nininger's reports, was suspicious enough to ask General Newman, who had now taken over for Farrell, to allow them to get tough and give Japanese officials an ultimatum: five days to hand over "full information, including present location, of any uranium-bearing stocks, refined or crude, which are presently in Japan or which were under Japanese control at the time of the war." They should also give a "complete report" on their efforts to find uranium, "together with the results of their search."

On September 29 Nininger was back in Japan at the Rikken, interviewing a Dr. Hata, a geochemist who had been involved in the Rikken's search for rare elements. He had been interviewed earlier and had told Nininger about the tin stocks the Rikken had gotten from Malaya and about river dredging in North Korea that had yielded small amounts of uranium-bearing euxenite. Now Nininger wanted to know the exact "location and amount of stocks of fergusonite and euxenite, both in Japan and elsewhere in the Empire," and wanted to get "an admission that Japan was interested in the extraction of U from these minerals."

One of the team wrote: "Dr. Hata knew of no large amounts of these minerals" but admitted knowing about the "fergusonite stocked in Korea." Hata told Nininger that interest in extracting uranium from such ores had not arisen until 1944, "when Dr. Nishina . . . saw the possibility of using U in connection with the development of an atomic bomb. However, Dr. Nishina announced in February 1945 that his efforts to extract U235 were a failure. Otherwise, all the fergusonite and euxenite would have been turned over for this purpose. Dr. Nishina's work was based on 1 kg. of U obtained before the war from either Merck in England or Kahlbaum in Germany."

The story was beginning to unravel, but the mission was suddenly ordered home. Perhaps that was the reason that even before Nininger had gone back to Hata, Furman (to judge from the date on the report —September 28) had already written the group's final report. Saying that "the investigations planned by this mission . . . can now be considered complete," he wrote that the Japanese atomic bomb effort "has been confirmed to be at the level of 1942 investigations in the United States. The geological and mining authorities have not been found to be engaged in the extraction of uranium-bearing ores of importance."

It was of "positive interest," he noted, that the Japanese had mined and stored the fergusonite in Korea. But it and the euxenite reported would have yielded only about 140 kilos (about 375 pounds) of uranium. The Americans had uncovered no other stockpiling, although he noted that the Japanese could have got more uranium from such ores "if expense" had been "no object."

In summary he concluded, "Normal research was conducted until 1943." Erroneously he wrote, "Activity was continued on a reduced scale after 1943. . . ." Tentatively he ventured, "Geological surveys apparently failed to disclose new sources of uranium to the Japanese within the territory under their military control." But he left open the possibility of amendment because many documents in Japanese and Chinese had been collected. "It is felt that these documents, especially those pertaining to geological matters, contain information which is of interest to the trust, both as a source of original information as well as evidence corroborating testimony obtained through direct interrogation." He recommended that two from the team accompany the documents to Washington to do the translations. In addition, a directive he had had signed by General MacArthur himself now demanded formal reports from the Japanese scientists on their nuclear research. These reports were due shortly, and should they reveal anything of importance, "it is recommended that [they] be immediately forwarded under separate cover to the attention of the Manhattan District [Project], Box 2610, Washington."

Furman was not yet through. On October 3 he interviewed Eiichi Takeda about Osaka University. His impression of its limited nuclear activities did not change. New information led him the next day to the Tokyo Shibaura Denki K.K., "Japan's equivalent to America's General Electric." A physicist there, Masamichi Tanaka, said they had been building a "2-million-volt Van de Graaff accelerator." Nothing too frightening. But then, on October 5, he was suddenly explaining to the War Department why he had not been duped.

It is not clear whether Washington had challenged some of the mission's findings or whether Furman, having come upon information implying that the Japanese had attempted to cover up biological warfare research, himself was raising the issue. He explained: "Lt. Col. Sanders is investigating the Japanese [biological warfare] activities. . . . His investigation came to my attention when it was learned that just at the time when he was about to conclude that the Japanese . . . activities were small . . . he was given a report . . . that revealed deep, large experimentation. . . . Up until this revelation, the subject officer had felt he had seen the requisite number of people in the field, had received from sources a logical corroborated [story] and . . . was ready to conclude his investigations." Sanders now felt he had been the victim of a cover-up and would have to start over again.

Furman's concern was: "How likely is it that the Atomic Bomb Investigation has been similarly prevented from getting . . . information?" Not much, he concluded. The mission had done a much more thorough job of investigation: had seen more principals, checked more documents. The Japanese biological warfare center was in inaccessible Manchuria, he noted, while the atomic bomb center was on the mainland, to which he and his group had access.

Nevertheless, he added, "Lt. Col. Sanders gave me the name of a Japanese Staff Officer in the Japanese New Weapons Division of the Bureau of Military Affairs, Lt. Col. Niizuma, who had been extremely cooperative and who appeared interested in doing all possible to present any desired information. . . . In lieu of calling in the proper Japanese Military, Navy and [government] officials and asking for direct reports on the military interest in Atomic studies," which would seem to have been the better procedure, Furman proposed that they consult Niizuma.

Seiichi Niizuma, a physics graduate of Tokyo University as well as an army officer, had been one of the early supporters of the uranium bomb project, although his interests had shifted to the death ray, of which he was considered one of the primary developers. He had actually become one of the administrative heads of NI when the project moved over to air force headquarters. His name later cropped up in a 1946 occupation investigation of an alleged plan by several former Japanese officers to make an atomic bomb with uranium from Fukushima Prefecture. He was "claimed to be a collaborator," the Counter Intelligence Corps report would say. In 1947 Kelly used him as a source on an occupation investigation of the wartime atomic bomb projects (indicating once again that the United States was still unsure of what had happened).

Furman questioned Niizuma the very next day. The Japanese officer lied, apparently believing that if the mission had not got anything from Nishina, he also would be safe in his attempts to throw them off. Furman wrote:

He said that the Army had approximately 10 laboratories for research of their own. . . . One of these Army laboratories was in the field of physics but no nuclear research had been attempted. . . . Niizuma said that the Army definitely had made no program. . . . He said that Nishina had no Army project and that he definitely was Japan's leading nuclear scientist. The Army had research work at the Imperial University at Tokyo and the Rikken. If we had checked with these two institutions, he felt we had knowledge of the latest Japanese developments in this field. He stated that he did not think we would have to check other Army officials on this, and he would be able to give us any necessary assurance.

Apparently they relied on Niizuma's assurances, for Furman now turned to the navy, discovering more activity than he had previously heard about. The navy had had a decidedly early interest in atomic research, Lieutenant Commander Miroshi Ishiwatari, Bureau of Naval Affairs, told Furman. As part of Ishiwatari's duties he had helped handle it. In the spring of 1944 the navy had decided to make a uranium bomb "and from that date attempted coordination of the research work being done by the Army. . . . It was thought at that time that if U235 could be concentrated at 10 percent or above, bomb or power possibilities would be likely." But the bombings and lack of uranium had stifled the program.

This was the first indication of a well-developed navy program, and Furman wanted to hear more. He requested "a full report of the Navy war interest and activities in nuclear physics research, including all documents from their Navy files that are available." Commander Kitagawa, who "has had direct liaison responsibilities with Arakatsu's work," was to prepare the report. "A report on uranium resources and stocks available to the Japanese" was "also forthcoming." Both reports were to be submitted to Colonel F. P. Munson, G-2, and then forwarded on to the mission.

Clearly there was more to be investigated. But now the mission was being terminated. Lieutenant Colonel Peer DeSilva, a security officer for the Manhattan Project, was going to remain in Tokyo until October 15. Anything that came in up to that time could be given to him. After that Furman requested that everything be sent directly to General Groves in Washington. Sometime around October 10 Furman and the mission went home.

Looking back recently, Furman stood behind the group's findings. "We never heard of any atomic bomb activity in North Korea, and it would surprise me greatly if there was any. We went to the university there at Seoul and talked to all the persons who should know. . . . You could also count all the scientists, and I think we had them all pegged. It was a new science and there was nobody over there. . . . It takes such a long time to build that expertise, I would doubt some guy previously untrained thought it all up by himself. . . ."

But he admitted the mission could have missed something. "They had some first-rate scientists. . . . We knew they could do it if there was an emphasis. . . . We didn't talk to any army officers. I'd be interested to hear what they say. We were very much aware of the fact that if we could do it somebody else could do it. . . . We were always suspicious that somebody could make it in their bathroom.

Every method we tried worked, so who is to say another method might not work that we hadn't thought of . . . ?"

Nininger was basically in agreement with Furman. He raised an additional objection to wartime progress on a bomb: Even if the Japanese could have got the uranium, he said, they would have needed huge plants to separate it. He was not familiar with Konan.

Combat Scientists gave the prevalent view of Japanese science during the war. Using Compton's Scientific Intelligence Survey as its basis, it stated:

> Japanese science had been poorly organized for war purposes. Many of Nippon's most outstanding research men had been educated in the United States. The Japanese High Command, fearful that this would influence their loyalty, did not give them high responsibilities in war work. The most important secrets were parceled out in such a way that men were commonly asked to work on components, or its intended use. In general, the Japanese were decidedly behind us in technological developments. They had made some progress in the critical field of nuclear energy; but apparently this was not directed toward its use in explosives. Their work had been aimed at developing atomic energy as a source of industrial power. There were such violent jealousies between the Japanese Army and Navy that joint responsibility for research, so common in America's war effort, was impossible. It was also apparent that the Germans had not shared their best secrets with this eastern end of the Axis, although they had aided Japan in training its military units. Late in the war they had attempted to compensate for this mistake by supplying the Japanese with some information about their rockets, guided missiles, and radar.

But the survey had not even been privy to the Atomic Bomb Mission's findings.

23

On the morning of November 22, 1945, without any notification, occupation troops rolled up in trucks to the various physics labs throughout Japan and began destroying the five remaining cyclotrons. They dismantled the machines, in some cases, using axes. Parts were dumped into Tokyo Bay; others were exploded with dynamite.

The move came as a complete surprise to the Japanese scientists, for just the preceding month, in accordance with what the Atomic Bomb Mission and the Scientific Intelligence Survey had requested, Nishina, Arakatsu, Kikuchi, Sagane, and the others had been given permission to continue using their cyclotrons as long as the work had no military or atomic energy purpose.

The destruction left some of the scientists in tears. As Nishina wrote in the June 1947 *Bulletin of the Atomic Scientists,* "Even today we absolutely fail to understand the reason for ordering the destruction. . . . A cyclotron may have been an important apparatus in the early studies on the creation of atomic bombs [but] however many cyclotrons one may have, no atomic bomb can be manufactured without the uranium material. . . ."

Nishina said he had planned to use his cyclotron to manufacture radioactive isotopes, which would help the country get back on its feet. Because of their minute size and traceability, the isotopes would have helped medical researchers follow the never-before-seen human metabolic process, agriculturalists better understand crop growth in order to increase production, and industrial scientists map precisely what happens to metal during friction and wear. These were only a few of the various isotopes' beneficial uses. Now there would be no such aids to Japan.

The seemingly wanton destruction caused an immediate international outcry. *Stars and Stripes* called it "stupid to the point of constituting a crime against mankind." *Time* likened it to burning Japanese libraries or smashing their printing presses. The cyclotrons *could* produce fissionable "material," noted Nishina, but it would take "months" of continuous operation to make even enough to "see," while it requires "pounds of such material to make one bomb."

What had prompted the sudden, vicious attack?

The orders had come from Washington. Of that, everyone involved, including General MacArthur, who reluctantly carried them out, agreed. But beyond that, nothing was ever conclusively determined. In his book *Now It Can Be Told,* General Groves said the order came from one of his subordinates, who made a "mistake." He was a "new man" and did not know the ropes. He never named the subordinate. In public, Secretary of War Robert Patterson took the formal responsibility. But he had never seen or approved the actual order, he said.

In the April–June 1978 *Bulletin of Concerned Asian Scholars,* University of Wisconsin History Professor John W. Dower said that "the U.S. War Department intimated that its actions had been based upon certain, unspecified intelligence findings." But MIT Professor Charles Weiner, writing in the April 1978 issue of the *Bulletin of the Atomic Scientists,* quoted a document that put the blame squarely back on Groves's shoulders.

What actually happened? The answer at this time can only be speculation. But here are some additional facts that might have a bearing. About the time Furman was leaving Japan, another report on the Japanese Navy's atomic program was handed in. Summarized in *The Comprehensive History of Japanese Science and Technology,* it disclosed that the navy definitely had tried to make a uranium bomb, not just atomic power, and had given Arakatsu at least 600,000 yen to do so. The project had succeeded in making uranium metal, which the Atomic Bomb Mission had mistakenly reported it had not, adding "the obtaining of fairly pure U metal is the key to the development of atomic power." In addition, it indicated that Arakatsu's program was still alive.

Furthermore, in a story carried on page 4 of the October 15, 1946, *New York Times,* Arakatsu, in an interview with an American Broadcasting Company correspondent, was quoted as saying he was making "tremendous strides" toward being able to make an atomic bomb and that Russia probably already had one. "The Japanese scientist laughed when told the United States did not intend to permit the secret to fall into other hands, asserting that any country which could afford production costs could be manufacturing atomic bombs very soon."

Were there other secret reports? Other such statements? Were War Department or Manhattan Project officials cognizant of other information that still has not come out?

Like the United States, Germany, Great Britain, France, and Japan, Russia had kept abreast of atomic developments in the 1930s and recognized the potential for an atomic bomb. It had even mustered a program of sorts until Hitler's attack in 1941 had diverted its scientific energies.

Once the Germans had been stalemated and put on the defensive, this interest returned, and the Russians also got a big break. Because of Communist sympathies, several persons at Los Alamos, including scientist Klaus Fuchs, began giving Manhattan Project secrets to the Soviets. In addition, the Soviets had a friend in British diplomat Donald Maclean, who was privy to American weapons development secrets at the highest levels. Through these sources and perhaps others still unknown, Stalin was kept highly informed about America's race to make the bomb and finally decided the USSR should keep pace. In 1943, he initiated a formal project headed by physicist Igor Kurchatov, according to *The Secret History of the Atomic Bomb*, edited by Brown and MacDonald, one of the few Western sources on the Russian progress.

Thirteen physicists were assigned to work under Kurchatov. "They did important work," according to Brown, "including experimental and theoretical calculations concerning the reactions involved in both nuclear weapons and nuclear reactors. They also did some important work on the production of uranium and graphite and on the separation of uranium isotopes."

When Stalin was informed of the American success at "Trinity," our first atomic bomb test, he ordered Kurchatov's program into high gear. Until a bomb had actually been successfully tested, he still had reservations, wrote Brown. But now Russia entered the race in earnest.

With the end of the war in sight in 1945, Russia was thinking just as much about getting German nuclear scientists as it was about all the other spoils it could get from the countries it moved into. It actually captured several such scientists and their labs, according to

Brown, which were removed, *in toto*, to the Soviet Union. The Soviets were masters at such mammoth removals. They had removed scores of entire war factories "from the path of the German invader in 1941," noted Brown, and had reestablished them "behind the Ural Mountains."

From the surrender of Japan onward, the program had begun to "leap," wrote Brown. "U.S. intelligence learned that they had obtained their first chain reaction on Christmas Day [1945], using a graphite uranium lattice that was almost a reproduction of the one on which Enrico Fermi obtained his chain reaction at Chicago in 1942." Brown stated that they exploded their first bomb on August 29, 1949. But the exact timetable is in dispute.

A January 8, 1946, a headline in the *New York Times* read: U.S.S.R. BOMB BETTER THAN U.S., indicating some were saying Russia already had one. On November 11, 1947, the French periodical *L'Intransigeant* reported that the Russians had successfully test-fired an atomic bomb in Siberia the previous summer. Washington countered, saying it had had no indication of the blast on its worldwide monitoring instruments and therefore believed the report was false.

And there were other such reports. . . .

Since its declaration of war on dying Japan on August 8, Russian troops had moved swiftly down from the north and in most cases had overrun Japanese defenses on the peripheries of their territories still held in Asia. Only in northern Korea had they encountered "appreciable resistance," said American intelligence reports I had found. This was because of the industrial buildup there. Everything that might help in the defense of the homeland, including factories from Manchuria and Japan proper, had been moved to northern Korea. Accompanying this had been a tremendous troop buildup there. Like the home islands, Korea had become a fortress ready for the siege. Most of the troops were in the North.

The area around Konan was perhaps the most heavily garrisoned in the entire country. In fact, according to U.S. Army Forces in Korea (USAFIK) Intelligence Summary No. 14, dated June 22, 1946, it was near Konan that the last battle of the war was fought. "The Hamhung Plain," said the summary, "witnessed what was probably the last dying gasp of the Japanese Empire when in late November a pitched battle was fought there between the Soviets and the reorganized remnants of the Japanese forces in Korea that had not surrendered."

This was nearly two months after the formal surrender. By that time the Russians had secured all other former Japanese territories under their control. These included Manchuria and the northern half of Korea down to the middle of the peninsula at the thirty-eighth parallel. Halted south of that parallel by prior agreement, all the United States could do was watch and listen. The Soviets would not let them in.

Intelligence gathered was uniformly grim. For instance, a letter sent in secret to American army headquarters on September 27 from a North Korean university professor, Kyu Yong Lee, said, "As you know already, in the northern part of Korea, we have a great many difficulties with the Russian Army." He cited, among other grievances, a Russian action which was to crop up continually in intelligence reports in the next few months: They were dismantling "and shipping to Russia" factories and factory parts "particularly in [Konan], Songjin, and Churgchin"—in effect, the lengthy coastal swath of heavy industry that Noguchi had built stretching from Konan north to the Russian border.

So secretive were the Russians about their activities around Konan, which they had ringed with an actual physical defense perimeter, that on August 29, 1945, according to a September 17 *New York Times* story, Yak fighter planes shot down an American B-29 that was attempting to deliver food and medical supplies to an Allied prisoner of war camp there. The Russians later apologized, claiming they feared the plane was a disguised Japanese bomber. The United States did not believe that, but attempts to gain more information failed. Even a special mission by U.S. diplomat Edwin Pauley, granted entrance into northern Korea to investigate the reports of factory scavenging and ill-treatment, was denied access to the Konan area. Something important was going on there, and the Russians did not want to divulge it.

Coupled with this were persistent rumors that the Japanese had conducted atomic bomb experiments in the Konan area, now called by its Korean name, Hungnam, and that perhaps the Russians had benefited from the experiments. There also were reports of uranium finds there. The United States did not put much stock into these rumors and reports until the spring of 1946, when repatriations began and the stories began to mount. At that time Colonel Nist, who was fielding most of the reports, decided that because of their uniformity, "a great deal of credence" should be attached to them.

The War Department appears to have agreed with him. On June

20, 1946, following the first reports of Russians guarding a uranium mine near Chuul, North Korea, MacArthur's headquarters in Tokyo sent an "urgent" message to U.S. Army officials in Korea requesting visitation clearance for a special team, including Major Richard R. Entwhistle, an ordnance officer, and Lieutenant George Yamashiro, a top translator. Both were with the occupation's economic and scientific division, and the purpose of their rush visit was to gather "scientific information urgently requested."

Exactly what that information was is not spelled out in the few documents I was able to gather on the mission at the National Archives. But the general thrust is clear. In a July 6 memo, Entwhistle noted that he had quizzed "various bureaus" of the occupation in Korea about the "processes, equipment manufacture and critical material production having a possible relationship to the production or investigation of nuclear energy." He had found little to support the idea that the Russians might be benefiting from any previous Japanese atomic bomb work.

He wrote, "The production of heavy chemicals is virtually at a standstill for want of raw material and essential intermediaries. ... The largest factories are located north of the 38th Parallel. There is no evidence that plants for isotope separation or uranium extraction or refining existed." He referred to a "letter received from Washington requesting the confirmation of pitchblende deposits. Plants for the refining of the rare element minerals did not exist except for the isolated case of Nippon Magnesite Chemical Industrial Co., Song Chin." This was Noguchi's plant at Joshin, as the Japanese called Songjin, about 100 miles up the coast from Konan. It is also the same area where the Chuul uranium mine was reported.

Entwhistle indicated that he found that black sands, which the Japanese had frequently mentioned as a possible uranium ore, had been "dressed and concentrated in Korea for shipment to Japan"— but little else of interest.

Bill Overstreet, of the U.S. Geological Survey and one of the Allied mineral experts in Korea at that time, remembered the mission: "It was a bunch of lawyers. Didn't know a damn thing about mineral resources. All they did was write memos. They were all very confused and the data [were] very poor in terms of quantitative statements about anything. We regarded it as one of those high-level delegations that . . . come in for three days, live it up," and then get the credit for what "we had worked like dogs for."

Even if the mission had been well received, it would have had a hard time checking on the alleged atomic bomb activities. Most of the secret Russian activity at Konan had ceased by this time. The Atomic Bomb Mission itself had not been able to get any information on North Korea. And it had conducted its investigation when information was relatively fresh, whereas this second fact-finding mission was trying to get information a year later.

Still, the reports of atomic activity at Konan persisted. But they never appear to have been challenged or clarified. I never found any evidence of a follow-up, although some of them clearly stated they were "brief" and "incomplete." By this time the United States was actively cultivating Japanese friendship, especially among the scientists. Kelly was one of the main exponents of this policy. His writings show that he saw his role as a conciliator, a mender of broken fences. Getting Japan back on its feet and in a position to contribute to the free world was the task. Why pry out information that was of little use now, the act of which threatened the goodwill?

By June 1947 intelligence reports on the question read like this:

Consistent rumors from the Hungnam [Konan] area have dealt with the possibility of atomic research being conducted there. It is believed that the research was in connection with "ENNUZETTO"—"NZ"— which was a Japanese effort toward what has been variously reported as new high explosives, rockets or jet propulsion. Project is said to be located within a building which was heavily guarded by special Soviet guards. Only certain Soviet and Japanese technicians are allowed in the project. The project is frequently visited by the Japanese scientist, Tamura. At night, a very bright glow can be seen coming from inside the project which appears to be the spark of a high voltage electric arc. The products of the project are reported to be removed every two months in three or four boxes—approximate dimensions 24" × 16" × 6"—and loaded on submarines berthed at Dock #4. It is reported that the project was moved by Japanese and German technicians to its present location during April and May 1947.

The intelligence summaries were confusing and inconclusive. Although they clearly indicated that American intelligence in Korea assumed the alleged atomic bomb factory had actually been a jet fuel factory, their tone was tentative. There were unanswered questions, facts that disputed the new assessment.

For instance, no one I talked to involved in the jet fuel project had heard the code name NZ. USSBS interrogations indicated the jet fuel project was code-named Rogo-Yaku—the only name by which Captain Mitsui, one of its directors, knew it.

In late 1947 and early 1948 occupation headquarters again ordered an investigation into Japan's wartime nuclear program. I found at Suitland some thirty pages worth of reports, dated from October 14 through February 10. They were addressed to Kelly, who had taken over the science and technology division of the occupation. They were written by Nishina, who by then had become Kelly's good friend.

They told of a more developed project than the Atomic Bomb Mission had been informed about. NI and its top secret, top-priority nature were revealed; so were extensive searches for uranium.

Meanwhile, I had happened upon some intriguing, albeit minor, facts: According to *The German Atomic Bomb,* the book by David Irving, the Nazis had disguised their nuclear program by calling it a jet fuel project. Nininger had even told me he had *heard* the two had exchanged atomic scientists. Had the Japanese disguised their own nuclear program by calling it jet fuel or, at least, used one to cover the other?

I found a description of the Eighth Army Technical Laboratory, the army lab which worked with NI at the end of the war. While the report, as expected, said nothing about the lab's nuclear activities, its last listed project was entitled "Researches on Rocket Propellant."

That was probably mere coincidence. But a section of a book by M. Shiraishi, given to me by Chisso company officials when I visited them, is illustrative of the continued uncertainty of the United States regarding Konan: M. Shiraishi had been a Chisso official at Konan at the end of the war. He wrote:

The Americans seemed to hear of the rumor that we were making atomic bombs. When I returned to Japan after the war, I was summoned at least three times to an intelligence agency which was located at Itabashi, Tokyo. . . . They started questioning me indirectly, asking if I was interested in atomic power; if I had any acquaintance among scientists. I answered that I knew Mr. Nishina for he was my junior in school. Then they asked if I knew some others.

They said, "We've heard of the production of secret weapons at your factory. What were you making?" I replied that we were producing iso-octane and hydrogen peroxide. "You must have made other stuff too? What about artificial graphite—carbon? Tell us the method.

Since you were making hydrogen at your factory, you must have produced heavy water?" In short, all questions boiled down to the issue of atomic bombs.

He said he was "released after . . . they confirmed my words." But about a year later a "young American physicist in his 30s came to see me. At Shiraishi's Yoyogi residence, the visitor asked, 'What did the Russians ask you when they came to the Konan factory? Did they question about atomic bombs, heavy water and artificial carbon? Were they interested in atomic bombs?' "

So the United States still wondered, and probably continued to wonder until, in 1949, it was confirmed that the Russians had made their own bomb, and then the question of what had happened at Konan no longer mattered. Once the Russians actually had the bomb, how they had got it became relatively unimportant for intelligence purposes.

24

Yoshio Nishina never fully recovered from World War II and its aftermath. He became an outspoken critic of war and of his country's attempt to use nuclear power for war.

"Japan must use atomic energy only for peaceful purposes," he wrote in a letter to the editor of the *Mainichi Shimbun* on February 17, 1947. He wanted atomic research to continue—but only under controlled conditions. "Japan must [first] revive her industry." Then "an international commission which will have control over atomic energy must be established. Japan must sign a peace treaty with the Allied Powers and be recognized as a peaceful nation of the world."

In order to help rebuild the country and thus put it into a position to resume atomic research and the "eminence" in nuclear physics "it had in the late 1930s," he took it upon himself to become one of the leaders in the country's economic rebirth. They should start at the most basic level: feeding, clothing, and caring for the ordinary Japanese; building life anew from house foundations up. He wrote:

Unless we have enough to eat and shelter to live in, we cannot do much work in science. We must develop our own new techniques by which we can utilize either the scanty natural resources in this country or materials imported from foreign countries and manufacture goods which will either be exported or consumed for domestic purposes. . . . This is the responsibility of Japanese scientists, who ought to do all our effort for the discovery of new means by which our peaceful industry will be made prosperous. This is not an easy task but it is well worth doing. . . .

It was a call to begin the enormous effort that eventually produced such great economic success for the Japanese. The only trouble for Nishina was that this switch in his activities from scientist to political leader, rallying his country around applied technology, further complicated his life. As his son, Kojiro, told me, he was a physicist and teacher, at his best in the lab or classroom. He never completely adjusted.

For a while he wrote articles in the popular press. An occupation résumé summarizes the topics: "popular explanation on atomic bombs"; "to draw attention of scientists to the problem of rehabilitation"; "popular exposition of atomic energy control"; "to promote research and invention." It was his way of reaching the public. He felt it his duty. A letter he wrote to a prewar friend, I. I. Rabi, a Columbia University professor whom he had known in Hamburg, Germany, who had been awarded a Nobel Prize, expresses some of the pain and change he was experiencing:

> Here in Tokyo the war destroyed nearly everything. About 75 percent of our institute was burnt down by fire bombs and our two cyclotrons which escaped the fire were later destroyed and taken into the Pacific. In this condition it is not possible to conduct scientific researches. We must first till the soil in which science can grow, this is what I am doing at present.
>
> Our institute is to be dissolved by SCAP [occupation] directive and a new company is to be set up instead. I am now working hard as an organizer for our company, which is said to be unique in its kind in the sense that it will be solely engaged in scientific researches. I know how difficult it is here in Japan to run such a company at present, but such a work is evidently necessary for our recovery and I may have to drop physics entirely for some years to come—a sad thing.
>
> After all, everything we have been experiencing since the war may be said ultimately to become a building stone for a peace loving, civilized nation so that you may have a better neighbor than ever before and the ocean between us will be literally "Pacific."

He asked Rabi to use his influence in the United States to help Japanese science. He still had the idea of using isotopes to help basic research, but that research now had to be rethought. To General MacArthur, who would make all the basic decisions, he wrote: "We had planned to make . . . investigations by means of radioactive isotopes. . . . Owing to the destruction of our cyclotrons, however, this is no longer possible and recourse has to be taken to stable isotopes."

By now, April 1946, he had had time to envision an even broader research program than he had contemplated with the cyclotrons. In addition to investigations of photosynthesis, human metabolism, and crop growth, he hoped to use isotopes to determine which fertilizers worked the best and to watch "carcinogenic substances" produce cancer, which he hoped would give him "insight into the possibility of its inhibition." The isotopes would also help in the understanding of "the mechanism of chemotherapy," a then relatively new treatment for the disease that soon took his own life.

It was a broadly humanitarian program that Nishina envisioned, sincere and heartfelt. To see it realized—that is, to acquire the isotopes—he proposed that he go back to the separation and concentration work he had done under NI. His application, of course, made no mention of his wartime activities. It said, "Concentration of rare isotopes . . . is to be obtained by the method of chemical exchange reaction developed by H. C. Urey," the discoverer of heavy water. This was a distillation method, different from those he had tried on uranium. In essence it concentrated the isotopes by boiling off the host chemical—the same method used to concentrate deuterium. Drawings of the distilling apparatus accompanied his request, as did a drawing for a mass spectrometer, which he also hoped to be given permission to construct. It, too, he pointed out, would yield isotopes.

MacArthur approved the request, but with a stern admonition against any violation of occupation directives forbidding work on fissionable substances.

It is not clear from the documents I was able to collect at Suitland and elsewhere whether Nishina ever built the equipment. Just raising the money for the projects could have taken years. In the meantime, he "pioneered," according to Kojiro Nishina, the introduction of miracle-drug antibiotics, such as penicillin, into the ravaged country. A 1950 newspaper picture shows him receiving U.S. officials of the "world-famous Merck Pharmaceutical Company" in connection with a "proposed large-scale production of streptomycin here." In addition, he was being appointed to various newly formed scientific organizations, including the League of Science and Technique, the Science Council of Japan, and the Japanese delegation to the United Nations Educational, Scientific, and Cultural Organization

(UNESCO). More often than not, he was made the president or director. In those capacities he began speaking regularly on the peaceful rebuilding of Japan, occasionally traveling out of the country for conferences. A May 5, 1950, newspaper article in the files of the American Press Club in Tokyo called him "the dean of atomic physicists in Japan."

By 1947 the Rikken, because of its wartime activities, was under fire. It was on an occupation purge list. And since Nishina was now its president, he, too, in the words of a top-level occupation document, was "likely to be purged." It was not that he had done anything specifically wrong, said the "confidential" memo, dated February 4, 1947, but he had served on wartime boards that the occupation had listed as "militarist" and "war-mongering." One of these was the Nippon Shuppan Bunka Kyokai, an "organization made up mostly of publishers." One of the emperor's brothers was president. It was "under the supervision of the Information Bureau" and apparently was a watchdog over what was being printed—a censorship board. Nishina got wind of the proceedings against him and wrote his accusers: "I attended the board meetings now and then and expressed opinions on scientific publications from the standpoint of a scientist.... This I did in order to raise the status of science in Japan, and this was the absolute limit of my activity as a member of the board of directors. I never expressed my opinion on the 'thought' or political problems." Nor, he said, had he ever been involved in the "continued strife between the more liberal members and those with army background."

Nishina need not have worried. He had a friend in Kelly and Kelly's scientific and technical division, which could advise overall headquarters on its planned actions. General J. W. O'Brien, the military man with responsibility for the division, wrote:

Because of the destruction of the cyclotrons, Nishina is in a fair way to becoming a martyr of science. The Scientific and Technical Division does not wish to encourage this martyrdom. Purging him may add to his prestige. Nishina is considered by the world and by the Japanese scientists as one of the leaders of nuclear physics in Japan. He has been very useful to us in gaining information—information which would have been very difficult to obtain without the cooperation of Nishina and the Japanese scientists. The Scientific and Technical Division holds that the opportunity of getting this information is important and may be lost by purging scientific leaders.

The recommendation apparently was heeded. In 1948 the Rikken, in accordance with occupation guidelines, was dissolved as a company dependent on the government and reorganized as an independent joint-stock company. And Nishina was retained as president. His administrative responsibilities grew. New privileges came with the reorganization—for instance, permission to seek radioactive isotopes from the United States. Ironically, in view of what he had done during the war, he began dealing with the Manhattan Project-created Clinton Laboratories at Oak Ridge. If he had not been getting intelligence about Oak Ridge during the war, he was now getting information first hand.

Approximately nine months later, in August 1949, Nishina was preparing for perhaps the last truly happy time in his life. He had been selected to be Japan's representative to the General Assembly of the International Council of Scientific Unions to be held in Copenhagen, Denmark. The honor meant a return to the site of his prewar schooling at the Niels Bohr Institute. Men he had not seen for twenty years, some of them among the most distinguished scientists in the world, would be there. The trip was to take him to London and Rome as well. It truly was a journey back into the part of his life he considered the best.

In addition, he had been selected to take part in a month's scientific mission to American universities the following spring. In a letter to Dr. Kelly, Miss Yokoyama recalled that her boss was "so excited with the expectation to see Prof. Bohr again" that he left for the airport without his plane ticket and had to come back to get it, almost missing the plane and blaming her "for my neglect to remind him. . . . At that time I felt somehow he was unfair . . . because it was he who took out the ticket from the purse in order to phone you. . . . Old memories are dear and sweet and how I wish to be back to those days again."

When Nishina returned from Copenhagen in October, he wrote the Bohrs: "It is just a week since I came home from my long journey, the recollection of which gives me much delight, consolation and encouragement. I was very, very glad to see you and your family again, which I had never expected during the war to be possible and which I had always wished to do since the end of the war." He thanked them for making him feel at home, "forgetting the lapse of 21 years. Your boys who have splendidly grown up and been doing very well and your beautiful mansion and extensive gardens brought me back to the reality and made me think a great deal

on what has happened during the interval of these two decades."
He recalled carefree shopping trips with the Bohrs and thanked
them for presents they sent. "My wife was very, very pleased to have
those nice things. . . . In a few days I shall see all of our friends in
Tokyo and talk about you and your home." A "beautiful elephant"
figurine they had given him had been in a bag which was stolen from
his room in Hong Kong. But later both had been found—a sure sign,
he noted, of the luck the elephant was to bring.

In London, he concluded, "I saw news of the Russian atomic
bomb. . . . I hope an effective method of international control of
atomic energy will soon be established."

Back in Japan, little had changed. "In a cold and gloomy concrete
building on the outskirts of Tokyo," wrote an Associated Press
correspondent about Nishina's work, "a handful of Japanese scientists with more zeal than money or equipment are carrying out"
experiments on cosmic rays, Nishina's prewar obsession. The feature
described the tough conditions at the newly revamped Rikken, now
called the Scientific Research Institute:

> Under the direction of Dr. Yoshio Nishina, one of Japan's leading
> scientists, a few Japanese, their hands blue with cold, their equipment
> a rusty jumble of lights, pipes and wires which junior wouldn't have
> in his grade school chemistry set, are conducting continuous measure-
> ments of cosmic ray intensities, which Dr. Nishina says will aid
> meteorology. . . . As most Japanese scientists do, Dr. Nishina com-
> plained that a lack of funds is hampering Nippon's work in pure
> science. He intimated the Scientific Research Institute has to scratch
> vigorously to raise ¥150,000 monthly to pay his laboratory men and
> continue the experiments. At the black-market rate, ¥150,000 is
> equivalent to U.S. $250.

Values had changed drastically since the war had ended.
Nishina had one more respite: the month he spent in America
visiting scientists and institutions. The trip took him to the cities of
Washington, New York, Chicago, Houston, and San Francisco, to
Princeton and Harvard universities, and to the California Institute
of Technology. Then, on January 10, 1951, at 4:16 P.M., he died of
liver cancer at the Kawashima Hospital, Tokyo. The disease had
been diagnosed several months before. He had entered the hospital
in December and become critically ill right after the New Year.

Yamazaki, now a major scientist in his own right, wrote, "Dr.

Nishina . . . was a person rather apart from money-making, but he realized [the] need to raise funds . . . and gave up his own researches" to help the institute. Tomonaga wrote, "In his nuclear research laboratory, Dr. Nishina wanted to carry out his great plan of research, not only in pure nuclear physics, but also in its wide application to biology, to agriculture, and even to medical science. . . . However, the Pacific War broke out, and it became difficult for him to continue his research, much more so to carry out his new plans and new ideas. Thus his grand conception collapsed."

Tomonaga might better have used the word *exploded*. In my opinion, it was the atomic bomb that killed Nishina—literally and figuratively.

AFTERMATH

Noguchi had been dead six years, but America was finally about to receive a firsthand introduction to him or at least to the vast and powerful complex he had built. It was to be an introduction that we would never forget: brutal, shocking, one that would set the pattern for our Asian involvement right up into the present. In addition, it was to shed light on the question of whether or not Noguchi's complex had ever held an atomic bomb project, although the answer, again, would be buried in official secrecy.

The introduction was the Korean War and our defeat at the frozen Chosin reservoir—the reservoir Noguchi built.

When I had contacted David Snell about his story about the atomic bomb project at Konan, the only concrete piece of proof he could come up with was to tell me that during the Korean War, when UN forces had been at Hungnam in connection with the retreat from Chosin, a mysterious installation in the mountains around it had been discovered. He said Jim Lucas, a Scripps-Howard reporter, had written a story about it, which he (Snell) did not have, but which I could probably find.

As my last bit of research I tried to locate the story. First I called Scripps-Howard offices in Washington. Jim Lucas had worked there, but they did not have any of his stories. I was told to call headquarters in Cincinnati. Public relations man Jim Sagar at Cincinnati was at even more of a loss. "We don't keep any files here. I don't know why they told you to call us." I would have to find a newspaper which had subscribed to Scripps-Howard during the Korean War and go through it page by page.

There were none in Miami or in the newspapers microfilmed in Miami libraries. In order to find out anything soon, my only hope was to go through microfilms of the *New York Times,* which *was* available. It was possible it might have published something, too.

Since we were not at Hungnam until around November 1, 1950, I began with that date. Painstakingly I searched each page. The whole Chosin Reservoir story unfolded—but no mysterious installation. In the meantime, I found out who Jim Lucas was. He was a Pulitzer Prizewinning war correspondent. He had covered many battles and atomic bomb blasts. He had died in 1970—no chance to contact him. But like Snell, he was accomplished and had to be considered reliable. If he had written the story, as Snell said he had, then there must have been something to it—the "case" in the mountain, perhaps where the Japanese had assembled whatever they had made.

I read right through the December evacuation. Nothing. I was about to quit. Then, through my reading on the war, I realized that UN forces had actually arrived at Hungnam in late October. I put the microfilm for the last half of October on the machine and started turning. It didn't take long. There, on page 3 of the October 26, 1950, issue of the *New York Times* was a United Press story that instantly drew my eyes. NORTH KOREAN PLANT HELD URANIUM WORKS was the headline. The dateline was Hungnam, Korea. It read:

A vital Russian research-supply project, believed by United States atomic energy experts to have been a Soviet uranium ore processing plant, has been captured by the South Korean army near this northern east coast port. Authoritative sources in Washington said the United States Atomic Energy Commission had known about the plant for a long time. They indicated it would not surprise them to learn if a second plant like it were found in North Korea.

The huge factory was strongly fenced in and guarded by electric barriers. An American military adviser to the South Koreans and a United Press correspondent saw a building constructed along the lines of a Kansas City grain elevator. Behind it was a compound 100 yards long, 50 yards wide and crowded with a great concentration of high voltage wiring which apparently powered two huge machines that seemed to be the center of the intricate set-up. Sand bags had been piled around the machines and apparently they had been unhurt by United States raids.

Quickly going through other possible sources, I found that *News-week* had carried the story as part of its main roundup on the war in the November 6 issue. The report read: "The Korean Communists were equally sensitive about the nearby Pujon and Changjin [Chosin and Fusen] Reservoirs. These supply not only irrigation waters but electric power for the captured Hungnam area, including: (1) A bombed-out fertilizer plant, the Far East's largest, which formerly exported to Russia; (2) an unbombed uranium-ore processing plant, zealously guarded by high-voltage electric fences, which fed raw material for Russia's atom bombs. . . ."

It was obvious that neither the *Times* nor *Newsweek* knew the full implications of the find, for neither followed up with stories about Hungnam's history. The lid on Japan's atomic efforts was shut very tightly by this time. But on November 3 the *Times* buried in a corner of a back page a one-paragraph Associated Press item quoting army officials to the effect that the UP dispatch had been a mistake. It cautiously—almost disbelievingly—said, "Tenth Corps Headquarters said today no atomic energy installations had been found in northeastern Korea. 'Uranium ore plants or other plants connected with production of atom bombs have not been discovered in the Tenth Corps area of operations up to the present time,' the statement said."

That last disclaimer—"up to the present time"—sounded phony to me. The discovery of the installation at Hungnam was information that the American government did not want publicized. The denial was an attempt to keep the story out of the public eye, another episode in the continuing cover-up of part of the secret history of World War II.

EPILOGUE

Ten years after *Secret War* was published, I got another chance to research its sources. In 1995, the 50th Anniversary of the atomic bombing of Japan was being observed, and the book, which had been both praised and denounced in reviews, was being reissued. I expected the passage of time would have opened up new sources of information, especially about the Konan aspect of the story, and about what had happened to the uranium onboard U-234—two of the most intriguing unanswered questions.

Over the years, the Department of Energy, notoriously secretive, was opening more of its files, and, in addition, I had received a number of leads. After a few calls, including one to John Taylor at the National Archives, I was told there were indeed new files open to researchers. I decided a trip to Washington would be worth the effort. As Rich Boylan, one of the archivists at the Suitland Branch, told me on the phone, "In contrast to when you were here last, most of the World War II stuff is now in. [If you come to Washington] at least you'll be able to say you have checked everything through 1994."

Actually, that wasn't true. Checking "everything" would take years. But at least I could spot-check, zeroing in on selected boxes of newly available records that seemed promising. I decided on a one-week trip to D.C., but before I left, two new pieces of information entered the puzzle:

The first came from an article in the December 1994 edition of *Military* magazine, a publication based in Sacramento, California. The article was by Leon Thompson, a former medic in the 237th Medical Dispensary in Tokyo from 1947 to 1949. Thompson wrote that as a result of a friendship with an OSS officer, whom he identified only as "Mr. Papps," he had been taken into a secret room in General MacArthur's headquarters and shown what Papps said was an "actual diagram of the Japanese atomic bomb."

Three "American atomic scientists" were there going over the plans, Thompson wrote, and Papps "showed me some Japanese orders to use the bomb on the Allies when they came into Japanese waters. . . . It was really a shock to our atomic scientists to learn that the Japanese had nearly beaten us to the draw, and this is one of the reasons they would not let the story be told."

Through the magazine, I reached Thompson, 67, who lives in Kent, Washington, near Seattle. He had undergone cancer surgery, and was going blind and deaf. Because of his hearing problems, a friend of his had to relay the questions I posed to him on the phone. But Thompson was able to do his own talking. He said he believed he was one of only a few people who knew about this and feared that he would die before he could bear witness. He told me following strange details.

He had met "Mr. Papps," whose first name he had never gotten, by accident. He and a fellow soldier were sightseeing near the Japanese Imperial Palace on a day in 1947. Unbeknownst to them, Papps was in the same area and was being pursued by two men, whom Papps later identified as Russians. They were after something Papps had. Thinking the American military uniforms would stop the pursuit, Papps struck up a conversation with the two unsuspecting soldiers.

The Russians retreated and Papps, said Thompson, invited the two young men, who still didn't know what was going on, for drinks. They readily accepted, happy to meet someone who seemed to know his way around. While the other soldier got drunk and eventually left, Papps and Thompson became friends. Later that afternoon, Papps, who by then had identified himself as an OSS officer and said he "owed" Thompson, asked if Thompson would like to meet General MacArthur? Thompson said sure. But when they got to occupation headquarters, MacArthur was in important meetings, so Papps invited him instead to see his own office, which was just down the hall.

They entered via password through a secretive outer room that, at first, Thompson thought was just a wall. It had a peephole for photographing MacArthur's visitors. It was in this room that Thompson said he saw the three scientists, whom Papps introduced only with first names, which Thompson cannot remember, and which he suspects were code names. The scientists were studying the plans with magnifying glasses. The plans looked to him like huge "negative" blowups, arranged one on top of the other and somehow rear-projected onto a large tilted screen against a wall.

"I asked Papps if the [bomb] was good enough to work," said Thompson, "and he said, 'Yes, it is just like ours,'" It was crude, but "workable in what these three atomic scientists have so far found."

Papps and Thompson then went into a smaller adjoining office belonging to Papps, where Thompson says Papps showed him some boxes and a briefcase stuffed so full of Japanese war documents it wouldn't close. Papps told him they had come from a Japanese general who had escaped from Korea "just before the Russians captured the complex where he was working." After the war, the OSS had found out about the general, who was a civilian by then, and when he tried to sell the plans to the Russians, they raided his apartment and confiscated the documents.

"I wish I could remember the name of the general," Thompson told me.

When he asked Papps why the Japanese hadn't used the bomb, Thompson said he was told, "They were awaiting the arrival of a German submarine that was carrying a better triggering plutonium because the uranium they had was a much lower grade and not as good."

With the exception of the plutonium, which seemed unlikely, these last details sounded much like those I had found in intelligence reports about Konan-Hungnam. Was it corroboration? I knew the OSS had been disbanded shortly after the end of the war, but Thompson was insistent that Papps was with the OSS. Maybe this was a leftover unit, or Thompson was simply mistaken. I asked him to write everything down, especially details, and send it to me. He said he would. I'd check and see if I could find Papps and would get back to him when I'd returned from Washington.

The other new lead was closer to home: A local physician here in Los Angeles had told a friend of mine, who knew him professionally, that he was aware of the Japanese program at Hungnam. The doctor's name was William B. Engeberg, a 30-year family practitioner in Inglewood and past president of the Los Angeles County Medical Society.

I called Dr. Engeberg and he told me that in February 1953, during the Korean War, he had been a flight surgeon with the "95th

Squadron" at a secret base on the west coast of South Korea. His wing commander there, a colonel at the time, he said, headed a B-26 unit that included the unusual addition of fighters.

The implication, I guessed, was that this was a rare and special unit, probably privy to secret intelligence.

"He was an unusual guy," said Engeberg about the colonel, "very intelligent, very bright."

They became friends. One day, he said, the colonel told him, "I want you to fly right seat with me." Engeberg indicated he couldn't have refused if he'd wanted to. "He was my CO." Their mission was farther north up the Korean coast than Hungnam, said Engeberg, but the colonel made an unauthorized deviation in order to fly over the former Japanese industrial stronghold and told Engeberg, once they were over the destroyed complex, that he had information that Japanese atomic research had occurred there and that the Japanese had made some kind of device there and fired it off.

"It wasn't as good as ours," said Engeberg. "I don't think we'll ever know the full story."

Engeberg said the colonel was now a four-star general and that they kept in touch. But when I wanted his name and information about how to reach him, Engeberg said he'd have to contact the general first and get his permission. He still does clandestine work and is currently not in the United States, Engeberg added. "He doesn't like the limelight."

This was an indication that the Konan-Hungnam reports were still alive in operational intelligence circles after the reported finding (and subsequent denial) of a uranium works in the area in 1950, I asked Dr. Engeberg to please try and find the general so I could get his version and I'd get back with him when I returned from Washington.

I started at Suitland where the post–World War II Army intelligence files and records of occupation (SCAP) are housed. Suitland is where earlier I had found most of my information on the Japanese projects. I had faxed Rich Boylan to let him know which boxes I had looked at in 1979 and 1980, so he would know what I had not seen.

The very first boxes he brought out—from Record Group 331 (SCAP), Entry 150—had interesting new information. In "Box 1," in a manila folder labeled "Atomic Bomb File, Top Secret," there was a one-page report on Dr. Bunsaku Arakatsu, who had headed the secretive Japanese navy project at the end of the war. (He was the one I thought most likely to have spawned, knowingly or unknowingly, anything that might have occurred in Korea.) The report writer stated that he believed Arakatsu lied when questioned about his wartime nuclear activities.

Entitled "Report on Collection of Records at the Laboratory of Dr. Arakatsu, Imperial University, Kyoto," the document had no date, but appeared, from the information in it, to have been written shortly after November 20th, 1945—two days before the destruction of the cyclotrons.

Asked for negatives of photos he'd made at Hiroshima, Arakatsu had told Lieutenant-Colonel E. J. Drake, a member of SCAP's nuclear-investigating Science and Technology Division, that the negatives had been destroyed. Not believing him, Drake wrote he had "searched further and found a packet containing negatives which Dr. Arakatsu admitted corresponded to the prints."

Drake wrote that Arakatsu, in light of Drake's discovery of the negatives, when questioned further about "laboratory note-books" that were also supposed to have been destroyed, now volunteered that they "were probably in the possession of a former collaborator, Sonoda Masateria, who is now in Manchuria."

I had heard this "Manchurian connection" before, and I would see it again. Later, at the new College Park branch of the archives [in Record Group 77, Entry 22, Box 172] I would find a March 27, 1946, Manhattan Project report by Major Russell Fisher, Japanese atomic-bomb-project investigator, that mentioned several reportings of Japanese atomic research in Manchuria and elsewhere in China in the later days of the war. Fisher had been sent to Shanghai to investigate but had decided against entering Manchuria because, like North Korea, it was overrun with Russians at that time, and he felt they might find out what he was after. He was thus forced to rely on information supplied by former Japanese navy officers who claimed to have been involved in the activity.

Manchuria and Konan were, of course, connected by rail.

I went on:

Box 2 of the SCAP records, Entry 224, mentioned that Noguchi's company was making heavy water for Arakatsu, and reported that Army investigators had impounded "360 cc" of heavy water from his cyclotron lab when they had searched it in 1945.

A 1946 document back in Box 3 of Entry 150 said flatly that the Economic and Scientific Division was trying to "disprove" the reports of a Japanese atomic explosion at Konan-Hungnam, and further documents in Box 1 of 150 quoted both Arakatsu and Kikuchi as saying the Konan stories were "false" and "fantastic." (Curiously, both professors used the same identical terms, according to the investigator.)

But subsequent directives in the same boxes ordered reinvestigations in 1947 and 1948 of Japanese wartime atomic research, indicating that SCAP still did not know exactly what had happened. In fact, SCAP was continually ordering reinvestigations of Japanese wartime atomic research and discovering new facts at least up until 1949, according to additional documents that I found.

For instance, according to records in Box 2 of Entry 224, it wasn't until June 1949 that the Special Project Branch, the small unit within the Science and Technology Division charged with the actual monitoring of Japanese atomic research, learned the origin of the heavy water confiscated from Arakatsu's lab and subsequently received its first-ever information on Noguchi's wartime production of heavy water in mainland Japan.

Supplied mainly by former Noguchi company employees, Saburo Tashio, director of one of the Noguchi labs on the mainland, and Masao Kubota (not otherwise identified), the reports state that although "our records were burned during the 1945 air raids," recollections from memory were that the company was first asked to provide heavy water to "Prof. Chitani, Osaka U, for use as tracer in chemical reactions. . . . By the end of 1942, using glass electrolytic equipment, we were able to produce 8 liters of 1.2% heavy water per month. . . . In Jan. 1944, 3 step constant volume continuous electrolysis equipment . . . was completed (and) by April 1944 . . . it became possible to produce approximately 50cc of 90% or purer heavy water per month."

The reports said nothing of Noguchi's heavy water production in Korea, which was not subjected to Allied bombing. But they did say that once the war started, Nishina's Riken was to receive "100 cc/month of 100% (deuterium)" but never did because "experiments with (Nishina's) cyclotron did not reach the stage of necessitating large quantities . . ."

This was the first connection of Nishina and heavy water that I had seen, as well as of Noguchi to Nishina, and suggests that the full story of Nishina's involvement has not been told.

Box 3 of Entry 224 yielded a high mark of my two days at Suitland: an interrogation of a former engineer at the Noguchi Konan complex, Otogoro Natsume, conducted on October 31, 1946. "Subject" of the interrogation was listed as "Further questioning re newspaper story about atomic bomb explosion in Korea."

In attendance were head of the Science and Technology Division, Dr. Harry Kelly; an interpreter, "T/4 Matsuda;" and a "Mr. Donnelly," identified only as "5250 TIC." He apparently was some sort of intelligence officer and, judging from their questions, the interrogators had more information about the Konan-Hungnam story than was in the newspaper.

Natsume, a chemical engineer, according to the interrogation, had been imprisoned by the Russians and then released to run a Konan plant until he escaped "on a small sailing boat" in December 1945. He told the investigators he'd heard the rumors about the atomic bomb explosion at Konan but knew nothing about it.

According to the transcript, the following exchange then ensued:

Kelly: "We have evidence that there was some kind of explosion there."

Donnelly: "We haven't actually found anything concrete. Last few days we have been talking with people here in and around Tokyo and asking them about report[s] of decomposition of hydrogen peroxide and asking them if they knew about it or which plant it was."

Kelly: "Did any of the plants have accidents during the war?"

(Natsume through Matsuda): "There were none."

Donnelly: "Ask him if he knows anything about the NZ plant making hydrogen peroxide."

Matsuda: "He says that he heard about the factory but it was under the Navy and highly secret. He had never been in it."

Kelly: "What was the name of the plant?"

Matsuda: "He says just NZ plant."

Donnelly: "Ask him what NZ plant made and what does NZ mean?"

Matsuda: "He doesn't know."

A few more questions about the ownership and location of the plant, then:

Kelly: "About how many chemists worked up there?"

Matsuda: "He says there are so many classes of chemists. Do you mean University Graduate?"

Kelly: "Yes."

Matsuda: "He says that there are two factories under management of this company—one in Konan and one in Honbu. There are about 700 chemists altogether (approximately 300 at Konan)."

In a lengthy exchange, Natsume indicated that most of the scientists, engineers, and workers at Konan were arrested and then later released to go back to work. But six key technical people from NZ, whom he later named, were not released and he had "no idea" what the Russians were doing with them except that they were being held in the "secret plant."

Kelly: "Has he got any idea as to how we can get these secret plans?"

Matsuda: "The six men mentioned are the only ones who knew much about the secret plant."

Donnelly: "Ask him where the naval officers were stationed up there—in what plant."

Matsuda: "In [the] NZ plant."

Kelly: "How was it that the Russians knew which men to get— only the six who knew the secret?"

Matsuda: "They more or less interrogated and they picked out the engineers and all the assistant engineers. And in a Japanese office, they had all the lists written up."

Asked by Donnelly if there were any others who had escaped Konan after the Russians had occupied it, whom the United States could interrogate, Natsume said there was only one, a "Mr. Sakaguchi."

Kelly concluded the five-page interrogation by having Matsuda tell Natsume, "We thank him. If he thinks of anything more pertinent to help us make a more complete report on this matter, I wish he would come back in and tell us."

This, like the memoir of Hasagawa, was firsthand witness to Konan. It was intriguing. Kelly said they had information about an explosion there. Natsume said that even though he was in the complex, the NZ plant was so secret and guarded he knew nothing about it. Kelly was clearly interested in the secrecy.

Where was the followup?

I searched the rest of the boxes but little in this regard turned up. Interviews of South Korean scientists conducted by the Branch's Major Entwhistle prior to the Natsume interrogation (in July 1946) were negative. The South Koreans, who had not been in Konan during the war or after, doubted the stories. An August 8, 1946, "Top Secret" SCAP report to the Joint Chiefs of Staff, which I later found at College Park, reflected that South Korean doubt. Citing Entwhistle's July research, it said, "The Japanese did not conduct any research in atomic nuclear physics or isotope separation in

Korea. Prospecting for sources of radioactive material was the limit of their activity in this sensitive field."

But why then did Kelly, the head of the Scientific and Technology Division, and Donnelly question Natsume so intently nearly three months later?

An explosion? Secret plans? NZ?

Clearly something new had tweaked their interest again. But the rest of the Suitland files I was able to go through did not yield the answer.

Instead, they produced the following marginal information:

· That a year later—on or about october 30, 1947—Dr. Kelly and the Scientific and Technology Division were still trying to gently pry from the known Japanese atomic researchers what they had done during the war.

A report on that date about a conference for that purpose, said, "The Japanese (scientists in attendance) were given the following brief outline of what was requested:

"a. Approximate date at which interest was first shown in the atomic physics research by the Army and Navy. The interest may be even just preliminary conversation.

"b. Methods proposed to carry out plans.

"c. Who was to carry out the research budget.

"d. Results of work and research.

"e. Reports in fields of Physics, Chemistry, Biology and Mining as relevant [sic] to the subject."

These were *not* the questions of an organization that already had received satisfactory information on the Japanese wartime projects. And, in fact, later, at the Laguna Niguel, California, branch of the National Archives, I was to find a November 28, 1945, letter to Secretary of War Patterson from Vannevar Bush, director of our overall scientific effort, signaling just how delicately we were treating the Japanese atomic scientists.

Reacting to the destruction of the cyclotrons just a few days earlier, which had taken him by surprise, Bush said he had "understood" that there was a "general plan of treating the Japanese scientists somewhat gently, inasmuch as they were rendering us extraordinarily complete information on their war activities."

We definitely were looking to get something back for our kindness.

Returning to the marginal Suitland finds:

·The Japanese may have lost at least one of its atomic researchers in a laboratory accident, which was information about the Japanese program I had never heard before.

According to a "Top Secret" memo from Army intelligence, dated December 6, 1945, the *Nippon Times* had reported that on August 15, 1944, Masaharu Odan, a physics researcher at Tokyo Imperial University, had been badly wounded in a chemical explosion while working on experiments "utilizing atomic energy in the construction of military arms."

Quoting the August 25, 1944, article, the memo said Odan, a graduate assistant at the university, "was fatally wounded in his chest and abdomen in an explosion at 4:25 P.M. He was immediately taken to hospital but died on the way. Thus, he died in his line of duty, having contributed enormously toward the improvement of arms."

It did not say what specific work he was doing, or for whom.

·A repatriated Japanese Army lieutenant, identified only as "Suzuki," who said he had been a physics student of Yoshio Nishina, among other teachers, had informed U.S. Army intelligence in China that the Japanese "knew in November 1944 that US had perfected [the] atomic bomb."

Did this add credence to the stories of Tojo knowing about our program or to what Alcazar de Velasco had told me?

Several times during this research trip, I would find indications, beyond those I had found previously, that the Manhattan Project had not been as secret as General Leslie Groves had always liked to believe.

For instance, Manhattan Engineer District files I was later able to see on microfilm at the Laguna Niguel, California, branch of the National Archives, had a copy of an American newspaper article, apparently written in 1943 or 1944, which stated in its headline that both the United States and Germany were "working on the Atomic Bomb."

The article said the information came from a "high Army Air Forces officer" at a press conference, and went on to state, "Fragmentary reports that the United States is developing atomic explosive techniques in West Coast plants came recently from members of Congress, but yesterday's disclosure marked the first time a War

Department authority has ventured to talk about the highly secret project. It is believed the projected bombs would utilize the terrific explosive power resulting from disintegration of atoms, which has long been the subject of major laboratory experiments and research." Accompanying the article were secret memos by Manhattan Project officials about how such a disastrous leak could have occurred, how to discipline the officer, and mostly how to mitigate the effect of his statements; ultimately, it was decided to deny them.

I made one more important find at Suitland—probably the most important of the trip. It was elaborated on in documents I later found at College Park. The find was this: The Japanese apparently spent much more money on their atomic bomb efforts than, as far as I know, has ever been reported—100 million yen more, according to Manhattan Project documents.

The huge outlay—approximately $25 million wartime U.S. dollars (a considerable sum for a comparatively small and less wealthy nation like Japan at that time) was made around 1945 to aid the surreptitious and sometimes frenetic efforts of Arakatsu and the super-secret, late-war Navy project officers, according to the documents I found.

The documents, some 35 pages of mostly two- and three-page "Top Secret" reports, some of which were also marked "Control" (meaning they could only be seen by certain persons who were cleared for top secret), were found at Suitland in Record Group 331, Entry 1947–1951, Box 2, and at College Park, in Record Group 77, Entry 22, Box 172.

Here is the story they tell (along with some background to the documents which helps shed light on why the Japanese atomic effort has remained so buried and little known):

As the immediate postwar period commenced, the Manhattan Engineer District, still run by General Groves and overseen by the War Department, was coming into inevitable conflict with SCAP and its monarchal head, General Douglas MacArthur. Groves was single-minded, primarily interested in keeping atomic secrets within America and away from Russia, while MacArthur, who certainly shared those views, had a host of other immediate concerns, not the least of which was to forge a workable governing system in Japan while at the same time lift his defeated subjects out of the postwar mire and into a bulwark against communism.

He tried hard not to needlessly antagonize them.

Consequently, Grove's parochial War Department–backed directives—roughshod control of Japanese atomic scientists, location of
radioactive materials and ores in Japan, and the like—were not being
attended to as the Manhattan Engineer District (MED) wanted.

As Major Russell A. Fisher, the MED representative sent to Japan
to correct the problem, wrote back to the War Department in a May
1, 1946, report: "It was found that at this time (January 1946, when
Fisher had first arrived) little coordinated action had been under-
taken (between SCAP and the War Department) except for destruction of Japanese cyclotrons in accordance with specific Joint Chiefs
of Staff instructions."

Often at odds with MacArthur's staff, Fisher nevertheless began
changing things. He created, he wrote in the same report, the Special
Projects Unit. It was specifically to watch the Japanese physicists.
And because, he added, "It is not possible to say whether (the
Science and Technology Division's) coverage of . . . laboratories is
in any sense complete in view of their . . . uncoordinated activities,
and the absence of many reports," he embarked upon an investigation of the Japanese physicists himself.

His main purpose was not history, but to find and confiscate
uranium and other atomic "assets" before the Russians got them.

"There are considerable numbers of Russian officers accredited to
SCAP," he wrote in a March 27, 1946, letter to Colonel W. R. Shuler
of the War Department, "and various Russian technical and economic missions . . . (which) are moving about Japan with apparent
complete freedom. The CIC has been watching them and I have
requested that particular attention be given to any evidence that they
are interested in Japanese nuclear physics or scientific personnel in
Japan."

(The picture of Russians running amok in Japan recalled the story
Leon Thompson had told me before I had left for Washington.)

It was while he was embarked on this investigation that Fisher
received information that, in the spring of 1945, Arakatsu had been
supplied with "approximately 100 kilograms of uranium oxide" by
the Navy. Unlike the MED's previous investigator, Robert Furman,
who had headed the Alsos mission into Japan right after the surrender and had left quickly without much followup, Fisher got from
Arakatsu, who pleaded mostly ignorance about the uranium, the
names of Arakatsu's Navy liaisons and began tracking them down.

According to a March 8, 1949, memo at Suitland, the former Navy
Commander Tetsuzo Kitagawa, whose memoir I had earlier ac-

quired, was the first to be interrogated about the matter—and with surprising and incriminating results.

It appears Fisher and whoever was with him decided to be cagey and play dumb, not tell Kitagawa specifically why he had been summoned. "When asked about his principal activities in the last year of the war," wrote Fisher, Kitagawa willingly volunteered about his work with "rocket fuels employing hydrogen peroxide," particularly the problem of "stabilizing (the) hydrogen peroxide for use in Japanese copies of the Messerschmitt 163 rocket fighter airplane."

(It will be recalled that Japanese plans for the "Defense of the Homeland" called for "fission" bombs to be placed in kamikaze jet planes to be sent against the U.S. invading fleet.)

But when questioned about the "nature of the Japanese Navy's project headed by Professor Arakatsu," wrote Fisher, Kitagawa "became noticeably cautious. At first he said only that there was a project to study the possibility of utilizing energy (like an engine as opposed to a bomb) from uranium."

And when they asked him about the 100 kilograms of uranium oxide, he "stated that no chemical supplies had been provided by the Navy, as none were available in Japan. [However] When informed that we already knew of some material supplied, he revised his statement."

In other words, Fisher was implying that Kitagawa lied—or, perhaps in terms more appropriate to the early postwar situation of fear and mixed loyalties, he was at least "not forthcoming."

Eventually, under "repeated questioning," the former Japanese Navy officer supplied more information, most of which is generally known, except for the following details:

·The Japanese Navy had supplied the "pure iron for the core of Arakatsu's cyclotron in 1943."

·Arakatsu had requested 1,500 kilograms of uranium compounds from the Navy, which was the impetus for the frantic search.

·The amount of uranium Arakatsu did get, which was still unclear, "probably came from Shanghai, since the bill of lading indicated that."

Nobody kept any written records, Kitagawa told them, and that was all he knew or remembered.

"Toward the close of the interview," concluded Fisher, "the discussion returned to the rocket fuel project, to the apparent relief of

Kitagawa." He did happen to have a written report on that, and he'd be happy to supply Fisher with it.

Fisher wasn't interested. Instead, he told Kitagawa to write up a report on the "uranium project, including dates, materials supplied and all other pertinent information," and be back with it within a week.

Former Admiral Sasagawa, whose intriguing report, "Investigation of Uranium Ores, 1 April 1945," I had previously located, was next on Fisher's list, having been mentioned by Kitagawa. Sasagawa, whose first name is nowhere on any documents I have found, was commanding officer of the "Special Material Unit" of the Japanese fleet at war's end, according to the documents. But he told Fisher that he'd come into the job late, after crucial decisions had been made, and the better man to talk to about the matter would be Lieutenant Commander Tetsuya Takao, former head of Special Material Unit's chemical section, the man who handled the "requisition, procurement and delivery to Dr. Arakatsu."

Fisher appears to have accepted that.

On March 13, 1946, the day after interviewing Sasagawa, Fisher wrote a report on Takao, who he obviously had immediately gone out and found. Takao told him, Fisher wrote, that upon hearing Arakatsu's request for uranium from Kitagawa, he "remembered" a Japanese lab in Shanghai called the Shanghai Natural Chemical Research Institute where he felt large amounts of uranium oxide might be available. Uranium oxide was used in the ceramics industries and there was a black market for it there.

The Japanese Navy gave the project top priority and Takao said he was able to arrange through the "Finance Dept. of the Navy Ministry" funds to buy the uranium oxide on the black market. "When questioned as to why the Navy did not confiscate the material . . . he said said since this material was not from one source, it would have been impossible to gather it other than to make an inviting offer."

By May 3, after considerable more investigation, Fisher was writing a top secret "Memorandum for the file," which I found at College Park, that said in part, "approximately 130 kilograms of uranium compounds, mostly yellow oxide, were purchased through black market agents in Shanghai . . . for the fantastic cost of One Hundred Million (100,000,000) yen. Approximately 100 kilograms of uranium material was shipped to Arakatsu in May 1945. This was impounded by U.S. forces in November 1945. The remaining 30 kilograms remained in Admiral Sasagawa's custody until taken over by (Fisher) in March 1946."

It is not clear whether Sasagawa had lied about what he had or how Fisher had found out about the 30 kilograms, since Fisher's first interview with the admiral mentioned nothing about the uranium in his possession. But Fisher subsequently went to Shanghai to continue his investigation, and an earlier "Summary Report" to Colonel Shuler in Washington, written from Shanghai and dated March 27, 1946, contained what appeared to be (judging from the other documents) the extent of his knowledge on the extravagant uranium purchase:

"During the winter of 1944–45, a procurement agent connected with the Japanese Naval Base headquarters in Shanghai purchased and delivered in Japan approximately 275 lbs. of uranium compounds, mostly yellow oxide. A total fund of one hundred million Yen [Yen 100,000,000] invasion currency, was expended by the Japanese Navy for this purpose.

"Source of purchased material was stocks of uranium salts in China remaining from pre-war shipments procured for use in the ceramics industry from European producers. Japanese purchaser employed black market agents in Shanghai to collect uranium material. Purpose of Japanese Navy procurement of uranium salts was to supply experimental material for Navy sponsored atomic energy project conducted at Kyoto Imperial University, under direction of Dr. Arakatsu.

"Original requirement specified by Arakatsu was for 1500 Kg, of which 130 Kg. [approximately 275 lbs.] were procured and shipped to Japan. Chemist, Dr. Okada, on staff of Japanese sponsored Shanghai Institute of Natural Science Research, acted as advisor to Navy on procurement of uranium in China.

"This information is derived from civilian scientists and Navy technical administrative personnel in Japan and special informants in Shanghai. Information is considered basically reliable."

(One of the reasons I highlight the fact that the information was considered basically reliable is that I've noticed a tendency on the part of some U.S. evaluators to downgrade credibility when the sources were Asian, especially Chinese and Korean, although I have been told by others in intelligence that the information was often accurate. So part of the problem of getting information from East to West may be bias.)

Fisher's aim, as already stated, was to find the uranium, not to pursue Japanese wartime activities for history's sake. It appears that mission was accomplished. A top secret message from Tokyo, dated March 23, 1946, and sent to the War Department, says solely, "Approximately 275 pounds Uranium Oxide in unopened bottles impounded to date. Request disposition."

An attached memo to "Gen. Groves" from Colonel Shuler, dated two days later, refers to the cable, and adds, "After checking with Jannarone and General Nichols, Colonel Field in the State, War and Navy Coordinating Committee has been advised to ship the lot to me personally. I will then ship it to the Madison Square Area. The principal reason for this decision was to keep the Russians from acquiring this lot of uranium oxide."

But what about the rest of the uranium?

Although I didn't emphasize it above, Takao had told Fisher in the March 13 memo that "He had learned that the 100 million yen was paid for . . . 500kg of uranium oxide," although Fisher said at the end of the report that when questioned further, Takao "could not make up his mind whether it was 500 or 50kg."

As Fisher himself had written, 100 million yen, or about $25 million in 1943 exchange rates (according to a Magic summary conversion table I have) is a "fantastic" amount for the teetering Japanese war machine to have spent on anything at that crucial time in their fight. Twenty-five million dollars then was like $100 million today. They must have wanted—and received—something substantial for their money. Was 275 pounds of uranium all they got? Was it then shipped home to a beleaguered island fortress that was being bombed mercilessly and from which many other pieces of the war machine that were still valuable to the Japanese military like the jet fuel project, were being evacuated to safer places like Korea?

I don't know the answers. But such a huge outlay indicates that the Japanese certainly gave a high priority to the uranium project, at least at the end of the war, which is contrary to what most apologists for the Japanese have always insisted.

Further information in the Fisher documents possibly shed more light on what could be other previously unknown aspects of the Japanese nuclear effort on the Asian mainland:

"During the war," Fisher continued in the March 27, 1946, report, "a small chemical plant was operated in Shanghai by a White Russian named Alex Shornik, which among other chemical products, produced metallic uranium by reduction of uranium salts. Consumers of metallic uranium were said to be Japanese who shipped material to Manchuria for use in steel metallurgy. Reports indicate that probably not more than 25 lbs. of metallic uranium was produced . . . Reports on existence of plant and its products are considered reliable."

In addition, he wrote, "It is reported that Chaing Kai-shek [the Chinese leader at the time] has stated that China must develop . . . atomic energy. [In connection with this, Chinese authorities were] instructed . . . to secure the assistance of Japanese scientists and technicians capable of work in this field. . . . [The authorities were] 'extremely shocked because the Russians had taken away all the plants in Manchuria in which Atomic energy research was being done.' "

While Fisher expressed skepticism about the plants existing in Manchuria, which, presumably—if they did exist—had been in the hands of Japanese occupiers, he conceded, "It is, however, confirmed that the Chinese Central Government has issued an order blocking all shipment of uranium material out of China."

So uranium metal, an essential to any nuclear bomb project, was reportedly being made in Japanese occupied Shanghai, where choice uranium ore was known to be in abundance, and the Chinese were now to be added to the list of sources reporting that the Japanese conducted atomic research in Manchuria.

Were the Japanese they hoped to employ from the Manchurian plants? Were they from elsewhere on the Asian mainland?

If so, where? And what had they been doing there?

More unanswered questions.

The final document in the Fisher bunch—final in the sense that it was dated December 10, 1946—was a top secret "Memorandum For the Commanding General, Manhattan Engineer District" about the stepped up "Control and Surveillance of Atomic Energy Research and Development in Japan." Only it dealt solely with Korea, listing various uranium or stockpiles discovered there, and noting that, "Despite the statement in the previous report that all plants known to have dressed or refined radioactive material had been visited and that stockpiles now reported represent the total stockpiles now existent, new plants and additional stockpiles continue to be uncovered. . . ."

In other words, they were still running into surprises.

I couldn't tell where in Korea the report referred to—North or South—or what specifically had prompted the investigation there. It was probably simply a survey in compliance with the stepped up

Joint Chiefs of Staff directives to get control of the Japanese and their research. But following listings of the various types and tonnages of ores uncovered was a list of facilities the report said were under "surveillance." These included *unnamed* "Rare metal ore dressing and refining plants . . . Oil refineries . . . synthetic petroleum plants . . . Heavy chemical industries" and "Chemical machinery manufacturers."

The only facilities *specifically named* were Osaka and Kyoto Universities, where Arakatsu and the Navy project had originated, and "Nagoya Imperial University," the place where the Snell story had said the Konan atomic bomb project had originated.

It was the first time I had ever seen Nagoya mentioned in connection with any Allied investigations of the Japanese atomic bomb effort.

Had investigators found out something they previously had not known?

I was frustrated when I returned home from Washington. Basically, I had spent almost all my time looking for new information on Konan, finding other tidbits, but without solving that basic mystery. The other area of research I thought might have opened up—what had happened to the uranium oxide from U-234—I had neglected. Now I didn't have answers to either.

When I had left Suitland for College Park, I asked Rich Boylan, who had considerable experience in these matters, why he thought I was having so little luck finding any more information about Konan-Hungnam, especially what finally had been determined about it. Boylan, who had been upbeat about my chances when I had first arrived, said he now thought that the records about Konan had been "taken out of his files and made top secret."

There were still classified records at Suitland which had to be security cleared with other agencies before researchers such as myself could see them. Up until a few years ago, many of those records were subject to such clearances, and lengthy Freedom of Information Requests (FOIAs) were often the only ways to get access to them, if ever.

Ever since Suitland had begun receiving sensitive documents, numbers of them had been removed periodically by agencies like the CIA or DOE and filed away, never to be seen by anyone except high level officials with the proper clearance.

It was this kind of removal that Boylan was talking about.

"[The period where the Konan-Hungnam issue came to a head— 1946–50] was the time of the Rosenbergs [the atomic spies], McCarthy [Senator Joseph and his Communist witch hunts]," he said. "Atomic secrets were our most important secrets. Officials didn't want them known. [And] the agencies were changing. [There was confusion in that. Records could have been lost.] Manhattan to AEC [Atomic Energy Commission] and then DOE [Department of Energy]."

Based on what I'd found before, he said he felt the information, if it existed, had been put "somewhere for 'need to know only.' "

He had no other ideas.

Even before I'd asked him, I'd begun to feel that the information about the Konan rumors I'd uncovered so far was really only the peripheral stuff around a core group of more important documents, such as firsthand reports, interrogations, and final determinations. The documents in my possession had the flavor of higher-ups or interesteds in other agencies reacting to what had been learned.

Where was the stuff they were reacting to?

The more I thought about it, the more I began to believe that this core material would be in intelligence files, like the CIA keeps, and then, finally, in those agencies set up in our history for atomic secrets: Manhattan. AEC. DOE.

I'd probably gotten most of what Manhattan had, however, because the MED began to fade with the war's end, and the reports about Konan, Japanese atomic research in Manchuria, even China, began to trickle in *after* the war.

The CIA—or military intelligence in Korea that eventually would be feeding the CIA ("eventually" because the CIA was not yet created)—would be the most likely to have picked up the information on Konan. That was their job—to know what was going on in the world hostile to America, which North Korea certainly was. And then the atomic agencies would have had the most reason to store it. It was their job to keep tabs on uranium, atomic research, developments, etc.

But then, when you learn the fragmented history of such agencies, the possibility of finding buried or hidden documents becomes that much more complex. The CIA wasn't chartered until 1947. Its forerunner, the OSS, would have probably done the actual collecting and then would have had to have passed the information on to the CIA at the exact time its first members were concentrating on the agency's birth. There was also friction between the two agencies as the baton was passed. Throw in other factors, like the bias I think was there, and the possibility for discard, misplacement, misinterpretation, or near unretrieveable lockaway was strong.

Similarly, Grove's Manhattan Engineer District had gone unwillingly over to the AEC, and then that larger organization had experienced great birth pangs and turmoil as it had taken over the role of defender of our atomic secrets.

Perhaps five years after I had completed *Secret War* in the 1980s, the CIA did respond to my Freedom of Information Act (FOIA) request for information about Konan by stating flatly that it had none. I can't find the letter but I remember thinking, How ridiculous. I have at least eight top-level intelligence documents discussing it, one of them from the "Central Intelligence Group," and they have nothing? The CIA keeps intelligence on nuns. Either they are inept or lying, which, at CIA, can be done in good conscience because of what is perceived as the national interest.

Actually, a matter as simple as the information having been gathered by the OSS would be justifiable grounds for denying knowledge of the subject of a request. Administrators of FOIA requests at the various intelligence agencies often use a ridiculously strict interpretation of the law to deny many claims. If, in fact, the information had come from OSS and I said, as I had, in my request, that I believed the CIA had the information, they could arguably deny they had the information on the basis that it was OSS information, not theirs.

I've seen worse, and I've filed a lot of FOIA requests.

I got similar denials of any information on Konan-Hungnam from representatives I contacted by phone at DOE, both in my first search in the early 1980s, and this time. I never did file an FOIA request at DOE, which is the much stronger way to look, because officials are then compelled by law rather than just cursorily checking, or doing you a favor at their leisure, as is often the case otherwise. But I never quite settled on DOE as a prime contender for having the information until this search.

When I finally did decide to look harder at DOE, I got more discouraging information:

Roger Anders is historian for the DOE's Office of Human Radiation Experiments, the Energy Department's newly set up unit to aid Americans who were experimented upon by our government without their knowledge in order for us to find out how radiation affects humans. (At the beginning of the Cold War we did things like that, thinking it was in the national interest.)

Prior to that, he was a general historian for the DOE.

As a result of his Human Radiation Experiments work, Anders told me that he has discovered in the last few years that key intelligence files—those for the old AEC, which kept our atomic records from 1947 through 1974, and those of ERDA (Energy Research and Development Administration which took over briefly for AEC)—have been destroyed.

This is the period that any Konan records would have been put in those intelligence files.

"Somebody just chucked 'em," he said, "probably in the late 1970s and early 1980s" when the DOE was taking over. He didn't know why. It could have been simple house cleaning to get more space. "The regulations governing such destruction were broad enough then. The rules to retain were such that when someone wanted to destroy documents, they could."

He didn't like it, he said, but that's the way it was. They're gone.

So it looks like the answers to both questions—what happened at Konan and to the uranium oxide onboard U-234—might be harder than ever to find. Not impossible, because there could be other repositories with the information, agencies which received copies, or had their own interest in the information.

But I had to wrap it up. My time and resources were running out—again.

One of the last aspects of my research arrived in the mail in March 1995. Wondering if the Harry S. Truman Library in Independence, Missouri, could shed any light on the questions I was interested in, I had called there and talked with Archivist Randy Sowell. He'd checked but found only a few pertinent items, one of which was Edwin Pauley's June 1946 report to Truman about his thwarted attempts to see Japanese assets in northern Korea.

While I'd been aware of the Russian's refusal to let Pauley come into the Konan area, seeing the actual denial in typed print—"Soviet refusal of admission to the two most important areas surrounding Chongjin and Hungnam was expressed in the personal negotiations held at Pyongyang"—made a renewed impression.

What were the Russians afraid of letting him see?

The jet fuel project? Bombed out fertilizer plants? The fact that they were dismantling plants and shipping them back home? Those possibilities were already known by America—and the Russians knew it. For instance, they had allowed him to see the dismantling in the other areas he visited.

The refusal didn't make much sense to me unless there was something at Konan that they didn't want America to know they had. Uranium or atomic works—since we didn't think they had either, and since that was the main poker chip in world power politics at that time—would have fit that bill.

But that is just speculation. All I really know is that Konan was special to them and they guarded it like no other place the Allies were near.

I ran into numerous reports of uranium ores in Korea, including, again, the pitchblende reported at Chuul (or Ju'ul, it has never become clear) Hot Springs, North Korea, which had intrigued me since I first saw it in 1979–80. In RG 331, 1945–50, Box 3 at Suitland, the North Korean ore site was the subject of a SCAP report made in response to a War Department request and gave details which bore on my current search.

Titled "Uranium Deposits in Korea," it said, "In the latter part of June 1946 [at the height of U.S. investigation into the Konan reports], a report was received by . . . G-2 Office, XXIV Corps, that a rich uranium deposit existed at Ju'ul Hot Springs . . . north of 38 parallel. The informant was not certain whether the deposit was fergusonite or pitchblende. Except that the deposit [was] discovered during the Japanese occupation and has been attended with the utmost secrecy. . . ."

The report, basically, brought me back to where I was when I had finished my initial research in 1980—could this have been a source of uranium for Konan?

Wrapping up:

Neither Leon Thompson nor Dr. William Engeberg got back to me with any more corroborating information. Thompson's sister, Clara McDonald, whom I reached in Houston, said he'd told her "almost all of that" (what he'd told me) when he returned back from Tokyo in 1949, but she "didn't pay too much attention to it."

She could provide few details.

On September 8, 1985, *The Seattle Times / Seattle Post-Intelligencer* published, a lengthy feature on Thompson by Sunday columnist Don Duncan which included much of what Thompson had told me. But I was bothered by the fact that my book had come out that previous spring, and while I certainly wasn't accusing him of lifting the story, he could not provide any proof that he had told his tale to anyone other than his sister prior to the book's publishing.

So what do I really believe about Konan?

There is not enough evidence yet to believe the Japanese made an atomic bomb. The explosion spoken about in the Snell story and followup American intelligence documents—if an explosion occurred—was probably just some sort of preliminary test similar to those conducted by the Manhattan Project prior to its development of the bomb. For instance, it could have been a large conventional explosion, perhaps trying to find out what kind of force and/or detonation mechanism was needed to initiate the fast fission reaction. Or it could have been a very rudimentary nuclear device, or a test only to scatter harmful radiation from some non-fast reaction source, an early nuclear weapons idea that had occurred to America as well.

(Interestingly, objections that any such radioactivity given off in the area of Konan would have been detected by Allied monitoring in 1945 appear to be contradicted by additional documents I found at Suitland. The documents by Army Adjutant General Edward F. Witsell, dated June 3, 1946, and two from SCAP headquarters general W. F. Marquat, dated December 4, 1947—indicate that we had neither capacity nor the equipment set up to detect "foreign" radioactivity in that area until after the Russians were reported to have exploded their first atomic bomb in 1947.)

But I do believe that the Japanese went a lot farther in their program than those in the know, if they are still alive, have told the outside world, and than those few who have previously researched the project have been able to find out. The recent revelations about what Fisher found out—the lying and hesitancy of Arakatsu and Kitagawa, and the huge appropriations for the Shanghai uranium—have furthered that belief.

In addition, another late-war document I found this trip clearly indicates that, contrary to the conventional history that Japanese atomic efforts were bombed into extinction by spring 1945 (a history contradicted by a post-bomb Magic intercept), the project was continued and heightened even after the Emperor's August 15 surrender:

"G-2 Periodic Report No. 208," dated March 24, 1946, which I found at College Park, says that a letter "written by a member of the Physical and Chemical Research Institute (apparently Nishina's Riken)" to "a member of the Physics Department, Osaka Imperial University" disclosed that on 31 August 45 (a half month after the surrender), the chairman of the Scientific Research Conference had ordered atomic research discontinued but that recently he had given approval for continuing experiments."

Something substantial was going on in the Japanese Navy in the way of atomic research at the end of the war. The Magic intercept spoke about it. Arakatsu, the Navy's scientist, lied about it. Kitagawa lied about it too, and then nervously didn't want to discuss it. Admiral Sasagawa, who had authored a report about finding uranium, also told Fisher he knew nothing about the project. The largest outlay of the war for the fission bomb had only recently been made—a huge, 25 million yen outlay—and it was for work on the Asian mainland.

If something wasn't going on, why had the cyclotrons been destroyed so abruptly? I do not believe it was because of an accident, as was claimed at that time. I ran into too many references to the War Department "order" to destroy the cyclotrons than to believe that story. Although apologists like to dismiss the Japanese atomic efforts as almost laughable, SCAP certainly didn't, even after the initial postwar investigations revealed very little.

Listen to Major Joseph O'Hearn, one of the U.S. officers who destroyed the cyclotrons, in a November 27, 1945, top secret report to the chief of the Economic and Scientific Section (found at Suitland):

"In the course of my recent mission in connection with the destruction of scientific equipment related to research in Atomic Energy, a number of factors were uncovered which convince me that further intensive investigation of this field is essential. These factors are as follows:

"a. There are a number of other devices, such as Van de Graff static generators, Cockroft high tension generators, Wilson Cloud Chambers, etc., existing and in some cases operating in laboratories throughout Japan, and these are at least as closely, and possibly more closely, related to Atomic Energy research than the destroyed cyclotrons.

"b. Certain Japanese scientists have stated quite openly that they are currently engaged in Atomic Energy research. Others have been reported to be so engaged. They are using equipment other than cyclotrons, at laboratories not visited by my party nor to my knowledge by any other agency.

"c. My mission uncovered a hidden supply of Uranium not previously known. . . . Full details are not yet available . . . but I believe the material . . . is Uranium Oxide, from which Uranium can be readily separated."

He concluded by stating that "investigation of the above matters should not be handled by "the Scientific Division of ESS [Economic and Scientific Section]" because, he said, the division did not have "competent" scientists at the time, and its personnel "are entirely Australian, and Australia is not a party to the Atomic Secrecy."

Even before that, in March 1945, when the Manhattan Project was first beginning to wonder what the Japanese were doing in the way of trying to make a bomb, a Manhattan District report from its Intelligence and Security Division (which I found at College Park in Record Group 77, Entry 22, Box 173) had concluded that "the Japanese scientists are capable of creating something similar to the (Manhattan Project) but they probably do not have the resources."

Indeed, back in October 1944, according to another document in the same group at College Park, Dr. Phillip Morrison, in an amazingly prophetic report, wrote that he thought the Japanese physicists knew much more than they were being given credit for in the late-war euphoria of certain victory.

"Even admitting that newspaper stories are completely unreliable," he stated in the "20 October 1944" document, "I must still point out that the best newspaper account of the (atomic bomb, which the U.S. was still working on at the time) was given in a Japanese broadcast reported in many American newspapers about 4–6 weeks ago. This broadcast not only included the usual stories of the terrible destructiveness, etc., of the atomic bomb, but added the significant and sensible detail that the site of the explosion would be surrounded by a radioactive fringe within which it would be impossible to live. Such a report can be based only on a piece of definite information from someone who knows at least the fundamentals of the problem."

Such indications of increased atomic activity at the end of the war and Japanese competence are contrary to the old view of what had happened in Japan. But they can't just be dismissed. Nor can the many top-level intelligence reports giving the Konan-Hungnam stories credence. Now those reports are paired with others about research in Manchuria and elsewhere in China. At the very least, I want to see what the United States finally determined about these new questions and newly mined perspectives. And then I would want to evaluate that determination against everything else I know.

In recent months, the incredible story of how the Japanese had performed horrible biological warfare experiments upon prisoners in

Asia, including Americans, and had been able to keep it secret until just recently, has left me with a new appreciation of how such things can be buried for so long.

In some of the experiments—conducted in the same Manchuria where the atomic research is reported—the prisoners were actually cut open without anesthesia so that Japanese doctors, they are now confessing, could view the disease they had implanted in its "fresh" state.

The American government collaborated in this. The thinking was that we needed the research in order to deal with situations that might later affect us.

If this was covered up with American help—for 50 years, no less—why would it be any less likely that Japanese atomic research during the war would have also been covered up?

Atomic research was more important to us than biological research.

But speculation about Konan is really beside the point. Konan is just an intriguing degree question. How far did they really get? The most important point of my research, I think, is that the Japanese, in fact, tried to make the bomb, got farther than the Germans did in the sense that they were after the fast reaction while the Germans appear to have been only on the slow reaction track. And certainly, as all the documents about their coming "Defense of the Homeland" indicate, the Japanese would have used the bomb in their defense had they been able.

They are not solely the victims of the bomb, as they have been portrayed for so long. They were willing participants in its use, and only losers in the race to perfect it.

But their story, which has been ignored—or kept secret, as the case may be—for so many years, has much to teach us.

As Joseph S. Bermudez, Jr., a *Jane's Intelligence Review* analyst who writes on subjects such as North Korea's current program to develop an atomic bomb, told me: What we forget is that while the Japanese atomic bomb effort wasn't as big or as large a program as ours, it was a "serious program by their standards. We tend to take less seriously Third World programs, comparing them to ours. We don't think they can do as well. We are very prejudiced. . . . We never considered Saddam Hussein's missile program a threat until the Gulf War. Then we woke up. We've done the same thing to the Egyptians."

Bermudez believes that in a world where many Third World powers—or even terrorist groups—are now going to try and acquire nuclear weapons, studying the Japanese World War II attempt to produce an atomic bomb will give worried governments and policemen valuable information.

"The Japanese effort is how rudimentary governments—or people under siege—go about it," he said. "We can learn from it. None of these developing nations are going to (use the same costly steps) we did. They're going to do it like the Japanese did it."

In a February 8, 1994, paper he produced, entitled "Democratic People's Republic of Korea: Nuclear Capabilities" (portions of which were delivered to a Senate subcommittee on Chemical and Biological Weapons on February 9–10, 1989), Bermudez confirmed the Japanese discoveries of uranium ores in North Korea, Jun Noguchi's and Russia's exploitation of Hungnam, and recounts the possibility of Japanese atomic efforts at Konan as part of the history leading to North Korea's atomic program.

We still live in a dangerous age of nuclear proliferation. We don't have much information about how the knowledge to build an atomic bomb is acquired—except by the rich Western democracies. But few who make a nuclear bomb in the future will do so with a Manhattan Project. Most will go about it like the Japanese did, so their effort should be studied for what it tells us about how those with smaller resources and means head toward the inevitable end.

Consequently, the unanswered questions from the Japanese project need to be answered, either by researchers following my lead by going back to the documents, or by the Japanese fessing up to what they haven't told us—if that is possible.

Many of the participants are now dead, and those with the crucial secrets, I fear, were so small in number that there is little chance that they are still around. This is especially true for those who might be able to shed light on what happened at Konan.

The Japanese, as they have so often stated, probably did not keep written records.

But there is more to be learned. Of that, I'm sure.

SOURCES

BOOKS

Alcázar de Velasco, Ángel. *Memorias de un Agente Secreto (Memories of a Secret Agent)*. Barcelona: Plaza y Janes, S.A., 1979. (Translation)

Allen, G. C. *Japanese Industry: Its Recent Development and Present Condition*. New York: Institute of Pacific Relations, 1940. (Noguchi)

————. *Japan's Economic Recovery*. New York: Oxford University Press, 1958. (Noguchi)

Allen, Louis. *The End of the War in Asia*. London: Hart-Davis MacGibbon, 1976. (General)

Bertram, James. *Unconquered*. New York: John Day Co., 1939. (General)

Bisson, T. A. *Zaibatsu Dissolution in Japan*. Berkeley, Calif.: University of California Press, 1954. (Noguchi)

Brooks, Lester. *Behind Japan's Surrender*. New York: McGraw-Hill, 1968. (General)

Brown, Anthony C., and Charles B. MacDonald. *The Secret History of the Atomic Bomb*. New York: The Dial Press, 1977.

Childs, Herbert. *An American Genius: The Life of Ernest D. Lawrence*. New York: E. P. Dutton, 1968.

Clark, Ronald. *The Man Who Broke Purple*. Boston: Little, Brown, 1977.

Coffey, Thomas M. *Imperial Tragedy*. New York: Pinnacle Books, 1970. (Japanese atomic project)

Cohen, Jerome. *Japan's Economy in War and Reconstruction*. Minneapolis: University of Minnesota Press, 1949. (Noguchi)

Compton, Arthur H. *Atomic Quest*. New York: Oxford University Press, 1956. (General)

Cross, J. A. *Sir Samuel Hoare: A Political Biography*. London: Jonathan Cape, 1977. (Espionage-Velasco)

Farago, Ladislas. *Aftermath*. New York: Avon, 1974. (Espionage)

————. *The Game of the Foxes*. New York: David McKay, 1971. (Espionage—Velasco)

Gallagher, Thomas. *Assault in Norway*. New York: Harcourt Brace Jovanovich, 1975. (German atomic program)

Glasstone, Samuel. *Sourcebook on Atomic Energy.* Huntington, N.Y.: Robert R. Kreiger Co., 1979.

Grajdanzev, Andrew Jonah. *Modern Korea.* New York: Institute of Pacific Relations, 1944. (Noguchi)

Groves, L. R. *Now It Can Be Told.* New York: Harper & Row, 1962. (General)

Hammel, Eric M. *Chosin.* New York: Vanguard Press, 1981. (Korean War)

Han Woo-keun. *The History of Korea.* Honolulu: East-West Center Press, 1971. (Noguchi)

Hays, Carlton J. *Wartime Mission in Spain.* New York: Macmillan, 1946. (Espionage)

Hiroshige, Tetsu. *The History of Science in Japan.* Tokyo: Chuo Koronsha, 1973. (Translation) (Japanese atomic programs)

Hirschmeier, Johannes. *The Origins of Entrepreneurship in Meiji Japan.* Cambridge, Mass.: Harvard University Press, 1964.

Hoare, Sir Samuel. *Complacent Dictator.* New York: Knopf, 1947. (Espionage)

Holmes, W. J. *Double-Edged Secrets.* Annapolis, Md.: Naval Institute Press, 1979.

Hoyt, Edwin P. *Raider 16.* New York: World Publishing Co., 1970. (U-234)

Hyde, H. Montgomery. *The Atom Spies.* New York: Atheneum, 1980.

Ienaga, Saburo. *The Pacific War 1931–1945.* New York: Pantheon Books, 1978.

Irving, David. *The German Atomic Bomb.* New York: Simon & Schuster, 1967.

Kiichi, Yoshioka. *Jun Noguchi.* Published by a private company, 1962, and obtained on loan from Fuji International Consultants, Tokyo, through the International House Library, Tokyo. (Translation)

Kirby, Major General S. Woodburn. *The War Against Japan,* Vol. 5: *The Surrender of Japan.* London: Her Majesty's Stationery Office, 1969.

Kramish, A. *Atomic Energy in the Soviet Union.* Stanford, Calif.: Stanford University Press, 1959.

Kuneta, James W. *City of Fire.* Englewood Cliffs, N.J.: Prentice-Hall, 1978.

Lewin, Ronald. *The American Magic.* New York: Farrar Straus & Giroux, 1982.

———. *Ultra Goes to War.* New York: Pocket Books, 1978. (Espionage)

Liebow, A. *Encounter with Disaster.* New York: W. W. Norton, 1970.

McCune, Shannon. *Korea: Land of the Broken Calm.* Princeton, N.J.: D. Van Nostrand Co., Inc., 1966.

———. *Korea's Heritage: A Regional and Social Geography.* Rutland, Vt.: Charles Tuttle Co., 1956.

Marshall, Byron. *Capitalism and Nationalism in Prewar Japan.* Stanford, Calif.: Stanford University Press, 1967.

Masterman, J. C. *The Double-Cross System in the War of 1939 to 1945.* New Haven, Conn.: Yale University Press, 1972. (Espionage—Velasco)

Millot, Bernard. *Divine Thunder.* New York: Pinnacle Books, 1972.

Mitchell, Kate. *Japan's Industrial Strength.* New York: Institute of Pacific Relations, 1942. (Noguchi)

Montagu, E. *Beyond Top Secret Ultra.* New York: Coward, McCann & Geoghegan, 1977. (Espionage)

Nakayama, Shigeru, David L. Swain, and Yagi Eri, eds. *Science and Society in Modern Japan.* Tokyo: University of Tokyo Press, 1974.

Pacific War Research Society. *The Day Man Lost.* Palo Alto, Calif.: Kodansha, 1972. (Japanese atomic projects)

Payne, Stanley G. *Falange.* Stanford, Calif.: Stanford University Press, 1961. (Espionage)

Petit, D. Pastor. *Espías Españoles: Del Pasado y del Presente (Spanish Spies: Past and Present).* Barcelona: Editorial Argos Vergara, 1979. (Translation)

Robertson, Peter. *The Early Years: The Niels Bohr Institute 1921–1930.* Copenhagen: Akademisk Forlag, University of Copenhagen, 1979.

Rozental, S. *Niels Bohr: His Life and Work as Seen by His Friends and Colleagues.* Amsterdam: North-Holland Publishing Co., 1967. (Nishina)

Schoenberger, Walter S. *Decision of Destiny.* Orono, Maine: University of Maine Press, 1962.

Schumpeter, Elizabeth Boody, ed. *The Industrialization of Japan and Manchukuo 1930–1940.* New York: Macmillan, 1940. (Noguchi)

Seth, Ronald. *Secret Servants: History of Japanese Espionage.* Westport, Conn.: Greenwood Publishers, 1975.

Speer, Albert. *Inside the Third Reich.* New York: Macmillan, 1970. (Espionage)

Sugai, J., et al. *Nippon Kagaku-gizyutusi TaiKei (The Comprehensive History of Japanese Science and Technology),* Vol. 13. Tokyo: Dai-ichi Hoki Shuppan, 1970. (Translation) (Japanese atomic projects)

Suh, Sang-chul. *Growth and Industrial Changes in the Korean Economy 1910–1940.* Cambridge, Mass.: Harvard University Press, 1978. (Noguchi)

Sunoo, Harold Hak-won. *Korea: A Political History in Modern Times.* Published jointly by the Korean-American Cultural Foundation, Columbia, Missouri, and Kunkuk University Press, Seoul, 1970. (Noguchi)

Thiesmeyer, L., and John E. Burchard. *Combat Scientists.* Boston: Little, Brown, 1947.

Thomas, Gordon, and Max Morgan-Witts. *Enola Gay.* New York: Stein & Day, 1977.

Thomas, Hugh. *The Spanish Civil War.* New York: Penguin Books, 1965. (Velasco)

Thorpe, Elliott R. *East Wind Rain.* Boston: Gambit, 1969. (Espionage)

Toland, John. *The Rising Sun: The Decline and Fall of the Japanese Empire.* New York: Random House, 1970. (Japanese atomic projects)

Tuge, Hideomi. *Historical Development of Science and Technology in Japan.* Tokyo: Kokusai Bunka Shinkokai (Society for International Cultural Relations), 1961.

Turner, L.C.F., et al. *War in the Southern Oceans.* New York: Oxford University Press, 1961.

Yamamoto, Yoichi. *The True Story of the Japanese Atomic Bomb.* Tokyo: Sozo, 1976. (Translation)

Yohan, E., and O. Tanin. *When Japan Goes to War.* New York: The Vanguard Press, 1936.

Yomiuri Shinbun (newspaper). *Showashi no Tenno (The Emperor in the Showa Era).* Tokyo: Yomiuri Shinbun, 1968. (Translation) (Japanese atomic projects)

ARTICLES

Alcázar de Velasco, Ángel. Interview in *El País* (Spanish newspaper), September 30, 1978. (Translation)

Arakatsu, Bunsaku. A UP interview with him in the October 15, 1945, *New York Times,* p. 4, "Japanese Believe Russia Has It [an atomic bomb]."

———. Articles on "Photo-fission," including "of Uranium and Thorium Produced by the Gamma-rays of Lithium and Fluorine Bombarded with High Speed Protons," in *Proceedings of the Physico-Mathematical Society of Japan*, June 1941, August 1941, March 1943, January 1946.

Blair, William M. "Big U-boat Arrives with High General." *New York Times*, May 20, 1945.

Bronfenbrenner, Martin. "The American Occupation of Japan: Economic Retrospect," *The American Occupation of Japan: A Retrospective View*. Lawrence, Kan.: Center for East Asian Studies, The University of Kansas, 1968.

Browne, Malcolm W. "Japanese Data Show Tokyo Tried to Make World War II A-bomb." *New York Times*, January 7, 1978.

Campbell, Louise. "Science in Japan." *Science*, Vol. 143, February 21, 1964.

Compton, Karl T. "Mission to Tokyo." *Technology Review*, Vol. 4., November–July, 1945–1946.

Condon, Jane, and Nancy Faber. "An Author Accuses the Japanese of Horrifying Medical Experiments on World War II P.O.W.s." *People*, Spring 1982.

Dower, J. W. "Japan's Atomic Weapons Research." *The Daily Yomiuri*, August 11, 1979.

———. "Science, Society and the Japanese Atomic-Bomb Project During World War Two." *Bulletin of Concerned Asian Scholars*, April–June 1978.

Feinsilber, Mike. UPI story in *Miami Herald*, May 30, 1978, "Hiroshima Left Japanese Pushing for Own A-Bomb."

Gray, Charlie. Compilation of stories broadcast by Mr. Gray about the surrender of German submarines at Portsmouth, New Hampshire: "Surrender at Sea." Published by WHEB, Portsmouth, June 1945.

Hasagawa, Hideo. Memoir about the last days of Konan, Korea, under Japanese control. Published in *Nippon Kaigun Nenryo-shi (The History of Fuel Development in the Japanese Navy)*, 1972. (Translation)

Heisenberg, Werner. "The Yukawa Theory of Nuclear Forces in the Light of Present Quantum Theory of Wave Fields." *Progress of Theoretical Physics*, Vol. 5, No. 4, July–August 1950.

"Japan's Hidden Physicists," early 1950s, found in file in Record Group 331, box 7418, National Archives, Suitland, Md.

Kelly, Harry C. "Yoshio Nishina—Scientist and Humanist." *PHP*, April 1971.

———. Article on, in *Science*, Vol. 169, July 31, 1970: "Harry C. Kelly: An Extraordinary Ambassador to Japanese Science."

———. "Commentary: Japanese Science and Technology." *Research 3*, 1950.

Kennedy, Robert G. "Nazi U-Boats Came Here." *Portsmouth Herald*, May 17, 1975.

Kigoshi, Kunihiko. "On the Viscosity of the Uranium Hexafluoride." *Bulletin of the Chemical Society of Japan*, Vol. 23, No. 2. July 1950.

Kitagawa, Tetsuzo. "My Memory of the Atomic Bomb." *Safety Digest* of the Japan Safety Society, Vol. 25, August 1979. (Translation)

Kobayashi, M. Preface to The Physical Society of Japan's *Progress of Theoretical Physics*' commemorative issue on Yukawa's discovery of the meson theory, July–August 1950.

Koizumi, Ken. "Yoshio Nishina." Shizen, Tokyo, 1976. (Translation)

Mansfield, Ambassador Mike. Interview: "Japanese Should, Can and Will Do More on Defense." U.S. News and World Report, November 16, 1981.

Marquina Barrio, Antonio. " 'To,' Espías de Verbena" (" 'To,' Spies for a Night Festival"). Historia, December 1978. (Translation)

Masazumi, Harada. "Minamata Disease as a Social and Medical Problem." Japan Quarterly, January–March 1978. (Some history of Noguchi's company)

Mitsui, Matao. Interview in a Japanese magazine, possibly called Culture Critic, December 1979. (Translation)

Nishina, Yoshio. "Fission Products of Uranium by Fast Neutrons." Letters to the editor in Physical Review, October 1, 1940, February 1, 1941, and April 15, 1941.

———. "A Japanese Scientist Describes the Destruction of His Cyclotrons." Bulletin of the Atomic Scientists, June 1947.

———. Further pertinent work under his guidance in the letters section of the Physical Review in "Some Experiments on the Relative Cross Sections of the (n,a) and (n,p) Reactions Produced by Fast Neutrons" (October–December 1940) and "On the Probability of Asymmetric and Symmetric Fission" (October–December 1950).

Norling, Bob. "Ex-U-Boat Officer Here for Visit; First Saw Portsmouth as POW." Portsmouth Herald, July 9, 1954.

Oppenheimer, J. R. Letter about the Klein-Nishina formula, reprinted in Robert Oppenheimer: Letters and Recollections, Harvard University Press, 1980.

O'Toole, Thomas. "How Spaniards Ran Spy Ring for Japan in U.S." Washington Post article run in Miami Herald, September 11, 1978.

Parrott, Lindsay. "Five Cyclotrons Wrecked in Japan." New York Times, November 24, 1945, plus other NYT articles on the same subject on November 26, 29, December 5, 6, 14, 15.

Paul, Anthony. "Inside North Korea: Marxism's First 'Monarchy.' " Reader's Digest, February 1982.

Price, Willard. "Jap Rule in the Hermit Nation." National Geographic, October 1945.

Saville, Allison W. "German Submarines in the Far East." U.S. Naval Institute Proceedings, August 1961.

Shapley, Deborah. "Nuclear Weapons History: Japan's Wartime Bomb Projects Revealed." Science, Vol. 199, January 13, 1978; and subsequent letters to the editor about same, February 17, March 24, April 21, and May 5.

Shiraishi, Muneshiro. "Memories of Mr. Noguchi," in Chisso Company booklet about the company's history. Given to me by Mr. Shiraishi at the company's Tokyo headquarters. (Translation)

Shobei, Shiota. "A 'Ravaged' People: The Koreans in World War II," The Japan Interpreter, Vol. VII, No. 1, Winter 1971.

Snow, C. P. "How the Bomb Was Born." Discover, August 1981.

Stephenson, R. J. "A Brief Account of the Physics of the Atomic Bomb." American Journal of Physics, Vol. 13–14, 1945–1946.

Suzuki, Tatsusaburo. "Memoir on the Research of How to Make the Atomic Bomb." Journal of the School of Chemical Warfare (Tokyo), No. 7, 1963 (possibly May 30). (Translation)

Tomonaga, Shinitiro. "Dr. Yoshio Nishina, His Sixtieth Birthday." *Progress of Theoretical Physics,* Vol. 5, No. 6, November–December 1950.

Weart, Spencer. "Secrecy, Simultaneous Discovery, and the Theory of Nuclear Reactors." *American Journal of Physics,* Vol. 45, No. 11, November 1977.

Weiner, Charles. "Retroactive Saber Rattling?" *Bulletin of the Atomic Scientists,* Vol. 34, No. 4, April 1978.

Williams, Dan. "Ghosts of Japanese Atrocities Haunt School." *Miami Herald,* May 13, 1982.

———. "New View of History Opens Old Wounds." *Miami Herald,* August 7, 1982.

Yagi, Hideji. Interview in *Nagasaki Shimbun,* September 26, 1945. Obtained from a file in Record Group 243, PTO-373, National Archives, Suitland, Md.

Yamashita, Nobuo. "Japan's Uncompleted Atomic Bomb." *Kaizo* (Special number), November 15, 1952.

Yamazaki, Fumio. "Dr. Yoshio Nishina Passed Away (a Memoir)." *Journal of the Scientific Research Institute,* Vol. 45, July 1951.

DOCUMENTS

"Atomic Bomb Mission, Japan—Final Report, Scientific and Mineralogical Investigation." This is the full 160-plus-page report filed by Major R. R. Furman, under Brigadier Generals Farrell and Newman, for the War Department (Manhattan Project) on Japanese work on an atomic bomb. Its last pages were written in October 1945. I found it in the National Archives, Suitland, Md., branch, Record Group 331, file box 7409. Included in it is a four-page "Summary Report, Atomic Bomb Mission, Investigation into Japanese Activity to Develop Atomic Power," which can be obtained from the National Archives Modern Military Branch, Washington, D.C., in Record Group 243 (USSBS), Sec. 2., 3f(14). The title *summary* is a misnomer for there is new information that follows the summary, which is dated 30 September 1945.

1947–48 reports on Japanese wartime research, including atomic, ordered by occupation headquarters and made through the Scientific and Technical Division. Compiled mainly by K. Shimizu, director of Japan's Scientific Education Bureau at that time, and Dr. Nishina. Obtained in the "Research, Wartime (Japanese)" file, box 7416 (and possibly 7419), Record Group 331, SCAP, National Archives, Suitland, Md. Approximately 40 pages.

"Investigation of Nuclear Research in Japan," a four-page section of the Foreign Intelligence Supplement No. 1 to *Manhattan District History, Book 1: General, Volume 14: Intelligence and Security* (Record Group 374), obtained from the National Archives Manhattan Project section.

"Japanese War-Effort Plants and Installations in Korea. Part 1. The Noguchi 'Konan' Enterprises and Financially Vulnerable Noguchi Militaristic Interests." By Carpel L. Breger, September 22, 1942. 30 pages, plus maps and drawings. Obtained at the National Archives, Modern Military Branch, OSS file (R.G. 226) and numbered 21872.

"A Preliminary Survey of the Holdings of the Japanese Economic Oligarchy." Compiled by the Foreign Economic Administration, Enemy Branch, Japanese

Special Services Staff. 82 pages. National Archives OSS collection (R.G. 226), #140182. (Noguchi)

Konan and the atomic connection: The main documents so far have been unearthed at Suitland. They include: The Snell story, from R.G. 331, box 7419, "Magazine and News Articles" file; Bid Sheets 564353, 564354, 564355, from the Military Intelligence Division I.D. files, R.G. 319, Box 3635; Bid Sheet and Military Intelligence Section report #403527, R.G. 319, Box 91; Headquarters, United States Army Forces in Korea, Intelligence Summaries #12 (21 May 46), #14(22 June 46), #39 (30 June 47), and #42 (1–15 August 47), all from R.G. 319, Box 739.

Konan and Noguchi in general: Numerous documents were unearthed, mainly from the National Archives OSS files (R.G. 226). These include: 125214, XL 20379, 130787, XL 11902, 19686c, XL 13147, 124929, 93176, 114936c, 111301, 29516, 70913S, 124795c (which is very extensive on Konan), and SL15827. Also, R.G. 243 (USSBS) Interrogation 128; and at Suitland, M.I.D. file 22616, dated September 15, 1942.

Konan at end of war and beginning of Russian occupation: Suitland has a fair amount in the intelligence summaries by United States Army Forces in Korea. In particular, see 22 June 1946 and 1–15 August 1947. Also, Report #11, "Japanese Ordnance . . ." file, box 841, R.G. 319. At the Modern Military Branch, the following OSS documents are pertinent: 128137R, 132218, 144285, XL26109, and XL44644. Also, USSBS interrogations 312 and 313 (R.G. 243, Sec. 8).

Entwhistle mission to Korea, summer 1946: 20 June 1946 "urgent" message from CINCAFPAC to CG USAFIK, signed by Major General W. F. Marquat. I got it at Suitland, R.G. 331, Box 7413, "Outgoing Radio Log" file. Also Entwhistle report, dated 6 July 1946, "Interviews with Bureau Heads, Economics Department USAMGIK." I found it in SCAP, R.G. 331, box 7419, "Korea, Gen." file.

Uranium in the Japanese Empire during the war: I found numerous reports of such, primarily at Suitland. The most pertinent are: R.G. 319, Box 3635, I.D. files 564331–564340, 564342, 564357–564358; R.G. 319, Box 739, Headquarters, United States Army in Korea, Intelligence Summaries North Korea, 15 June 1947 and 15–30 August 1947. Also from Box 739, I.D. files 564340–564356. And R.G. 331, boxes 7428 (China), 7431 (Interrogation Report 17432), 7433 (memo on Manchuria). Finally, R.G. 338, Box 1061, MIS Summary 1721, dated 28 January 1942. At the Modern Military Branch, OSS files (R.G. 226) 26511c, 115578, 70913, 124808, and L40069.

"The Atomic Bomb," by Yoshio Nishina. Report by him about what he saw at Hiroshima and Nagasaki, including some of his calculations and studies of same. National Archives, R.G. 243 (USSBS), P.T.O., 13 b (4). 8 pages.

Nishina biography prepared by himself for the occupation. 15 pages. Suitland, R.G. 331, Box 7438.

"Reorganization of Rikken Institute of Physical and Chemical Research." Report to occupation about the institute with much pertinent information, including history. There are also several documents about the Rikken in USSBS.

"The Present State and Future Outlook of Researches in Certain Branches of Science in Japan," by Yoshio Nishina. Article prepared for the occupation forces. Suitland, R.G. 331, Box 7433.

Letter from Nishina to occupation forces defending himself for being on a black-listed wartime committee. Dated May 15, 1947. Suitland, R.G. 331, Box 7416, "Rikken Institute" file.

Alsos list of "Scientific Intelligence Targets, Japan and Japanese Occupied Areas." Dated 27 April 1945. Includes many of those involved in the Japanese atomic effort. 40 pages. I got it from the Navy and Old Army Section of the National Archives, Washington, R.G. 38 (ONI), box 10, File A-l-k, Reg. # 25588.

"Technical Intelligence Report Number 20, subject: National Research Council of Japan." Prepared by Major Russell J. Baldwin, 18 January 1946, Office of the Chief Ordnance Officer (Occupation), Japan. Lists those involved in atomic programs during the war. I got it from National Archives, Washington, Navy and Old Army Section, ONI, Box 35 (R.G. 38).

"Japanese Survey of Atomic Bombing of Hiroshima and Nagasaki," by M. Kimura and E. Tazima. Suitland, R.G. 331, Box 7409, file 120.

Translation of Report Prepared by Direction of Admiral Sasagawa, CO Special Material Unit, Fleet Adm HQ, "Investigation of Uranium Ores, 1 April 1945." 5 pages. Suitland, R.G. 331, Box 7428, "Technical data" file.

"The Field Observation at Hiroshima on the Radioactivity Induced by Atomic Bomb," by Professor Bunsaku Arakatsu. 10 pages. Suitland, R.G. 331, Box 7409.

"Inquiry into the Atomic Bomb at Hiroshima," by Captain Matao Mitsui (Navy), dated September 1945. This is Mitsui's report to his navy about the blast. He headed the team that was first on the site and was also involved in the navy's atomic bomb project. He gave it to me when I interviewed him in Japan. 12 pages, including recommendations of how they could make an atomic bomb.

Biographical sketches and data about the members of the navy and army atomic bomb projects: Numerous, primarily from Suitland and the Harry Kelly archives at the University of North Carolina State. In particular, a three-volume work, "A Short Biography of Japanese Scientists," which he asked the scientists themselves to compile when he was with the occupation. At Suitland, among others, see R.G. 331, boxes 7431 and 7439.

Magic intercept about "researches into the atom" at an undisclosed location: National Archives, R.G. 457 (Far East Summary), SRS 508, No. 508, 10 August 1945.

Alcázar de Velasco and TO spy ring: Numerous, but primarily from Magic intercepts (R.G. 457) at the National Archives, the FBI, and State Department via Freedom of Information Act requests. Also the Canadian Public Archives. Some of the most pertinent Magic citations are: SRS 847 (January 24, 1943), 573 (April 16, 1942), 586 (April 30, 1942), 691 (August 22, 1942), 675 (August 9, 1942), 697 (August 28, 1942), 706 (September 6, 1942), 787 (November 25, 1942), 849 (January 26, 1943), 865 (February 3, 1943), 878 (February 13, 1943), 944 (April 23, 1943), 984 (June 2, 1943). At the State Department, a telegram from the U.S. London embassy, dated October 6, 1941, to the Secretary of State is important, as is another to the Secretary, dated July 20, 1943 (894.20210/224c Ps/t2). At the National Archives, Modern Military Branch, which also houses the Magic documents, USSBS report on Japanese intelligence (Sec. 8, lr[1.]) was helpful, as were OSS reports 62917 and 55215.

"Report on Interrogation of the Crew of U-234 Which Surrendered to the USS

Sutton on 14 May, 1945 . . ." Dated 27 June 1945. 7 pages, from D.C. Allard, Naval Historical Center, Washington Navy Yard.

"Manifest of Cargo for Tokio on Board *U-234.*" Translated from German, 23 May 1945. Also from Allard.

Report of the USS *Sutton* on the capture of the *U-234.* 10 pages. From the Library of Congress. Also from the Library of Congress, the *U-234*'s war diary. Approximately 50 pages.

"Blockade-Running Between Europe and the Far East by Submarine 1942–44." A Magic summary dated 1 December 1944. Approximately 15 pages.

Uranium from Germany to Japan: Several sources, among the most pertinent the intercepted communications on file at the Modern Military Branch, National Archives, with the following descriptions: SRA 01576, Tokyo to Berlin, 7 July 1943; Tokyo to Berlin, 24 August 1943; Berlin to Tokyo, 1 September 1943 (SRA04221); Berlin to Tokyo, 20 November 1943 (SRA 05501); and Tokyo to Berlin, 15 November 1943 (SRA06420).

Diary kept by Tadashi Takeuchi, which is part of *Nippon Kagaku-gizyutusi Taikei,* Vol. 13 (Sugai et al.), which I had translated. It has many diagrams and charts.

"Report of Scientific Intelligence Survey in Japan," Vols. I, II, and III. Dated September–November 1945. At the same time the Atomic Bomb Mission was investigating only Japan's atomic activity, this larger survey was investigating all other aspects of Japan's wartime scientific effort. The two sometimes crossed paths. With appendices, well over 100 pages. I got them from the Navy and Old Army Branch, National Archives, ONI file A-l-k #25588 in Box 35 (R.G. 38).

"Recommendation for 'Science and Technology' Monograph," dated 10 March 1949 and signed by L. H. Battistini. This appears to be an official occupation history of Japan researches over the century, including World War II. It contains material about the Atomic Bomb Mission and about the atomic projects. Suitland, R.G. 331, Box 7428.

"Hiroshima and Nagasaki Occupation Forces," a Defense Nuclear Agency Fact Sheet, obtained at the agency's Washington office. It describes the Atomic Bomb Mission. 33 pages. Dated 6 August 1980.

"Personal History" of Tokuyasu Shikanai in which he describes working on a joint army-navy atomic bomb project late in the war. Suitland, R.G. 331, Box 7433, "Miscellaneous" folder.

"Atomic Discharge to be Used Against Aircraft," OSS report XL6282, dated 1 February 1945. From National Archives, Modern Military Branch.

OSS Report (R.G. 226, National Archives), XL 20426, which discusses possible passengers on *U-234.*

Military Intelligence Summary (MIS) 1277, "Jap Air Plans for Invasion Defense." Dated 3 October 1945. Suitland Archives, R.G. 338, box 1052.

MIS Report, "Japanese Research on High-Frequency Electric Wave Weapons." Dated 24 June 1949, Suitland Archives, R.G. 319, box 841.

INTERVIEWS

Alcázar de Velasco, Ángel, "TO" spy net.
Furman, Robert, Atomic Bomb Mission.
Iimori, Satoyasu, Army Project geologist.

Kigoshi, Kunihiko, Army Project.
Kigoshi, Yascazo, Japanese attaché, Berlin.
Lansdale, John, Manhattan Project security (by mail).
Mitsui, Matao, Navy Project.
Munekata, Eiji, Chisso Corporation (Nichitsu).
Nininger, Robert D., Atomic Bomb Mission (mineralogical investigation).
Nishina, Kojiro, Nishina son.
Nishina, Yoichiro, Nishina son.
Old, Bruce Scott, Naval liaison with Manhattan Project.
Overstreet, Bill, U.S. Geological Survey, Korea.
Shiraishi, Muneshiro, Chisso Corporation.
Suzuki, Tatsusaburo, Army Project (by letter).
Takeda, Eiichi, adviser to Army Project.
Tamaki, Hidehiko, Army Project.
Yamamoto, Yoichi, Army Project.
Yokoyama, Sumi, secretary to Dr. Nishina.

NOTES AND SOURCES FOR EPILOGUE

Although I have cited within the text where I found each document mentioned, the following is as complete a citation as I can give for the epilogue's most important documents:

The 1946 Fisher mission, Arakatsu's and the Japanese Navy's obfuscation of the facts, and the 100 million yen expenditure at the end of the war for uranium: Most of the documents can be found at the College Park, Maryland, branch of the National Archives in its "Records of the Commanding General, Manhattan Project, Special Liaison Branch, Foreign Intelligence Section, 1944–46." The specific numbers for the files are: Group 77, Entry 22, Box 172, File 42.7002. While Box 172 has most of the documents, Boxes 160 and 163 also contain some. Suitland also has documents telling some of the same story in its SCAP Records for 1947–51 (Record Group 331), Economic and Scientific Section (Entry 224), Nuclear Physics Correspondence Files, Box 2.

Noguchi heavy water for Arakatsu and Nishina. These documents, mostly one and two page top secret memos from George Yamashiro, a Science and Technology Division investigator who signs them only "G.Y.", are also at Suitland in Record Group 331, Entry 224, Box 2.

Interview by SCAP with Konan chemical engineer Otogoro Natsume. It is a five page document at Suitland which can be found in Record Group 331, Entry 224, Box 3.

Arakatsu believed lying to SCAP investigator Drake is a one page document at Suitland entitled "Report on Collection of Records at the Laboratory of Dr. Arakatsu, Imperial University, Kyoto." It can be found in Record Group 331, Entry 150, Box 1.

The account of Japanese atomic researcher Masaharu Odan being killed during experiments in 1944 is contained in a U.S. Army Forces Pacific Counter-Intelligence "Check Sheet" found at Suitland in Record Group 331, SCAP, Box 1, "Atomic Bomb" file.

Intelligence that the Japanese knew of America's atomic bomb in November 1944 was found at Suitland in Record Group 331, Entry 224, Box 1, "Research, Nuke, Japan" file.

In addition to those mentioned in the text, I would also like to thank the following: John Weber and Lawrence Deneault, my publisher and editor at Marlowe for their understanding and support; Physicist Peter Zimmerman of Great Falls, Va., who believes the Japanese were at least closer to making an atomic bomb than the Germans; Dr. Gerald L. Looney of Redondo Beach, Ca., a historian of the Russian atomic bomb who has kept me informed of possible leads; Archivists Rick Ray and Diana Leafe of Albuquerque's National Atomic Museum, Marge Ciarlante at College Park, Bill Doty at Laguna Niguel, Randy Sowell at the Truman Library, and Will Mahoney of the National Archives' main branch in downtown D.C. Also, James Corey, a nonproliferation scientist at Albuquerque's Sandia National Laboratories; Jerry Cook of LaJolla, Ca., who has also supplied me with leads; and Michael J. Ravnitzky, a Minnesota development engineer.

INDEX